A SHAKY DC

The Škoda works raid
16/17th April 1943

Peter Wilson Cunliffe

A SHAKY DO
The Škoda works raid
16/17th April 1943

Peter Wilson Cunliffe

Regards Peter W. Cunliffe

A SHAKY DO
The Škoda works raid
16/17th April 1943

Peter Wilson Cunliffe

© Copyright 2007 Peter Wilson Cunliffe

British Library Cataloguing-in-publication Data
A catalogue record for this book is available from the British Library

ISBN 978-0-9557957-0-1

First edition published 2007 by
Accycunliffes Publications

Printed in the United Kingdom

Cover photo The Macfarlane crew in front of a Lancaster at Syerston

DISCLAIMER

The information in this book is true and complete to best of my knowledge. All recommendations are made without any guarantee on the part of the publisher and author (P.W.Cunliffe), who disclaims any liability incurred in connection with the use of this data or specific details.

Contents

Acknowledgements

First and foremost I would like to thank the veterans of Bomber Command who helped with this book. We owe them great debt!

Backhouse H. J. 35 Sqn; Baird Jock 103 Sqn; Beardsall Ken 103 Sqn; Bury Nat 207 Sqn; Collier Geoff 12 Sqn; Cottrell, Ken 158 Sqn; Dashper, Fred 61 Sqn; Dean, Ken 51 Sqn; Dennis, Ray 78 Sqn; Duncan, Ian 419 Sqn; Fitt, Peter 467 Sqn; Goodwin, G.R. 77 Sqn; Harrell Bill 44 Sqn; Hernamon, Harold 467 Sqn; Hughes, Harry 102 Sqn; Hurrel, Stan 78 Sqn; Jackson, Roy 100 Sqn; Jackson, Tom 419 Sqn; Johnson, Tony 427 Sqn; Knott , Syd 467 Sqn; Langsford, Phil 78 Sqn; Lashbrook, Wally 102 Sqn; Martin, Alfie 102 Sqn; Lawrence, Charles 12 Sqn; Mitchell, Fred 103 Sqn; McQuaker, Ron 158 Sqn; Moller, Jack 156 Sqn; O'Toole, Walter 10 Sqn; Patterson, John 61 Sqn; Pegrum, Jack 207 Sqn; Pennington, John 44 Sqn; Petrie-Andrews, Joe 35 Sqn; Scholes, Graham 158 sqn; Stephens, 'Steve' 106 Sqn; Thakray, Tom 10 sqn; Wingham, Tom 102 Sqn; Woodgate, Albert 44 Sqn;

I would also like to thank many sources, helpers and relatives of veterans.

Abbotsford Times Canada
Archives of the Aisne
Archives of the Somme
Australian National Archives
B.B.C. People's war web site
Bardua, Heinz Germany
Benkel, Uve Germany
Boiten Theo, Netherlands
Canadian National Archives
Chorley, W. R. (Bomber Command Losses)
Dhielly Danny, France
Dunn Peter, Australia, 'Oz at war'
Edward, Eric Aus
Egan, Keryl Aus
Evening Herald Bristol U.K.
Fell, Eddie
Friend, Tony, Australia
George Jim, 467 sqn Assoc.
Glynne-Owen, Raymond 207 sqn.Info.
Griffiths, Elspeth (Sedbergh School)
Halliday Hugh, Canada
Harrison, Greg (100 sqn research)
Hipkins, Maj.Jon
James, Chris Canada
Jean-Marie Dubois, Chièvres Belg.
Jonasson, Chuck Canada
Krátký, Dr. Vladislav Škoda Museum
Martyn Errol, (New Zealand)
Meister, Ludwig
Menges, Peter Germany
Michel Leprêtre, France
Moore Sandra Nth Ireland
Nanton Lancaster Society
Naylor, Peter, R.AF. Retd.U.K.
New Zealand National Archives
Norman, Bill 640 Sqn historian
Pearson Ray, U.K. research helper
Penant, Reynaut Belgium

Pilon, Jean-Luc Canada
Potts, Wally
R.A.F. Air Historical Branch
R.A.F Museum, Hendon
R.A.F.Web.org
RAF Linton-On Ouse Memorial room
Redgwell Flt. Lt. 12(B) Sqn R.A.F.
Régis Decobeck Belgium
Rueter, Stephan Germany
Savé, Phillipe Belgium.
Smith, Clive U.K.
Smith, Steve U.K.
Spoden, Peter Germany
Tambouret, Paul, France
Ten Squadron Association
The National Archives U.K.
Thorburn, Gordon, 9 sqn Author
Govearts, Wim, Belgium
Volman, Norbert Germany
Williams, John, Australia
Wing Co. Mawby R.A.F. Retd.
Yorkshire Air Museum, Elvington

http://www.467463raafsquadrons.com
http://www.elsham.pwp.blueyonder.co.uk
http://www.rafcommands.com/
http://www.worldwar2exraf.co.uk/index.html
http://www.ozatwar.com/ Peter Dunn's web site
http://www.rafweb.org

The Max Fischer story. WW2 People's war; is an on line archive or wartime memories contributed by members of the public and gathered by the B.B.C. the archive can be found at
http://www.bbc.co.uk/ww2peopleswar

A Shaky do. The Plzen raid April 16/17th April 1943

Dedication
This book is dedicated especially to
Flight Sergeant William Waller Dawson
61 squadron R.A.F. and the crew of Lancaster W4317 QR-R
And to all veterans of Bomber Command
and U.S. 8th Air Force in World War II.

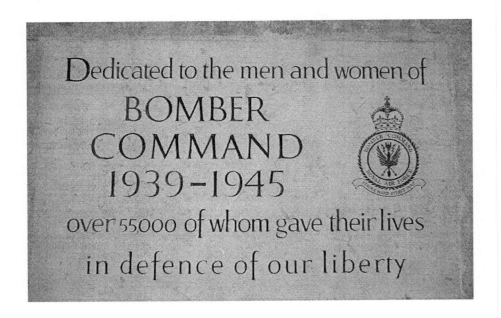

Bomber Command plaque Lincoln Cathedral

In loving memory of

William Waller Dawson

Killed in action 17th April 1943

For the Lord himself will come down from heaven, with a loud command, with the trumpet call of God, and the dead in Christ will rise first. After that we who are still alive and are left will be caught up together with them in the clouds to meet the Lord in the air. And so we will be with the Lord forever. Therefore encourage each other with these words.
1Thessalonians Chapter 4v16-18

A shaky do-The Skoda works raid 16/17th April 1943

Introduction

I first visited the graves of my Uncle's crew several years ago and also many other Commonwealth war graves sites over the following years. When I stood before the tombs of so many brave men it so moved me that I was determined to do something to honour them and all they did in the defence of our freedom. In the process of writing this account I have had the privilege of corresponding with and meeting some extraordinary people. Some of the airmen I interviewed have also become personal friends. This I consider to be a very high honour indeed.

The record of this raid does not make pleasant reading for the most part, but I felt it necessary to record even the unpleasant facts for the sake of the historical record. I hope that this story of the Plzeň raid and the men who flew on it will help to ensure the remembrance of these loved and lost. I also hope it will spur us all on to work and pray for peace.

****

The crews of Bomber Command, Harris' Old Lags, made a major contribution to the defeat of Nazi Germany by keeping tied up a million fit men who would otherwise have been in the front line, but instead were forced to defend every city in Germany. The enemy were kept guessing as to where they would be struck next. The strategic bombing offensive also tied up half of the German anti-aircraft guns which otherwise would have prevented an allied advance on the ground. The bombing of German industrial cities caused massive damage, requiring vast manpower to repair the damage. These men would otherwise have been fighting at the front. Albert Speer Germany's armaments minister stated that due to the vast numbers of troops, guns and ammunition drawn away from other theatres particularly the Russian front, this constituted a second front in early 1943. It was also vital to keep Stalin satisfied and prevent him from signing a pact with the Nazis.

R.A.F. Bomber Command mined every major enemy port, caused serious damage to the U-boat pens and sank or badly damaged many heavy warships. On top of that they seriously degraded the enemy's supply lines. They also gave the British people and her allies a great boost in morale to know that the enemy was being hit every bit as hard and more, as they were. It is a shameful fact that Bomber Command crews were not awarded a campaign medal. Even worse, they were vilified from certain quarters by what one veteran called 'the shiny a****' brigade of hind sighted journalists.' The joke is that they sit today in offices judging those who fought, whilst the fabric on the seat of their own pants becomes polished by many hours writing about wars, rather than fighting in them.

The crews of Bomber Command fought night after night under heavy fire and extreme conditions with grievous losses. For example of any 100 airmen who flew, 55 were killed on operations or died as result of wounds; 3 were injured on operations or active service; 12 were taken prisoner of war; 2 were shot down and evaded capture; 27 survived a tour (Approx. 30) of operations. Approximately 3,500 Australians died in Bomber Command in the Second World War. 10,000 Canadians, over 1,600 New Zealanders, nearly 1,000 Poles also gave the supreme sacrifice. Many other nationalities such as Americans, French, Belgians, Czechs and South Africans also died in the service of Bomber Command. It is also often forgotten that many ground crew were also killed.

Veteran Eddie Foster of 467 squadron commented in his memoires;

Many people cowering in air raid shelters in Berlin (or indeed London) would have visions of airmen aloft laughing gleefully as they dropped their bombs. The truth would be very different. They were young men who had become involved in a war that was none of their making and at that time would be suffering similar fears, sometimes terror, as were the unhappy civilians below. They were forever aware that violent and horrendous deaths were occurring in the skies around them and that their own demise might well be imminent.[1]

Another veteran wrote to me in 2006 saying;

'At the time we just got on with the job and tried not to think of the loss of so many crews. But now it makes me very sad.'

This account is not intended to be a glorification of war nor a vilification of the German people as a whole. After all they suffered as grievously as any anyone at the hands of the Nazis. Regarding German aircrew, the crews of Bomber Command had in general great respect for their adversaries. Bomber Command veterans have until recently met in friendship with their counterparts in the Nachtjagd (night fighter force). I have made many German friends who have helped in the research for this book, including German aircrew and civilians who were on the receiving end. I have never talked to a Bomber Command veteran who took delight in the loss of lives below them. But they had a job to do. There was 'every bit as much terror above as below', as one Pathfinder pilot and veteran of this raid commented.

If anyone requires evidence as to the difficulty of hitting any target accurately at night over long distances and under fire, then it is available in full measure regarding this raid. It is pure folly to look back over the years and morally criticize the method or the means by which the allies were to defeat the most evil regime in modern history and thus safeguard their own civilization.

Another veteran of the Plzeň raid asked me why I had chosen to write about an operation, which was a failure. My answer was that the men who flew on this operation were nonetheless worthy of remembrance and gratitude.

The German arms industry was hit hard during raids on Essen on the 5/6th of March, 12/13th of March and 3rd/4th of April 1943, which heavily damaged Krupp's factory. Like the landings at Arnhem, had the Plzeň raid been a success, it would have considerably shortened the war and saved many lives.

****

---

[1] Eddie Foster Navigator 467 sqn. http://www.467463raafsquadrons.com/Pages/TrueTales/eddiefosterstory.htm

Plzeň

The town of Plzeň is a very old one, known to have possessed a castle in 976 A.D. and was founded in 1290 by King Wenceslaus II of Bohemia. A brewery was in existence in the year 1307, and in 1468 an early printing press was operating in the city.

In November 1839 Emil Von Škoda was born in Plzeň, Bohemia. Škoda studied in Germany and then returned to Plzeň where he bought a small machine factory. There he began to produce weapons for the Austrian Army. The Škoda Works was to become the dominant heavy industry centre of Bohemia and the Austrian Empire being the country's steel making centre. The works were one of Europe's great armaments producers, rivalling Krupp's in Germany and Vickers in Britain. Škoda produced armour plate, heavy guns for the Austrian navy, also field and heavy artillery for the Austrian army. Of course the city is well known for the internationally famous beer (Pilsner), which has been exported worldwide. Chemicals, cement and ceramics have also been manufactured there.

British shareholders had benefited financially from their investment even as German forces rolled across Europe in the summer of 1940 using weapons manufactured at the Škoda works.

Attacks on the target began as early as 27/28th October of 1940 when 8 Whitleys from 51 Squadron were in action. Only one crew reported bombing. On the 19/20th November, 11 Whitleys from 58 Squadron and 8 Hampdens from 5 group, were tasked to attack the Škoda Works. No one found the target although the works were claimed to have been heavily bombed. Czech agents confirmed that on the night of the raid, three aircraft were missing[2] and the nearest R.A.F. bombs had fallen over fifty miles from the city.

On 25/26 April 1942 six Stirlings carried out a long-range attack on the Škoda factory, cloud covered the target but 5 Stirlings bombed and one Stirling was lost. Another attack followed on 4/5 May 1942 when five Stirlings went to Plzeň, one Stirling was lost.

In April of 1943 the Škoda work force had reached sixty-seven thousand. The core and traditional product line was guns of various calibres ranging from 3.7 cm and higher, anti-aircraft guns 8.8 cm and heavy guns up to 21 cm. Using all the work force available and extending the working hours to seventy-two per week, the management succeeded in boosting the works output to 2,677 guns in 1943, which represented 5.4% of the total production in German territory. The Škoda works was a major repair centre for tanks, both for the German army and their allies - Rumania (Romania) and Bulgaria. For the aircraft industry, thousands of castings for Argus AS10 and Focke-Wulf 190 engines were produced, as well as automated machine tools for the ammunition industry, submarine parts etc. As Plzeň was considered relatively safe against the ever-heavier raids, much investment activity was evident in view of expanding production, primarily of guns.[3]

On the night of 16th/17th of April 1943 the largest force so far was sent to destroy the Škoda works. It is this operation which is the subject of this book. A force comprising 327 aircraft codenamed operation 'Frothblower' set out. 271 aircraft were also tasked against Mannheim, (operation 'Chub') the other major target and diversionary raid. On the same night a force of 11 aircraft from 91 Group dropped Nickels[4] in the Rouen area, with one aircraft returning early. Three of the force encountered enemy aircraft but all managed to evade the attacks and return safely to base.

---

[2] TNA UK AIR27 ops records squadrons
[3] Dr. Vladislav Krátký, Škoda Museum, Plzen
[4] Propaganda leaflets

Chapter One
Target for tonight

The Škoda works raid was code named 'Frothblower'; perhaps someone's humorous reference to one of Plzeň's most famous products, Pilsner beer! It was to be a maximum effort 'Goodwood' operation.' The combined Mannheim and Škoda operations comprised five hundred and ninety eight aircraft. On the Plzeň raid alone this entailed three hundred and twenty seven aircraft and some two thousand three hundred airmen. The aiming point was to be the locomotive construction sheds.

The regular complement of a Lancaster and Halifax Bomber crew numbered seven. These were, pilot, bomb-aimer; flight engineer; navigator; wireless operator; mid-upper gunner; and lastly the rear gunner also known as 'Tail end Charlie.' Crews were often supplemented by an additional crew member under training.

To put a 'Goodwood' maximum effort into the air required large numbers of ground personnel including armourers, W/T mechanics, electricians, instrument fitters, engine fitters, spark plug testers, air frame fitters, riggers, radio mechanics, W.A.A.F. drivers and parachute packers, to name but a few. Before the raid the aircraft had been air tested and engines run up, then fuelled and armed. The effort that the ground crews put in to maintain a major bombing operation was enormous and they took great pride in their work. For example a Merlin engined Lancaster or Halifax had 96 spark plugs and 148 valves which needed cleaning and resetting often. No mean task!

Later in the afternoon the crews would be briefed for the night's operation. No doubt a groan went up from all the crews as they saw the ribbon stretch across the large wall map to Plzeň. The raid meant a round trip of some 1,600 or more miles across territory heavily defended by night fighters, flak and searchlight concentrations.

The briefing would be given by the met officer, followed by the flying control officer who would advise about the start up and taxi sequence to ensure the smooth take off of all bombers. The intelligence officer would then advise the crews of the route, the position of way marker flares, enemy flak, radar and fighter concentrations. The target marking method would also be explained. This would be followed by a briefing from the squadron and station commanding officers. The navigation leader would then address the men and synchronize watches. Finally there would be a word from the base commander. After this they would collect their escape aids and then go to the mess for the pre-flight meal. Having eaten, flying clothes would be donned.

Each Lancaster and Halifax was armed with eight .303 Browning machine guns mounted in turrets. There were two guns in the front turret (normally manned by the bomb aimer); two in the mid-upper turret and four in the rear turret. An exception to the eight-gun armament was many Halifaxes having the front turret removed and faired in. The 'Z' or Tollerton fairing (Tollerton Aircraft Services made the first conversion) was introduced in place of the rather protuberant Bolton Paul nose turret. This nose fairing was officially known as Mod. 398. It was also known as the "Z-fairing" because of the additional fuselage framing required to support the sheet metal covering. Slight differentiations in outline shape existed between the original conversions and later factory installed nose fairings. Invariably two forward horizontal windows were installed to restore some degree of forward vision. The 'Z' fairing existed on Halifax B MkII Series 1 (Specials). On still some others the mid-upper turret was removed also to improve aero-dynamics and bomb load! In these cases the redundant mid-upper gunner manned an observation blister or cupola placed in the ventral position, to keep an eye out for fighters approaching from behind and below. Indeed this was the direction from which most fighters attacked.

A Shaky do. The Plzen raid April 16/17th April 1943

Pennington ED611 (left side) and Shearman W4949 (Right side), 44 sqn crews ride to their aircraft on 16th April 43. Shearman and all but one of this crew were lost on ops to Oberhausen 14/15 June 1943. Shearman wears a moustache. Photo Pennington

When all preparations had been made, crews would walk, cycle or be driven out in vans to their aircraft. This was the time when crews felt most pensive as they gathered at the aircraft. Mid-upper gunner Bill Harrall in 44 sqn 'J' Johnny recalled,

'We then had time to think about what might happen to us but once we got on board the aircraft we had a job to do.'

Bill is second from the left in the photo above.

After pilot and flight engineer had done all their customary checks and perhaps a ritual 'watering' of the tail wheel or a particular routine of their own, they boarded their aircraft.

The roar of engines broke the silence and aircraft taxied in due order around the perimeter track as aircraft turned onto the allocated runways and lined up to await the green signal from the flight controller, to go. The few minutes prior to take off could also seem like an eternity.

Bomber Command Order Of Battle Plzeň (Škoda Works) 16/17th April 1943

Group	Squadron	Base	Type	Strength
1 Group	12	Wickenby	Lancaster	9
	100	Grimsby	Lancaster	10
	101	Holme On Spalding Moor	Lancaster	15
	103	Elsham Wolds	Lancaster	16
	460	Breighton	Lancaster	15
3 Group	115	East Wretham	Lancaster II	8
4 Group	10	Melbourne	Halifax	11
	51	Snaith	Halifax	17
	76	Linton On Ouse	Halifax	10
	77	Elvington	Halifax	15
	78	Linton On Ouse	Halifax	10
	102	Pocklington	Halifax	14
	158	Lissett	Halifax	16
5 Group	9	Bardney	Lancaster	8
	44	Waddington	Lancaster	12
	49	Fiskerton	Lancaster	7
	50	Skellingthorpe	Lancaster	10
	57	Scampton	Lancaster	13
	61	Syerston	Lancaster	13
	106	Syerston	Lancaster	14
	207	Langar	Lancaster	10
	467	Bottesford	Lancaster	15
6 Group Canadian	408	Leeming	Halifax	12
	419	Middleton St. George	Halifax	15
8 P.F.F.	35	Gravely	Halifax	10
	83	Wyton	Lancaster	12
	156	Warboys	Lancaster	10
Total Lancasters	197	Total Halifaxes	130	327 Total

38 airframe losses were recorded on the Plzen operation. 199 KIA, 52 pow, 13 evaders

271 Aircraft were tasked against Mannheim & 11 aircraft of 93 Group dropped Nickels in the Rouen area

In praise of the Halifax

In the fighter war the Spitfire often claimed all the accolades, the Hurricane being overlooked. Likewise in the bomber war the Lancaster receives much justified praise whilst the Halifax is often forgotten by the writers of history and the makers of documentary films. Her crews however will rightly defend her magnificent efforts and speak of her with pride and affection. Over 6,000 Halifaxes were built and between 1941 and 1945. They made over 75,000 bombing sorties and dropped 227,610 tons of bombs; more than a quarter of all bombs dropped on Germany by the Royal Air Force. She was also extensively used for special operations, glider towing and Coastal Command operations.

A Shaky do. The Plzen raid April 16/17th April 1943

The plan

The official plan was to fly at a much lower level than the normal 15-20,000 feet, at around 1500-ft through the main night-fighter belt across France. Certainly the ops records of 103 squadron state that, 'by command', they were to cross the fighter belt at 1,500 feet as did W4845 of that squadron flown by Sgt. Rudge. Sgt. Fletcher was flying Lancaster ED557 'Y' of 100 squadron. She flew between 500 and 2000 feet as flight engineer Sgt. Clarke noted in his log book.[5] He was on only his 3rd operation.

It was a night chosen for its full moon which it was hoped would facilitate accurate low level target location and aid navigation by enabling the bomb-aimers to pick out vital pinpoints en route. The moon would be 90% full and above the horizon during the operation. Of course a bomber's moon was also a night-fighter's moon! There were two major turning points to keep the enemy guessing as to the intended target. All groups would follow the same route. It must be stated that on the raid report track map, 5 Group is shown crossing the Pas de Calais area on the outward journey. However no evidence has been found that this was the case. Furthermore all five group aircraft investigated by the author did as the raid report stated follow the same route as the other groups. No route coordinates were mentioned in the raid report for any aircraft travelling just south of the Pas-de-Calais. It would also seem illogical for a large force of aircraft to merge in to another force in mid stream!

Before the force had even received the green light to go, at least five aircraft failed to take off. Flying Officer Evans captain of 50 squadron Lancaster ED470, didn't take off due to a member of the crew being ill. The same fate met ED491 captained by Huntley. ED769 'I' of 103 squadron, captained by Squadron leader Prickett, had unspecified mechanical problems. Squadron Leader Thiele's 'O' of 467 Squadron failed to take off due to problems with the port outer engine. Yet another aircraft from 10 squadron failed to make the start due to a defective flap jack. 78 squadron's Dowse and crew had problems with their allotted aircraft and so transferred to DT773, the reserve aircraft. 467 squadron and Bottesford also had the problem of an outbreak of diphtheria. All personnel were tested and those showing a reaction were inoculated. However, there was a war on and this medical drama did not stop the squadron from putting up a maximum effort of 15 aircraft.

So hundreds of aircraft from 27 squadrons were given the go ahead at around 21:00, with the Northern England based aircraft from Four and Six groups, setting off around 20:30. The throttles would be pushed to full power, the flight engineer helping the pilot keep the four throttle levers pushed forward so he could concentrate on the critical take off run. The heavily laden Lancasters and Halifaxes heaved into the sky to climb according to the official brief to about 13,000 feet or so. They would then push the nose down to pick up speed and cross the French coast around Cayeux and on into enemy territory.

Sgt. Brown on Halifax HR720 commented;

'We had a dream flight out. High over the French coastal defences and then dropping down to a few thousand feet for the West-East end of the trip. It was a clear moonlit night and Bert Doel settled down in the bomb aimer's position, as far as I can recall, some form of topographical map and a small light. For what seemed an age and must have been several hours he map read. I confirmed from my plotting, our track was perfect.'[6]

---

[5] RAF Museum archives Hendon MF100012/11
[6] Bill Chorley, In Brave Company

The average height flown was between ten and twenty thousand feet and most of the combat reports and night-fighter claims indicate an altitude of at least nine thousand feet. Many aircraft however, did fly very low indeed both on the outward and return journeys.

The drone of almost six hundred heavy and medium bombers would be heard crossing the French coast around Cayeux and then continuing on to the first turning point, a position North of Beauvais. They would then cross the region of the Aisne. Many flak positions would have to be faced. Another serious threat was the many night fighter stations from Juvincourt, St. Dizier, Leon-Athies, Florrennes etc. Onward they would go across the River Meuse, (49°27'N-5°12'E) and then the Mosselle (49°23'N-6°12'E) taking an hour from the coast to reach this point. The River Saar (49°21'N 6°42'E) was next and eastward into Germany. Way point Position 'B' was east of Saarlouis and north of Saarbrücken. The Plzeň force would then cross the Rhein at 49°14'N-8°24'E and aim to go through the 'gap' between Mannheim and Karlsruhe. In fact defences would still exist between these two cities. In the region of Bavaria they would then make a sharp turn north east at the last turning point at position 'C' west of Straubing on the Danube (Danau) and then make the final run up to the target at Plzeň.

The diversionary Mannheim force would follow the same route to Cayeux and a parallel track from Position 'A' near Beauvais until 49:20N 08:35E a position just half a mile north of the present day motor racing track at Hockenheim. Here they would part company with the Plzeň aircraft turning onto heading 328° for the run in to their target at Mannheim. Because both the Plzeň and Mannheim forces flew very similar tracks inbound and came up against the same defences I have included in the book some detail about a few Mannheim aircraft where relevant.

Mostly the fighter opposition would be twin engine Messerschmitt BF110s and Junkers 88s, with some Messerschmitt 210s. These would be waiting at beacons and designated boxes for the bombers to enter their area. This was known as the Kammhuber line and the system of defence known as Himmelbett. This consisted of a grid system stretching across the Low Countries and France. Fighters would patrol individual boxes within the grid, searchlight batteries attempting to pick out individual bombers with their radar guided master lights. They would also indicate the direction of the bomber stream in co-operation with the fighters. Würzburg radars would pick up the bomber stream at long distance and direct the fighters to within visual range their targets. This was known as G.C.I. Ground controlled interception. A few fighters would have had early examples of short-range air to air radar. If possible the night fighters would pick off the bombers which were adrift at the edges of the main stream or approach aircraft the gunners of which were less vigilant.

****

Enemy coast ahead

The Plzeň force would have started to funnel into some sort of loose stream over the south coast of England at Dungeness. The route then headed to 50:10N 01:30E (Cayeux) and on to 49.37N-02:05E (Position 'A' Beauvais/Amiens) – 49:20N 07:00E (Position 'B' near Saarbrücken) – 48:55N 12:30E (Position C on the Danube) - Plzeň - 49:50N 05:50E (Position 'D' Luxemburg) – 49:37N 02:05E (Beauvais/Amiens) – 50:10N 01:30E (Cayeux).

The outbound route after position 'A' north of Beauvais, went in a straight line East across France to the north of Saarbrücken and then continued on to a point in the Regensburg area at Straubing on the Danube. Yellow target indicators were to be dropped here by the pathfinders. Navigators would dead reckon from this point and time their run up to the target

PLZEN TRACKS TO AND FROM TARGET

Germany

Plzen

Dobrany

Pos C

Straubing

Regensburg

R Danube (Danau)

Munchen

Nurnberg

Wurtzburg

Darmstadt

Heilbron

Stuttgart

Mannheim

Karlsruhe

Ludwigshafen

Worms

Koblenz

R Rhein

River Rhein

Kaiserslautern

Koln

Pos B

R Saar

Saarbrucken

Bitburg

Trier

Metz

Pos D

Luxembourg

Belgium

Sedan

River Meuse

Bruxelles
(Brussel)

Phillipeville

Mons

Laon

River Aisne

St Quentin

Reims

Noyon

Amiens

France

Calais

Dungeness

Cayeux

Pos A

Beauvais

Plzen force route via positions A, B, C, D.

Distance from Pos. A to Pos.C = 471 miles (759 Km)

Navigator's log 207 sqn. 16/17th April 1943

TIME	RQD. TRACK (T)	W/V USED AND D.R. DRIFT	Course (T)	Course (M)	NAVIGATIONAL OBSERVATIONS (Pin-points, Fixes, Position Lines, Actual T.M.G., Actual Drift, G/S and. W/V, Manoeuvres, etc.)	GENERAL OBSERVATIONS (Met. Conditions, Bombing, Intelligence, Enemy Action, etc.)	R.A.S.	HEIGHT & A. TEMP	T.A.S.	D.R. G/S	DIST. TO RUN	D.R. TIME	E.T.A.
2215					WATCHES SYNCHRONISED								
2130					CHOCKS AWAY. DR Compass checked.	COMPASS CHECKED.							
Det 34					BASE AIRBORNE. DR	COMPASS ON.							
2142½	141	N.L	141	151	BASE S/C DEBDEN. Climbing	HT 3000' (ETA 2210)	164	4000	188	188	81	26	2205½
2156					FIX 51°23'N 00°6'W.	G/S = 198 MPH							
2206					FIX 52°02'N 00°12'E								
2208½ /159		220/5	163	173	DR DEBDEN S/C DUNGENESS	HT 11000' (ETA 2235)	164	11000 –7	204	196	80	27½	2233
2209					FIX 51°34'N 00°21'E	START AIRPLT.							
2202					FIX 51°24'N 00°35'E	TMG = 163° G/S = 193							
2227					W/V = 163/05 TR 445								
2230½					DR 51°00'N 0.0°42'								
2234	151	220/5	150	164	DUNGENESS (S/E) circling	HT 17000'	164	17000 –20	214	206	102	30	23
2238					DUNGENESS S/C A.								
2241½					NAV LIGHTS OUT	IFF off							
2245					FIX 50°36'N 01°05'E	BOMBS FUSED							
2249					FIX 50°2'8'N 01°09'E								
2253					FIX 50°1'N 01°16'E	increase W/S + 160.							
					TMG = 164 G/S = 186								
					W/V = 110/14U TR 645 (?)	river							
2303-120	120	130	120	130	crossing east TR 645	S/C A	168	18000	214	225	36	9½	23
2309½ /093	093	51/022	089	501	DR 49°52'N 01°23'E		176	14000 –7	222	236	221	53½	0103
238					DR A S/C B	increase IAS to cross fighter belt	186		230	240			
2331					following river same bearing attack probable Post 2							
2331					crossing same river								
					approx. 49°29'N 04°40' E								
2334					W/V = 276/26 Air plot. Travelling N for river suspect 7331 a/c low error on								
2348					DR 44°24'N 05°50'E	Climbing 15000	164	15000 –5		270	58	16½	0044½
2354					B/A believes we are crossing river (Moselle?)								
0002					River running || on STB.								
0003	144	27/13	144	151	River breaking away	S/B D (B/P)	168	25000 –17	310	270	240	66	0111

(Nat Bury)

20

Navigator's log 207 sqn. 16/17th April 1943 Cont.

Time	Remarks
0016	FIT POS. B. S/C (ETA 0111)
	F/AIR S/H's AHEAD. EVIDENCE of raid in progress
	Probably MANNHEIM. A/C to STBD. to
	clear it. Also to get back closer
0026	to track.
	Back on original course
	APPROX W/V 1235/211 A/H 167.
0033	Crossing RHINE
0037	Violent evasive action to avoid S/Ls.
	Avery accurate Flak. Suspect several
	hits.
0046	S/Ls evaded. 14 9500'
0050	A/S increased
0114 / 0035	DR C - no flares. s/c TARGET
0134	TARGET SIGHTED. A/C visually to STBD
0148	TARGET ATTACKED - C.B. A/C turning on
	GREEN 776. Overshot first s/c TARGET WELL
	Alight ES/1?. little flak.
0158	TARGET S/C CON POINT.
0213	DR 49°43'N 12°05'E. Increase A/S.
0221	DR 49°46'N 11°79'E. Increase A/S.
0228½	In 49°41'N 10°50'E.
0244	DR CON POINT. ETA D 0334.
0259	Crossing RHINE
	WELL P/ange'd town to STBD
0227½	Smoke rising to 12000'
	DR D S/C A.
0440	DIVERSION - TANGMER
0413	DR A S/C DUNGENESS
0417	VIOLENT EVASIVE ACTION to avoid searchlight
	A/C
0426	Unable to find coast.
0430	SPG U.S.
0446	Homing on SPG.
0450	SPG U.S.
0451	Crossing coast DUNGENESS ly. TBO
0453	IFF ON

(Nat Bury)

TIME	RQD. TRACK (T)	W/V USED AND D.R. DRIFT	Course (T)	Course (M)	NAVIGATIONAL OBSERVATIONS (Pin-points, Fixes, Position Lines, Actual T.M.G., Actual Drift, G/S and W/V, Manoeuvres, etc.)	GENERAL OBSERVATIONS (Met. Conditions, Bombing, Intelligence, Enemy Action, etc.)	R.A.S.	HEIGHT & A. TEMP.	T.A.S.	D.R. G/S	DIST. TO RUN	D.R. TIME	E.T.A.
0451	276				from rough B.G's BRIGHTON	(S9) BRS. B500 T.							
0505		—	276	286	DUNGENESS S/C TANGMERE.	NAV lights ON.	180	8,000	203	203			
0514	260	—	260	270	D.R 50°51'N 00°15'E.	S/C TANGMERE.			203	203	44	13	0527
0528					TANGMERE								
0540					TANGMERE B.S. landed.	✓							
0545					SWITCHES OFF	IFF OFF							
1115	?				TANGMERE CHOCKS AWAY	✓							
1119	?				TANGMERE Airborne	DR Compass ON							
1124	356	N.W.	356	007	TANGMERE S/C BASE	✓	186	4760	183	183	142	45	1209
1139					Crossing THAMES on track.	G/S=210							
1143					Drift= 6°S. Diff. recorded.	✓							
					W/U= 215/33 TR/615.								
					Homing to BASE								
1201					A/C lor BASE								
1202					BASE								
1209					BASE S/C BOTTESFORD								
1212					BOTTESFRD								
1216					BOTTESFORD landed								
1220					SWITCHES OFF.								

Signed.........................Navigator

MEMORANDA

SQUARE SEARCH

HEIGHT		W/V		VAR.		VIS.		T.A.S.	
Track T	Course M	D.R. G/S	DIST.	D.R. TIME.	T.I.T.	DIST.	D.R. TIME	T.I.T.	DIST.	T.T.T.
		2V			6V			10V	
		2V			6V			10V	
		4V			8V			12V	
		4V			8V			12V	

(Nat Bury)

Navigator's log 207 sqn. 16/17th April 1943 Cont.

FORM 441

SQUADRON...	A/C NUMBER...	LETTER... D DATE 16/4/43
CAPTAIN... S.G.T. STEPHENS	2nd PILOT... Sgt. Bury	
NAVIGATOR... Sgt. ...		
CREW... Sgt. Pegrum, Sgt. Rowput, Sgt. McDavitT, Sgt. Llewellyn.		
SPECIAL... Sgt. PILSEN		
ORDERS... all A/c return at 0210. Bomb 2000'		

	SUN		MOON		TWILIGHT	
	RISES	SETS	RISES	SETS	A.M.	P.M.

WATCH .... AT .... G.M.T. Fast / Slow RATE ....secs./hour Gaining / Losing

FORECAST WINDS

STAGE	FROM TO	,000 FT.		,000 FT.		,000 FT.		,000 FT.	
		FROM T.	SPEED	FROM T.	SPEED	FROM T.	SPEED	FROM T.	SPEED

Main log

FROM / TO	W/V USED	HEIGHT FT.	T.A.S.	RQD. TRACK (T)	COURSE (T)	VAR.	COURSE (M)	D.R. G/S	DIST.	TIME
A/B 2135										
BASE 2140 / DEBDEN 2210	/	3 / 17000	'55 / 166	141	141	10	151	186	81	26
DEBDEN (07-13) / DUNGENESS 2235	27%/15	1-16000	155 / 199	159	163	10	173	190	86	25
DUNGENESS 32-38 / A 2303	27%/15	16 / 18000	'55 / 212	151	155	9	164	208	102	24½
A / B 0001	279/15	18000	(160) / 220	045	098	7	105	230	221	58
B / C	279/10	18000	(160) / 210	091	097	5	102	226	248	68
C 0111 / PILSEN 0140	279/10	10000	(160) / 194	035	032	5	037	199	70	21
PILSEN 0147 / D	279/10	10000	197	271	276	6	272	187	340	1"49
D 0334		10000 / 1000	(170) / 215	265	265	8	273	245	169	47
D / A 0425	/	1000	(155) / 174	331	334	9	3.40	174	102	35
DUNGENESS		7000	(160)							
DUNGENESS 0430-0530 0458 / 0503-0545	/	7000	164	339	339	10	349	184	80	26

WEATHER FORECAST

A. 49°37'N 02°05'E
B. 49°20'N 07°00'B
C. 48°55'N 12°30'E
D. 49°50'N 05°50'E
EV.574 EV.575 - 2330-0130 0215-0330
A126 RWS X.160
ConP7. 0239
S ... red star

(Nat Bury)

at Plzeň and the late runners would see the target indicators in the distance. The run out from chocks away to target took about five hours.

Several aircraft turned back with various maladies even before the French coast at Cayeux. Halifax DK169 on a heading 275° and twenty miles from Skegness, ditched her bombs in sea due to the rear turret being unserviceable. 158 squadron Halifax HR780 returned from forty miles south east of Felixstowe and dropped her load in the sea not far from Lissett. She wouldn't climb.

DT689 of 419 squadron based at Middleton St. George, turned back at 22:53 hours from 50:26'N 01:20'E dropping her bombs twelve miles off the French coast with three of her rear guns out of action. At 22:56 101 squadron Lancaster ED377 returned with the starboard inner engine unserviceable from the Chelmsford area, and the North Sea received another few thousand pounds of explosives fifty miles north east of Skegness. Bomb loads were dropped in this way because it was a very unsafe thing to try to land an aircraft with over two thousand gallons of fuel and several thousand pounds of high explosives! Bombs and bombers were expendable, but crews took many months to train.

The enemy was now well and truly aware of the presence and direction of the bomber stream. Indeed Luftwaffe operators would have been aware of the imminence of a big raid by the number of air tests being conducted earlier in the day and would have also been monitoring the signals given off by the H2s and Gee[7] sets as crews switched them on.[8] Enemy long range radars would also have picked up large numbers of aircraft forming up over southern England. Observers on the French coast would keenly note their direction as they crossed the coast. Meanwhile, aircraft of the Pathfinder force 8 Group, under the command of D.C.T. Bennett had made their way well into enemy territory. It would be their job to mark the target. Flight Lieutenant Lang of 156 P.F.F. squadron, (Lancaster W4943) observed twelve 'ineffective' searchlights in the Beauvais area at 22:24 hours. Flying at 15,000 feet, 35 squadron Halifax BB320, turned back from just south of Cayeux at 22:40 with three guns out of action.

In an attempt to confuse the enemy regarding the intended target, the raid planners had plotted a significant change in direction of the track from a heading of approximately 150° at Crévecoeur le Grand (approximately thirty kilometres to the north of Beauvais) onto course of 090° true. This was known as position 'A'. For another two hours the Plzeň force would continue eastward through the night fighter belt and very many flak positions, before the next turning point.

Thirty five P.F.F. squadron Halifax W7873 'W', flying straight and level at 16,000 feet, saw some flak in the distance. At 22:56 hours she was suddenly hit by what the crew thought was a salvo of flak underneath the aircraft. The starboard inner engine immediately caught fire and began to burn furiously followed by the starboard outer going unserviceable. The flight engineer cut off petrol flow to the starboard inner and tried to feather it but was not able to do so.[9] The fire spread rapidly and there was no time to put the fire drill into practice before the aircraft was pulled onto its back by the drag from the port engines. She then began spiralling and losing height. The pilot Flight Lieutenant Owen gave orders to stand by to bale out. The flight engineer unplugged his inter-com and went to the forward hatch to open it but it was jammed. Eventually he opened it and went to get his parachute. By the time he returned the wireless operator and probably the navigator had baled out. After Flight Sergeant Allen had left the aircraft he saw it begin to break up. Upon landing, Allen and Bradley saw the aircraft burning furiously in the next field. P/O Cruickshank the bomb aimer,

---

[7] H2s was a downward-looking early ground radar and Gee a navigation aid enabling navigators to obtain a fix.
[8] Gee was a system of three transmitters sending a grid of signals which could be read off a screen and plotted on a lattice chart giving a reasonable positional fix.
[9] Loss report K1 AIR14/1442 TNA UK.

24

Sgt. Martyn the navigator, F/Sgt. Bourne the mid-upper gunner and Sgt. Young, the tail gunner were all killed.

In fact Owen's aircraft was the first Night fighter victim of the night as reported by Lt. Helmut Bergmann of Stb.III./NJG4 who stated in his combat report...

"Towards 22.53 hrs I was directed to an enemy aircraft flying at a height of 5.800 metres. Around 23.00 hrs I saw it 200-300 metres to my left and some 400 metres above me. I positioned myself underneath the aircraft which I identified as a Halifax and attacked from below and behind. Immediately, a fierce fire broke out between the two right-hand engines. The aircraft slowly went down. Around 23.03 hrs I saw the crash fire, the place of impact was 15 km NW Rethel near Sevigny."[10]

This was Lt. Helmut Bergmann's ninth victory. He and his crew, Uffz. Hauthal and Obgefr. Pritsch were to be especially busy this night.

Owen was taken prisoner of War and sent to Stalag Luft III.[11] Bradley and Allen were to successfully evade enemy captivity. Evaders and prisoners of war are listed in the appendix of the book.

Also of 35 squadron, Flight Lieutenant Cranswick had an eventful outward journey. In apparently clear skies, he was abruptly shaken to see a Messerschmitt Bf110 appear from nowhere, dead ahead and closing with breathtaking speed head-on. Instinctively pushing his control column hard forward, he felt the shock waves as the equally startled German pilot pulled up the nose of his aircraft and passed over the Halifax, missing a horrendous collision by literally inches. The vibration of its passing almost lost Cranswick control over his bomber, but he soon recovered and pressed on to his target. [12]

At 23:06 hours a main force aircraft, Lancaster W4949 'H' (44 squadron) had a brief encounter at 20,000 feet with what they thought was as a Messerschmitt Bf109 single engine fighter at 49.46'N 02'E over Poix de la Somme (now Poix de Picardy). On a course 097°, the rear gunner Sgt Akeister saw the enemy 1,000 yards below on the port quarter, and immediately opened fire as the fighter closed in to 700 yards, climbing to the port quarter above to make a dead astern attack. The rear gunner continued firing with a couple of long bursts and the enemy broke off the attack on the green quarter below and disappeared into cloud.[13] The temperature at that height was around -20°F. Despite the many reports of single-engine night fighters operating, it is unlikely that any actually did, the BF109/Fw190 experiments by the Nachtjagd Versuchs Kommando of Hajo Herrmann only started in May and June 43. These became known as Wilde Sau (Wild Boar) operations.

The night fighters were now airborne in numbers and prowling in search of outbound bombers. At 23:20 hours a Junkers 88 twin engine fighter approached Halifax HR787 'J' of fifty-one squadron on the starboard quarter below at about four hundred and fifty yards range. The Junkers was spotted by the rear gunner Sergeant Green whilst cruising at thirteen thousand feet at a ground speed of 194 miles per hour. The heading was 103° magnetic. The enemy had dropped red marker flares to indicate the track of the bomber and the fighter opened up with its nose armament and a two second burst. The Halifax rear gunner did not open fire and the enemy aircraft was not seen again. No doubt because the fighter realising he had been spotted, decided discretion was the better part of valour and turned away from the port quarter level, to find a less vigilant opponent. He had missed the Halifax causing no

---

[10] Dr. Theo Boiten
[11] Footprints in the Sands of Time, Oliver Clutton-Brock
[12] Bomber Barons, Chaz Boyer. Permission for use obtained from Pen and Sword Publishers.
[13] Combat reports AIR50/180 National Archives UK

A Shaky do. The Plzen raid April 16/17th April 1943

damage. The Halifax's rear gunner seeing the fighter turn away would not pick a fight if he could avoid it.

Bill Harrell a mid-upper gunner on 44 squadron kept his mind on the job and didn't engage in unnecessary chatter over the inter-com. He remembered an operation when he was standing in for another gunner on leave;

'The crew I was with were chattering away as if they were on holiday. This made me very nervous as their minds were not on the job.'

Crews never liked having an 'Odd Bod' on the crew. They were a close knit team and didn't like unknown quantities. Bill was later awarded the D.F.M. and also completed a second tour on 582 squadron, Pathfinders.

Searchlights were seen indicating the track of the bomber stream, when at 23:30 hours Flight Sgt. Virgo's 10 squadron Halifax (JB910) was at twelve thousand feet cruising in clear weather above some cloud. A few miles south east of Rethel, (49:28'N 04:25'E) rear gunner flight Sergeant Hill saw a Messerschmitt BF110 on the starboard quarter down, 300 yards away and six hundred feet below. The Halifax showing an indicated airspeed of 155 M.P.H. began to weave and as the enemy aircraft closed in underneath the rear gunner lost sight of him. The blister gunner Sgt. Tester (the mid-upper turret had been removed)[14] then sighted the enemy and instructed the captain to dive to port. The night fighter now only 300 yards astern opened fire with cannon and machine guns. At the same time, Sgt. Hill opened fire with several short bursts scoring hits between the fuselage and port engine on the BF110. The enemy then closed in to 100 yards, stalled and exploded. The port wing and engine broke off resulting in the fighter spiralling down in flames to crash at St. Menehould near Châlons-sur-Marne [15] (now Châlons-en-Champagne.) The enemy aircraft was flown by Fw. Rase of 6th Staffel NJG4. Rase baled out safely and was destined to survive the war but his bordfunker Uffz. Rolf Langhoff, was killed in this action.

Flight Sgt. Hill had fired 250 rounds of ammunition and the Halifax suffered a cannon shell through the port inner propeller and a small hole in the port wing tip. The crew were uninjured.[16] The bomb aimer this night was Jack Hulley a member of Tom Thackray's crew, standing in for the regular crewman. The Bf110 was claimed destroyed. Sgt. Hill was trained at 7 A.G.S. and 24 O.T.U. The blister gunner Sgt. Tester was trained at number 9 A.G.S.

Considering the ferocity of air combat and danger experienced every night by Bomber Command aircrew as evidenced above, I shall introduce an anecdote regarding the pilot of the above crew. Virgo a big blonde Australian and his crew were walking to their aircraft prior to a raid one evening, when a Warrant Officer on a bicycle saw them laughing and joking loudly with hands in pockets. The overeager W/O asked them where they thought they were going. A quick reply came from the big Aussy, "We're going on ops, you coming?" No answer came from the W/O![17]

A 9 squadron Lancaster crew, (ED836) also had a combat at this hour and area. This time flying at 11,000 feet on heading 130° Sgt. Turp's rear gunner Sgt. Shelmerdine, sighted a twin engine enemy aircraft on the starboard quarter at 500 yards. The captain commenced to weave and was on standby to corkscrew. When the enemy closed to 450 yards the corkscrew manoeuvre was begun. The mid-upper gunner Sgt. Silvester had also seen the enemy aircraft and as the fighter approached both gunners fired two 3-second bursts at 400 hundred and 250 yards respectively. Soon the enemy broke away; both gunners again fired 3-

---

[14] The 'blister' was ventral position manned by the mid/upper gunner.
[15] Dr. Theo Boiten. Location of crash
[16] TNA UK AIR50/194 combat report.
[17] Tom Thackray, 10 Sqn veteran and association newsletter editor.

A Shaky do. The Plzen raid April 16/17th April 1943

second bursts. The enemy aircraft was then seen to orbit on the port beam and then stand off at 700 yards. A final diving turn to port was executed by Turp and the fighter was lost to view.[18]

Another contact was made with the enemy at 23:30 hours in the area of Noyon with the bright moon on the starboard beam. Sgt. Carter the rear gunner on 77 squadron Halifax JB804, sighted a light in the air 2,000 to 4,000 yards on the port beam which was more than likely a decoy by the enemy. Suddenly a Junkers 88 twin engine fighter attacked from 800 yards closing to 600 yards and firing. The Halifax took evasive action and dived steeply to port, Sgt. Carter opening fire at 400 yards for two seconds. The enemy soon broke off the attack to the starboard beam.[19] The whole encounter lasted a mere six seconds and no damage was done to the aircraft, which was based at Elvington near York.

At 23:44 hours many aircraft were still making their way across France when observation posts in the Metz area had already passed a message on to Stuttgart air traffic control, warning of the advancing Bomber Command forces. It was taking aircraft about an hour to cross France with much attention from light flak and fighters. There was also the need to keep a close look out for other bombers. For those crews who flew low near the deck, the risk was less from fighters but increased from light flak and crashing into the ground. Tell tale shadows on the ground on a bright moonlit night such as this were also a problem. Higher up they missed most of the flak but would be silhouetted against the sky. It was important to maintain a position as near as possible within the main stream. To be a stray aircraft was to invite unwanted attention.

At a point somewhere between the French coast and Mannheim, Sgt. McRae's Halifax DT690 of 51 Sqn. was attacked by a JU88 fighter when flying straight and level at 9,000 feet. The fighter came in from underneath on the port bow firing one long burst of tracer and scoring many hits. The port outer engine was hit in the radiator and the exhaust blown off. A line of holes also appeared across the main plane between the inboard engine and the fuselage, the inner flap being badly damaged. A large two-foot square hole was made in the rudder and one bullet went through the rear turret just above the Sgt. Jones' head. The pilot Sgt. McRae tried to take violent evasive action but was prevented from doing so by the rudder damage and only managed a shallow dive to port. The rear gunner had seen the fighter dive away without firing. As he continued to rotate his turret the enemy attacked again but overshot and scored no hits. The fighter then drew level, turning away to starboard. As he did so, Sgt. Jones gave him a burst of 400 rounds at 150-200 yards scoring hits on his port engine which emitted blue flames. Sgt. Allerdice the flight engineer was standing on lookout in the Astro hatch and saw a yellow flash and a fire on the ground about six miles astern and to port. The crew thought it was the fighter crashing.[20] Possibly though, this was the enemy aircraft shot down by Virgo's Halifax as only one enemy fighter was shot down in this sector. Although the port outer was having serious trouble and the rudder a little sluggish, the other three engines were running well and the Halifax continued on.

[18] TNA UK AIR50/180 combat report. The aircraft is listed as ED480 'U' in this report.
[19] National Archives Australia A11305 206/7/AIR 466 Sqn RAAF combat reports.
[20] K35&41 AIR 14/1442 report TNA UK.

Chapter Two
Crossing the Rhein

The loss of another Plzeň bound bomber at the hands of a night fighter occurred at 00:03, a 408 squadron Halifax crashing at Louppy-Le-Chateau to the east of Châlons-Sur-Marne. All seven crew lost their lives. Lt. Friedrich Tober of IV./NJG4 probably was the victor in this combat. Tober survived the war.

Allied losses were already mounting with Lt. Helmut Bergmann of Stb. III./NJG4 claiming his second of the night, a Mannheim bound Wellington (HE501) of 466 squadron, captained by Tozer R.A.A.F. The aircraft crashed at Seraincourt at 23:56.

At 23:44 hours already between Karlsruhe and Mannheim, Sgt. Able's 106 squadron Lancaster (ED451) was at 15,000 feet. With the bright three-quarter moon on the starboard beam, the pilot saw an enemy aircraft on the port bow and warned the crew. Sgt. Barber the mid-upper gunner, soon identified the enemy fighter on the port beam at 330 yards range and saw it turn into the attack. Sgt. Barber opened fire with two long bursts as the pilot corkscrewed to port. The enemy did not open fire and was lost to sight on the port quarter whilst the wireless operator in the Astro-dome, saw another fighter (thought to be a Focke-Wulf 190) astern and above, closing rapidly in a shallow dive. As the fighter passed over the rear gunner's turret he gave it a short burst, the Lancaster was still corkscrewing.

Soon the mid-upper gunner saw another fighter (thought to be an Fw 190), possibly the one which attacked first, on the starboard quarter at 200 yards and opened fire with a long burst, claiming hits. The enemy did not open fire but turned away steeply from the starboard quarter passing below the Lancaster. As this fighter was breaking away, the rear gunner Sgt. Brown sighted the second at 300 yards on the port quarter. He immediately opened fire with three short bursts forcing the enemy to break away to port beam below without firing. He was not seen again. The Lancaster's gunners had fired 1,700 rounds in this action.[21]

Just south of the Luxembourg border with France at 23:55 hours, 158 squadron Halifax HR722 'C' skippered by Flight Lieutenant Donaldson, was making good progress doing 191 M.P.H. at 9,000 feet on a heading of 103 magnetic. The crew spotted a searchlight which appeared to be indicating the bombers' track. The rear gunner, Pilot Officer Willis then sighted two Ju88s, one with a red light and another with a white light in the nose, flying at the same height on starboard quarter at 660 yards range. The skipper plunged the Halifax into cloud and the enemy aircraft were lost. Only thirteen minutes later another JU88 was sighted astern and below at 600 yards which then closed to 400 yards. The Halifax dived and corkscrewed as the rear gunner fired a short burst and the enemy aircraft was shaken off. Shortly after this, the bomber was again attacked by a fighter with a red light in its nose on the starboard quarter level, at 75 yards range. The Halifax turned into the attack, the rear gunner simultaneously firing a short burst as the enemy broke away to port and was not seen again. The rear gunner had fired two hundred rounds.[22]

The corkscrew manoeuvre was standard evasive action when attacked by fighter from the rear. The aircraft was put in to a steep dive turning one direction, then pulling up steeply in the opposite direction. The gunner who first sighted the fighter usually called the Corkscrew. For example the rear gunner might call over the intercom, "fighter one thousand yards port quarter, range 1000 yards positioning for attack. Range 900 yards closing. Prepare to corkscrew port, range 600 yards, prepare to corkscrew port, GO!" If he had chance the gunner would get in a burst at the enemy. During this manoeuvre the other members of the crew would stay off the intercom unless absolutely necessary. Sometimes if the intercom was

[21] AIR50/208 combat reports TNA UK.
[22] AIR50/222 combat reports TNA UK.

out of action a system of lights was used by the gunners to communicate with the pilot as shown below;

Enemy aircraft sighted –Rapid A.A.A.'s
Enemy aircraft coming in on Port-series of DITS. When dits stop, turn to Port.
Enemy aircraft coming in on Starboard-series of DASHES. When dashes stop, turn to Stb.
Corkscrew -K. K. K.'s
Resume course -R.R.R.'s
All clear-One long dash
Send someone to rear gunner-slow N.N.N.'s

It was not unknown for certain crew members to float upwards in a negative 'G' state as the aircraft dived followed by a sudden drop as the aircraft climbed.

Crews had been flying at varied heights ranging from twenty thousand feet to one hundred feet but mostly at around 10,000 feet. Sgt. Tribe, a Canadian pilot flying 12 squadron Lancaster ED357, was flying very low indeed through the fighter belt across France. His flight engineer Geoff Collier remembers pulling up to miss church spires and recalls over-flying a factory from which emerged a surprised worker who threw some cinders on a spoil heap as he looked up at the Lancaster with a pipe in his mouth!

Flying 100 squadron Lancaster ED553, also on 'the deck', was American Flight Lieutenant Julian who had joined up with the Royal Canadian Air Force. He was warned by his navigator to watch his airspeed. Back came a calm response in classic southern drawl from the Texan,

"It's aw-right navigator aam jus' flyin' over a li'le hill."[23]

At 23:59 207 squadron Lancaster ED412 was observed to have crossed the river Moselle at 15,000 feet by navigator Sgt. Love. Fifteen minutes later he saw 'evidence of a raid in progress', with flak and searchlights ahead. In fact zero hour for the Mannheim raid was at 00:45 hours and Love had most probably seen the results of Plzeň aircraft dropping their loads early on an alternative target. Love was apparently quite a character who somehow managed to hang on to his navigator's log detailing the crew, aircraft code, observations and route to and from Plzeň,[24] much to the gratitude of this author! By all accounts he did not pay too much attention to detail when filling out forms. Indeed on the form for the 16/17th April raid he put the wrong aircraft code letter at the top of the form 441.

Flight Engineer Nat Bury comments;

'I am afraid, that although we had a first class navigator he was often in trouble for not including the aircraft letter or number and other omissions. In fact after one raid he was asked once by the navigator leader if the kite had flown itself, having omitted all our names from the form! Being Canadian he was almost a law to himself. Sadly he passed away in 2005.'

---

[23] Article 'Missing Škoda' Air Mail Spring 1993
[24] Form 441 Navigational Log of Sgt. Love, provided by Nat Bury 207 Sqn.

As numbers of aircraft crossed the Rhein they met increasingly heavy opposition and concentrations of flak. At 23:50 hours Flying Officer Elderfield's 50 squadron Lancaster ED784 'N' had got as far as Saarbrücken but was driven into cones of searchlights by two Messerschmitt Bf110s, heavily damaged by flak and forced to turn for home. At two minutes past midnight Sgt. Brook in 101 squadron Lancaster ED650, had loss of oil pressure in his port inner and bombed Saarbrücken suffering some flak damage in the fuselage and headed for home.

Sgt. Jock Baird the mid-upper on Sgt. Rudge's crew (Lancaster W4845 'Q') remembered;

'We were warned to slip by Saarbrücken, but went slap bang over this town and were quickly coned by twenty to thirty searchlights. We were around seven thousand feet at this point and Den Rudge our skipper threw our heavily laden aircraft around like a Spitfire and did break free. We sustained a bit of flak damage, but.... onward to Plzeň. During the above aerobatics we got so low I saw the slates shining on the roof tops. Being the mid-upper I had the best view of the crew.'

At 00:37 four minutes after having crossed the Rhein, a 207 squadron Lancaster (ED412) flown by Sgt. Stephens, was cruising at 15,000 feet when forced to take violent evasive action to avoid searchlights. They were shot up by flak, suspecting several hits, and in the process of evasion were down to 9,500 feet. It took the crew nine frantic minutes and a dive of over five thousand feet to evade the grasp of the lights! The bombers had now been in the air for about four hours.

Shortly after midnight at 00:16 hours, 158 Sqn Halifax HR758 became engaged in combat when well north of track to the northwest of Kaiserslautern.

According to a local police report;

A bomber aircraft flew low over Börrstadt going in an easterly direction above the village of Goelheim It was attacked by a German fighter (Bf110) and forced to turn off its course. It again turned and flew over Börrstadt and it was noticed that it was losing height; it was clearly seen to be a four motor bomber. Suddenly it burst into flames and at the same time witnesses report seeing two men bale out. The aircraft was still circling and suddenly there was an explosion, whereupon the aircraft broke into two pieces and crashed burning into the woods near Hahnweilerhof about two miles north of Börrstadt.

The attacking fighter was flown by at flown by Oblt. Gerhard Friedrich 10./NJG4. The Halifax was his 6th victory. However the night fighter was also brought down as the bomber had returned fire simultaneously at the attacker.[25] In any case the load of incendiary bombs (450x4lb, 90x4 'X' type & 24x30lb) and the port wing of the bomber had caught fire. The bomb aimer Pilot Officer Barrett, in an act of selfless bravery had held the forward hatch open for others to bale out, as it would not jettison. Sgt. Newdick, the mid-upper gunner received a blow on the head as he baled out and remembered little. When he reached the ground and released the toggle it fell away off the main harness strap! Fawcett the rear gunner was badly burned about the face and hands when escaping from the blazing turret.[26]

At the scene of the crash the Australian pilot, Flying Officer Jay, was found dead lying beside the burning aircraft. He was identified by his wristwatch. The body of bomb aimer, Pilot Officer Barrett was discovered 300 metres from the crash site at 08:00 hours on

[25] Info provided by Eddie Fell originally sourced from Kirchheimbolenden town archives.
[26] J. Alwyn Phillips' Valley of the Shadow of Death incorrectly identifies this enemy a/c as a BF109

the 17th of April, his parachute had not opened. He was identified by a cigarette case and I. D. tags. The German authorities buried these two men on the 23rd of April at 09:30 with full military honours. The mayor of Börrstadt, Herr Gilbrin spoke some appropriate words. Police constables Grasser of Rockenhausen, Schwartz of Börrstadt, Vath of Vinnweiler and the German home guard of Börrstadt and Imsbach were also present. Sergeants Ford and Newdick were apprehended at 01:00 hours. Sgt. Fawcett was captured near the crash site in the morning. Sgt. Holmes was also arrested in the morning by Pfc Karl Gresser at Gehrweiler and taken to Rockenhausen police station. Ford, Newdick, Fawcett and Holmes were handed over to Corporal Gehr at Börrstadt railway station 16:50 hours on the 17th of April. The navigator Scholes was captured at Langmeil and taken to Kaiserslautern in a lorry by an army officer. The five prisoners of war were taken to Dulag Luft interrogation centre and then to various prisoner of war camps.[27] The aircraft had been carrying 2,116 gallons of fuel when she set out. She also carried Tinsel and Mandrel electronic countermeasures equipment.

The aircraft was well north of track which again demonstrates the difficulty of navigating under combat conditions over long distances at night. The navigator had to keep very careful watch on airspeed and direction and time. Using Gee he could get a reasonably accurate fix up to a two or three hundred miles out. But the enemy would be trying their best to jam the signal. Astro-navigation was also used but not without risk. The navigator would take several star shots and average out the readings to obtain a fix. The danger in this would be that it would be necessary to fly straight and level for several minutes. An aircraft flying thus would be more at risk from flak and fighters.

Lt. Norbert Pietrek of 2./NJG4 was heading back towards a beacon, cursing the R.A.F. jamming that was blocking his link with the ground controller. At approximately 00:30 while still circling the beacon he spotted what he described as a 'barn door', a large, easy target in fact a Stirling four engine bomber (Mannheim op). The fighter pilot fired a few rounds which passed in front of the bomber which then commenced wild twisting and turning. Much too close for comfort, green lines of tracer from the Tommy's tail turret swished past him. Pietrek climbed and turned, in a steep spiral and pulled up. The bomber tried the same manoeuvre again but to the right and so on. Never could Pietrek have imagined that one could carry out such wild manoeuvres with such a giant aircraft as this!

In the frantic exchange of fire Pietrek managed to hit the starboard outer engine. It appeared to ignite but the flames then died down only to flare again. He continued to chase as the bomber sank ever lower. In the back of the Messerschmitt 110, wireless operator Fw. Otto Bauchens worked hard to fill the ammunition pans to keep the cannons firing. The stream of tracers from the bomber's mid-upper gunner kept him at bay. Eventually, though, he was able to in his own words...

'creep up on him from beneath, pull up and level out swiftly and ...fire a burst over the top of the fuselage. A ball of fire and the turret has disappeared. That's what you get when you cause so much trouble!' [28]

Pietrek put the last, fatal touches to the encounter with a burst that set the port outer engine on fire, only breaking off when he ran out of ammunition. The bomber by then was doomed. Pietrek then lined up alongside and watched the Stirling slide to earth. According to Chorley's Bomber command Losses, Stirling BU-A of 214 squadron crashed at Bonneuil les eaux. Was this Pietrek's Stirling? It has not been possible at the time of writing to confirm this. All the crew except one of the gunners managed to bale out and Pietrek did not report

---

[27] Some info also obtained form Australian National Archives A705/166/2032
[28] With permission Theo Boiten, "Nachtjagd".

seeing any parachutes. The loss report of [29] BK653 states their position was south of St Quentin at the time of the combat. If indeed BK653 was the Stirling Pietrek shot down, 7 of the 8 crew managed to bale out. Nevertheless the report fully demonstrates the ferocity of air combat in the night air war.

At 00:38 hours an aircraft was lost at Oggersheim area, Lancaster W4848 of 103 squadron flown by the crew of Jim Mooney R.Z.A.F. Mooney was born in County Antrim Northern Ireland, and had emigrated to New Zealand in 1939 joining up in November 1941.

A letter was sent to the Mooney family by Lothar Stattmüller, a 16 year old schoolboy assistant on a flak position. He gives his account;

'I was a 16 year old senior schoolboy assistant on the Grossraum Flak battery 1/902 between Ludwigshafen am Rhein and Mannheim. On the night of 16/17th April 1943 I was on my watch as telephone operator in the radar post on the site. Shortly after my duties were to end for the night we were notified of British bombers approaching in large numbers. A bomber stream was heading for Plzeň flying from west to east. My radar unit had identified the bombers very early. It was a full moon, as bright as day. The bombers could have followed the nearby autobahn. They came over the town of Frankenthal Pfaltz at about 00:15 and were illuminated in the beams of the battery searchlights.

Our 88 mm battery flak guns opened fire and the first salvo hit a British bomber which immediately caught fire and lurched forward in a steep dive. I think the pilot was killed when the aircraft was hit and his body slumped over the controls causing the aircraft to dive to earth. As we watched it became clear that the bomber was heading directly towards us and we dived for cover. The bomber hit the ground seconds later on the battery site and very near to the radar post. I was very badly shaken and was unconscious for several seconds.

When I regained consciousness it was obvious to me and my surviving comrades that the radar post was destroyed. Three of my comrades were killed. A good friend of mine lost his left foot.

At dawn we inspected the crash site nearby. The crash of the bomber had made a 25-metre diameter crater in the ground, big enough to put a house in. We found a parachute and were ordered to look for human remains. Later I found an escape map printed on silk, which showed the site of our battery! Three men had escaped, one was captured hiding nearby. Another was found on the ground with two broken legs. Another was found dead.' [30]

(In a letter to the author in February 2008 Lothar Stattmüller stated that the Lancaster was taking evasive action at 500-600 metres altitude and her gunners had fired at his position.)

---

[29] TNA UK report K22 AIR14/1442
[30] Peter Menges, German historian Ludwigshafen

Left: soldiers examine the crash site. Right: Sgt Jim Mooney Lancaster W4848 103 Sqn.

The Plzeň force continued on but the high rate of attrition was unrelenting. Halifax HR776 of 158 squadron captained by W/O Smith, had engine trouble and the port outer failed. They turned back onto 275° bombing Saarbrücken through a concentration of flak and searchlights from 11,000 feet, catching a glimpse of the river Saar and a line of incendiaries.[31]

At 00:17 hours yet another air combat ensued this time between Halifax DT637 'F' of 51 squadron captained by Pilot Officer Byres and two night-fighters. Flying at 15,000 feet at 49.15N-08.40E (approximately 15 miles east of the River Rhein) on course 104° magnetic, the bomber was stalked by two fighters (supposedly Bf109s.) one of which fired a machine gun burst from six to five hundred yards, the Halifax returning fire with three bursts totalling 500 rounds and was not damaged. Again the corkscrew manoeuvre combined with return fire was effective in fending off the attacker.[32]

At around 00:20 hours Halifax DT769 of 408 squadron and 6 Group, was attacked by flak at Saarbrücken when eastbound, the pilot's escape hatch blowing off. A couple of minutes later when 14 kilometres (9 Miles) West of Heilbronn, Flying Officer Kelly's 102 squadron Halifax (JB782) crew observed a Bf110 fighter flash across their tail at 12,000 feet from port to starboard. It then stayed at the same height as the Halifax on the starboard quarter. Kelly immediately corkscrewed as the enemy fired two streams of tracer, which passed underneath the Halifax, the rear gunner Sgt. Cosford simultaneously returning fire. The Messerschmitt Bf110 then moved from the starboard quarter at the same height to port quarter low, closing in to the port beam and then going underneath the Halifax. The fighter then broke off the attack to be seen no more.[33] The mid-under [34] observing the action reported that the enemy seemed to fly into the Halifax's bullet group, the rear gunner having fired four bursts. This action took place about ten miles west of Heilbronn, midway between Mannheim

---

[31] AIR27 /1048 TNA UK
[32] AIR50/189 TNA UK
[33] AIR50/205 TNA UK
[34] The ventral observation Perspex blister.

and Stuttgart. Stuttgart reported aircraft were in numbers passing through the Bachnang, Stuttgart, Nurtingen areas.

At approximately 00:25, 50 Squadron Lancaster ED691 'K', was flying at 19,000 feet still over France in the Châlons-sur-Marne area of France when they were attacked from astern and below by twin engine night fighters. The starboard wing and both engines were set on fire by the first burst. The third observable burst gave second pilot Trotman a cannon splinter in the leg, as it tore into the belly of the Lancaster. The skipper Harry Day tried all possible means to put the fire in the wing out; first attempting to feather the props, then the fire extinguishers, and diving.   None of which worked. He then gave the order to bale out. When Trotman jumped the whole crew had baled out except for the captain. As Trotman landed near the Châlons-sur-Marne he saw a 'Z' beacon flashing Morse code in white. He destroyed his chute and Mae West, then walked south until dawn arriving at the village of Rosay. There he rested and received civilian clothes and food. Information was also given to him about local troops, curfew and the airfield at St. Dizier. Walking an average distance of 35-45 km. per day Trotman made it to Switzerland and after a trek of approximately 400 kilometres, was arrested by the Swiss douanier on the 27th of April at Réclère. [35]

The beacon Trotman saw was probably a night fighter control rendezvous point. Six members of the crew were taken p. o. w. The pilot was killed. Holland, the navigator evaded captivity and after two days was helped by some locals but then fell into the hands of the gendarmes. The Germans took him to see the body of the pilot and the Gestapo. He was taken to Fresnes prison[36] near Paris, then Stalag Luft I and Stalag Luft III in October.

At 00:29 hours 100 squadron Lancaster ED564 skippered by F/L Milliken R.E., R.N.Z.A.F. was shot down by two centimetre light flak positioned near the grounds of the steel works at Dillingen. The records of the volunteer fire brigade Dillingen/Saar show the following entry;

After some planes already had passed by, the light flak of the Dillingen steel works opened fire. The first salvos hit plane which crashed burning, with its whole incendiary bomb load between Diefflen and Nalbach in fields south of the river Prims.[37]

Another account by an unknown author gives the following account;

17th April. At about 08:15 hours I visited the crashed plane on the Saarwellingen Bann near the river Prims. The plane was still burning. Due to the explosions parts of the plane covered an area of some 100 square metres .....[38]

The witness continued...

The plane crashed into the arable land. Perhaps it overturned beforehand. The fuselage still contained dead bodies and remains of the airmen testified to the force of the explosion. From the one part of the wreckage came green flames. The ship was loaded only with incendiary bombs which all burned out on the ground.[39]

---

[35] WO208/4273 escape and evasion report TNA U.K.
[36] Fresnes prison was used by the Germans to incarcerate British S.O.E. agents and members of the resistance. Conditions were poor and prisoners were often tortured.
[37] Stefan Reuter, Dillinger Geschichtswerkstatt via Eric Edward
[38] Ibid
[39] Ibid

An account from one mysterious source, *Brief an die Gefolgshaft des Rathauses der Gemeinde Dillingen-Saar.* (Letter to the adherents of the city hall of Dillingen –Saar) entitled Achievements of our home flak, states the following;

'A moonlight night welcomed us when we were woken by a siren and went to the air raid shelters. Everyone hurried to his duty. I was standing on the street together with some air raid wardens when the deep roaring sound of motors made us look up. "There's another! There it comes! 'Do you see it?'" my neighbour shouted. Indeed a four engine bomber passed above us at low altitude. After a few minutes a new engine noise comes from the west also at low altitude. On about the same latitude as the Forsthuaus, the home flak opened fire. The first salvo hit and the ship was burning, at first only a small fire but after only 100 metres it covered the whole plane.[40]

The accounted continues;

'But this wasn't the only one for the night a second plane was downed by them. Also their participation in the shooting down of a third plane was acknowledged by the leading department.'

Milliken had flown operations to Hamburg, München, Stuttgart, Essen, Kiel and Duisberg in Germany and St Nazaire (France) and La Spezia (Italy). Early entries in his diary were dramatic but optimistic. He recorded;

'Approaching this [the target], searchlights came very close to us, but our evasive action was more than they could cope with'

He wrote on March 4th 1943 regarding an operation to Hamburg.

The flak shells slowly climbed into the night sky like beads on a string to burst in vivid sparks in the distance. I found myself a very interested spectator of a very fine pyrotechnic display.' He continued..... *'The thought that I have been training for two years to drive through this also passed through my mind...I have no fear now and feel very confident about it all.*[41]

However another entry was more sullen.

'Sgt. Partridge is missing from last night's operation to Frankfurt (10th April). It was his first operation I had quite a long chat with him before he went away and gave him all the tips.'

Milliken wrote for the last time in his diary on the 12th of April;

'I took a long walk in the country........it was like going back home and I felt great sadness come over me at the time.'[42]

One of the other Lancasters mentioned was 100 squadron Lancaster (ED563). She was hit by flak too, crashing at around 00:29. In her final moments she had been seen by a witness to be circling at low level, then crashed into some high-tension wires and into a hillside at Rentrisch 5 miles north east of Saarbrücken. She was also captained by a New

---

[40] Eric Edward nephew of Milliken
[41] Ibid
[42] Ibid

Zealand pilot, Sgt. Atkinson. This crew were given a burial service by two German pastors and a full military honour guard.[43]

Sgt Wilkins' 101 squadron Lancaster crew on ED809 bombed their alternative target Karlsruhe, at 00:29 and had a tough time from searchlights and flak, the aircraft sustaining fifteen flak holes and the trailing aerial being shot away.

The primary target was still some way off, the first aircraft due not before 01:30.

---

[43] Stefan Reuter, Dillinger Geschichtswerkstatt

A Shaky do. The Plzen raid April 16/17th April 1943

Above: The Battle of Britain memorial flight Lancaster makes a flypast whilst lowering her wheels.
Photo ©Nicholas Joyce 2007

Below: The Yorkshire Air Museum 'Halifax III' on the pan at Elvington in 2007 (MK IIIs did not take part in the Skoda raid 16th April 1943)

A Shaky do-The Skoda works raid 16/17th April 1943

Above photo (Petrie-Andrews) Crew of W7779 TL-U of 35 Squadron Pathfinder force. L-R Sgt Morgan F/E, Sgt Berwick Wop/ag, Sgt Backhouse A/B, Sgt Petrie-Andrews Capt, P/O Armitage Nav, Sgt Dale M/U, Sgt Barnett R/G

Crew of Halifax JB898 Photo (S. Godfrey) L-R Sgt Blackhall RCAF Capt, F/S Norton Nav, Sgt Emmons RCAF F/E, Williams R/G (not on Plzen raid 16th April) F/S Godfrey W/op, Sgt Semper B/A

A shaky do-The Skoda works raid April 16/17th 1943

Sgt Peel 106 Sqn Lancaster ED708
(Photo Peel)

F/S Tillotson 467 Sqn Lancaster
ED803 (Photo George)

Sgt Foster 467 Sqn Lancaster
ED772 (Photo George)

Sgt Allerdice Halifax DT690 evaded
Photo (Family of Allerdice)

Sgt Simpson Halifax DT690 pow
(Photo Family Allerdice)

Sgt Trott 115 Sqn (Tony Trott)

P/O Dennis 78 Sqn Halifax
HR659 pow
(photo Dennis)

Sgt Moore 49 sqn ED597 KIA 16th
Dec Sept 43, 617 Sqn
(photo Murphy)

F/S Ward 460 Sqn Lancaster
ED711 KIA 17th April 1943
(Photo Hall/Dunn)

A Shaky do-The Skoda works raid 16/17th April 1943

Sgt Clark KIA Lancaster W4942
460 Sqn. Photo Clark

Wing Co. Warner C/O 78 Squadron
photo Naylor, Linton Memorial

Sgt Watkins KIA Halifax JB870
Mannheim op (photo Thomas)

Left to Right Flt/Lt *at time of photo* Raphael DFC KIA Peenemunde 18th Aug; Wing/Co Gomm DSO DFC (Lanc ED547)
KIA 15th Aug; Flt/Lt Desmond (Lanc ED504) KIA ops Essen 27/28th May (photo George 467 archives)

A Shaky do-The Skoda works raid 16/17th April 1943

Crew of ED357 L-R Front: Hildebrand (M/U), Tribe (Pilot), Collier (F/E)

L-R Back: Hill (R/G), Thompson (Wop/ag), Moore (A/B) (photo Collier)

12 Squadron airmen sit on top of a 4000 lb Cookie at Wickenby (photo Collier)

A shaky do-The Skoda works raid 16/17th 1943

Band Of Brothers, Skipper Bill Steel and crew of ED528 103 Squadron
(photos Mitchell)

Sgt Bill Steel Captain

P/O Noel Bayliss W/OP

Sgt Ken Fee RCAF A/B

Sgt Tom Beautyman F/E

Sgt Alf Birch M/U gunner

Sgt Fred Mitchell, Nav.

Sgt Fred Holland rear gunner

A Shaky do-The Skoda Works raid April 16/17th 1943

42

Top: Fred Mitchell makes a sky-dive in 2007 in honour of Skipper Bill Steel and his beloved wife Monica. Funds raised for Harrogate cancer unit. Bottom Right: Fred Mitchell heads for debriefing- One for the line book. Any landing you can walk away from is a good one! (Mitchell)

Fred Mitchell & his crew in 1943 (Kneeling) R-L Sgt Fee RCAF A/B, P/O Bayliss W/op Sgt Holland R/G, Sgt Steel Capt., Sgt Birch M/U gunner, Sgt Beautyman F/E in front of Lancaster ED828 (Photo Mitchell)

A Shaky do-The Skoda works raid 16/17th April 1943

43

(photo Collier)

Left:Flight engineer Geoff Collier. Right:Pilot Dave Tribe RCAF 12 sqn.
Lancaster ED357

A shaky do-The Skoda works raid 16/17th April 1943

44

(photo Tolchard)

Sgt G H Porter   Sgt D Doe
R/G   M/U   P/O L H Tolchard
RCAF   Capt.   F/O L R Hastings   Sgt W George
              F/S G W Coburn   Nav   W/op   Sgt A E Best
                    A/B   F/E

Lancaster ED448 (N.B.F/S Arnold RAAF was W/op on 16/17th April)

A shaky do-The Skoda works raid 16/17th April 1943

(photo Cox)

Brothers in arms and in fact, the Cox brothers; Left to right Ernie, John and Steve. Ernie gave his life on the Plzen raid 17th April 1943 flying Halifax DT561 of 51 squadron. Steve served in coastal command earning the D.F.C. D.F.M. & M.I.D. Brother John served as a navigator on ferry command in the Middle East

A shaky do-The Skoda works raid 16/17th April 1943

View of the starboard motors

Milliken RNZAF (ED563 100 sqn) in the pilot's seat (Photos Eric Edward)

Bomb aimer's position

A shaky do-The Skoda works raid 16/17th April 1943

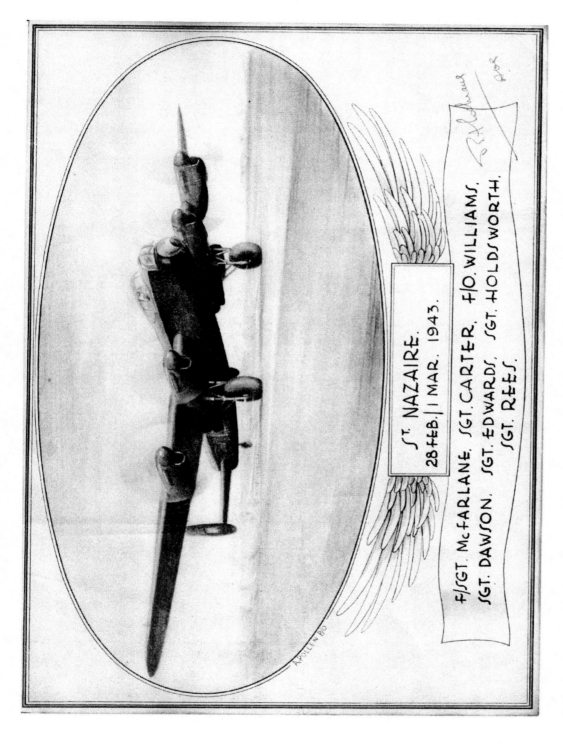

Aiming point certificate (signed by Cochrane A.O.C. 5 Group) awarded to the 61 squadron crew of W4317 QR-R all of whom were killed in action on 16/17th of April with the exception of Sgt Carter who was a stand in Flight Engineer on the St Nazaire operation of 28th Feb/1st of March 1943

A Shaky do-The Skoda works raid 16/17th April 1943

Chapter Three
Stuttgart and the Danube

S gt Musgrove, bomb aimer on 76 sqn Halifax, JB874 saw shells bursting in the air at Karlsruhe, Mannheim and Stuttgart en route.
Sgt. Bill Steel R.N.Z.A.F. and Lancaster ED528 'Z' of 103 squadron were harried by a fighter on the outward journey as navigator Fred Mitchell recalls;

I heard our rear gunner-Fred Holland-tell the skipper to break port and his guns fire, he maintained that he saw a night fighter but the mid-upper said he didn't see it. But then our 19 year old rear-gunner was a little trigger happy!

Further on the crew found themselves south of track and over Stuttgart's defences. They were suddenly caught by a blue master light (radar guided) immediately several white beams from slaved searchlights coned[44] them, flooding the cockpit as light as day. Bill Steel instantly put the aircraft into a steep diving turn to starboard and she was shot up by the 88mm flak guns. A fearful crump was felt accompanied by an orange flash as the aircraft staggered from the blast. Sgt. Steel ordered the flight engineer (Sgt. Tommy Beautyman) "standby to feather starboard props and activate the graviner extinguishers if needed." Still in a diving turn with the aircraft vibrating badly and now down to eight thousand feet, Steel decided to pull out of the dive and sideslip to port in order to escape the grasp of the searchlights. A shrill sound was heard over the sound of the engines, "sounds as if the port inner is going" Beautyman yelled over the intercom. The captain gave the order, "bomb-aimer, jettison bombs live, bomb doors open. Prepare to abandon!" Canadian bomb-aimer Ken Fee, grabbed his parachute pack from the stowage and knelt on the escape hatch cover on the floor of the Lancaster's nose. Making sure that the bombs were fused he pushed the two jettison bars on the bomb-aimer's panel and 'Z' Zebra heaved upwards as if with a sigh of relief as the three tons of high explosive were released. The 4000lb 'cookie' which was jettisoned started a fire The pilot assisted by the flight engineer struggled to control the aircraft, now firing on all four engines answered to the right rudder and jinked out of the searchlights and into the night sky with the full moon above. The Pilot gave the order,

"bomb doors close-cancel abandon drill-navigator give me a course back to base."

The time was around 00:20 hours. Navigator Fred Mitchell remembers,

'We were thoroughly lost after the manoeuvres Bill took to get out of the flak and searchlights we did not know it was Stuttgart until debriefing and backtracking my D.R. plot. We had nearly become guests of the third Reich!'[45]

His logbook carries the entry; *6th op. Plzeň Škoda arms factory, low level. Shot up by flak. Thirteen holes in aircraft.*
Fred was to add yet another 'op' to his tally, when on May the 12th 2007 at the age of 86, he did a tandem parachute sky-dive from ten thousand feet. This included a freefall of 7,000 ft. and a parachute drop of 3,000 feet in aid of the Cancer Unit at Harrogate Hospital, in memory of his old skipper Bill Steel who died in 2006 and of his beloved wife Monica.

---

[44] Several lights would follow the blue master light onto the object aircraft.
[45] Information courtesy Fred Mitchell 103 squadron

A Shaky do. The Plzen raid April 16/17th April 1943

Skipper Bill Steel had saved his rear gunner's life on another op when he heard him singing deliriously over the intercom, the nursery rhyme, 'Ba Ba Black sheep have you any wool?' The skipper realised something was up and sent someone aft to check on the gunner. Sure enough his oxygen pipe was leaking. It was not possible to repair it and they dropped their bombs and descended to a lower altitude. A good skipper meant a great deal to his crew!

At 00:30 hours a few kilometres north of Lachen-Speyerdorf was Halifax DK165[46] of 76 squadron based at Linton on Ouse. She was shot down by night fighter probably flown by Oblt. Jacob Bender of 7./NJG101. The fighter was seen to fire a three to four second burst of cannon fire at a height of 400-500 metres. This was possibly a further attack as the first contact was noted by the fighter pilot at above 3,000 metres. Only one member of Sgt. Webb's crew, mid-upper gunner Sgt. Mitchell survived to be taken p. o. w. He was trapped in the wreckage and heard knocking to draw attention to his plight and was shouting for help. He was duly extricated from the centre section of the Halifax and apprehended by the Luftwaffe. After the impact of the bomber several pieces of the wreckage were found. The site smelled strongly of petrol but no fire had started. The tail of the bomber was missing as were the rudders. Two of the crew members were found dead in their blue uniforms. Another eyewitness observed that the bodies had been crushed by the impact of the bomber with the ground. The crash place was close to a drainage channel called Erbsengraben. Six of the crew members were neither burned nor mutilated and could be identified by the Luftwaffe. Was there an eighth crew member not listed in the ops records or was this an error on the part of the witnesses? Other witnesses stated that the dead fliers were robbed by the civilians.[47] This may not have been as barbaric as it may appear. Times were very difficult and during the hardship of war people would do what it took to survive.

Canadian wireless operator Sgt. Ross was killed. He had been on only five operations; twice to Wilhelmshafen on 18th &19th of February with pilot Sgt. Griffith, Köln on the 26th of February again with pilot Sgt. Griffith, St Nazaire on the 28th February with pilot Sgt. Cresswell and finally Plzeň. Mitchell was then taken to Dulag Luft at Frankfurt for interrogation. One of the methods used was a fake Red Cross questionnaire. Later Mitchell escaped from a marching column when the Germans evacuated Stalag Luft IV on 8th of February 1945 with a Warrant Officer J. Akehurst.[48] They were recaptured at an aerodrome near Regenwalde after about fourteen days.

At approximately 00:32, 101 squadron Lanc. ED776 captained by Flight Sergeant Kelly was coned by searchlights took some flak and sustained damage to the starboard main plane. They dropped 7,000 lbs of high explosives on Karlsruhe from 3,000 feet as an alternative and headed for home.

At 00:32 hours a 4 Group crew observed 'one aircraft seen falling with one engine on fire and fire spreading rapidly at Stuttgart.' This was quite possibly JB908 of 77 squadron. An article in 'Ehningen – The chronicle of a Swabian village' by Karl Gleißner[49] states;

'Sure enough the enemy sustained aircraft casualties on the boundary of Ehningen, too. In April 1944 (sic) it was a four engine bomber, which swept before dawn like a burning torch very low over the village, before the aircraft crashed into the valley of Mauren. One of the crew members has baled out in good time and the airman went down safely to the ground near the "Limes Inn" (Gasthof Zur Linde). But four of his comrades fell to their deaths with their parachutes unopened and two crewmembers burned inside the bomber. One of the dead was laid out in the house of saddler Bader and then he was buried together with his

---

[46] W7813 is *incorrectly* noted in AIR27 TNA UK ops records as the aircraft shot down in this instance.
[47] Peter Menges
[48] General questionnaire for British/American ex-prisoners of war TNA UK WO344/221 24345
[49] Published by the Community of Ehningen, November 1965

comrades with military honours by the Luftwaffe at Böblingen.' (Article translated by Norbert Vollmann.)

Although this account contains some discrepancies, it is so similar to the circumstances of the loss of 77 Sqn. JB908, other researchers agree with the author this was JB908. According to Chorley's Bomber Command losses, three crewmen were taken prisoner of war; pilot Sgt. Wall, bomb-aimer Sgt. Tullett and Sgt. Johnson air gunner. Sgt. Robinson was found dead in the aircraft. Three crew had baled out at low altitude their chutes failing to open. These were Sgt. Pullen (flight engineer), Sgt. Fernee (navigator) and Sgt. Edgar (wireless op/ag).

By the Worms-Horchheim road, yet another seven aircrew lost their lives at 00:34 when Lancaster W4942 0f 460 squadron flown by Sgt. Williams, was shot down at approximately 9,000 feet by Ofw. Richard Launer of 10./NJG4. According to Herr Penk on whose land the aircraft came down, in her final moments flying west to south east, the Lancaster was at low level and coned by searchlights then hit by flak. Finally coming in at a shallow angle and bouncing before coming to rest, the fuel tanks exploding and catching fire in a field by the Worms-Horchheim road. Although she had her bomb load still on board they did not explode on impact. Two-unknown crew survived the crash but one died soon after and another later on the way to hospital. The pilot, navigator and bomb-aimer were Australians.[50]

At 00:40 106 squadron Lancaster piloted by American Pilot Officer Rosner landed back at base in England having turned around earlier due to a shuddering air-frame.

P/O Smuck's Halifax (DT769 of 408 Sqn.) having already been attacked by fighter and flak twenty minutes earlier, was again stalked by a fighter. The rear gunner fired at 600 yards range astern and to port and the fighter disappeared not to be seen again.[51] Smuck and six of the crew on the Plzeň raid were lost to a night fighter along with the same aircraft on ops to Aachen 13/14th July.

At 00:45 hours and at 9,000 feet, Flight Lieutenant Robinson in Lancaster ED716 of 44 Sqn. and his crew were on reasonable time but due to having no navigational aids and Astro-navigation being prevented by weaving, were 100 kilometres off track and ran into the full defences of München. They were unable to find a pinpoint and were engaged by flak and held in searchlights for more than five minutes. The standby to bale out had already been given and Sgt. Woodgate[52] the wireless op. had already clamped down his Morse key, sending out a distress signal. Fortunately the skipper managed to pull out of the dive at around 3,000 feet. The 4,000lb 'Cookie' was dropped but the two 1,000 pounders went too. The bomb-aimer claimed to have selected the correct switches for the cookie only. It was decided to continue on to the primary target in order to continue with the main concentration. The rear turret had also gone unserviceable earlier in the journey. Nickels[53] were dropped at the same time as the bombs on the east side of München. The aircraft was much damaged by shrapnel.

At 00:46 hours an unknown Five Group crew observed, 'one aircraft seen hit by light flak at 3,000 feet north of Stuttgart.' This was very probably ED711 'U' of 460 squadron based at Breighton.[54]

Looking up into the night sky was sixteen-year old Heinz Bardua. He was training as an aircrew volunteer on gliders and on the night of the raid was on fire watch in Stuttgart. He remembers clearly seeing a Lancaster bomber appear from the south at about 00.55 hours on

---

[50] A707/163/178/366 National Archives Australia
[51] AIR27/1797 TNA UK
[52] Sgt.Woodgate 44 sqn.
[53] Propaganda leaflets
[54] AIR14/3217 TNA UK

the 17th of April and receive direct hits from light anti-aircraft fire. The aircraft Lancaster ED711, was set on fire and jettisoned its bombs (1 x 4000 lb 'cookie' and 4 x 1000 lb) as an emergency procedure. The bombs exploded in the Upper Rosenberg Street area, killing one person and injuring fifty-eight. Some people had come up from the shelters thinking the danger of air raid had passed.

Even as the aircraft descended in flames, one of the ED711 gunners (probably the mid-upper turret) returned fire at a flak battery wounding one of the flak gunners. The bomber flew right over the city and the Feuerbach valley and cut down many trees for about sixty metres as she exploded on impact on the wooded Heukopf. The crash caused a large crater and spread debris over a large area. Heinz went to the crash site in the forest the next day and saw the partly burnt bodies of the eight crewmembers. The eighth crewmember was a '2nd dickey' or pilot under training, Sgt. Stewart. Later Heinz returned to the site of the crash and found much debris. At a later time he retrieved various items such as fragments of the navigator's maps and an English penny. The maps were later themselves destroyed, as Heinz's own family home was destroyed by bombing.

In 1947, the British authorities attempted to identify the exact crash site at Böblingen but could find no trace of a crash or any aircraft remains. In fact they had been looking in the wrong place. Böblingen was the place where the Luftwaffe unit was based which dealt with the crash, hence the place name, which appeared on the German documents.

Six of the crew of ED711 were previously involved in another danger filled incident on the St Nazaire raid in March of 1943 whilst flying Lancaster 'D' W4879. On that occasion just after crossing the French coast they were attacked by a Junkers 88. In the ensuing combat the mid-upper and rear gunners returned fire. The aircraft was badly damaged and went out of control diving before pulling out at four thousand feet. The rear turret, fuselage, tail-plane and starboard main-plane were all damaged by cannon fire. The rudder and elevator trim was shot away. Although 'D-dog' was difficult to control, the crew went on to the target but a bomb failed to release and Sergeant Ward struggled for half an hour to manually release it. Having succeeded he assisted the pilot with great difficulty, in controlling the aircraft. She then struggled back to England and crash-landed at South Cerney Gloucestershire. The Lancaster was written off but no injuries were reported. White and Ward were awarded the Distinguished Flying Medal.

Well on the way to Plzeň but behind time at 01:01 hours, Sgt. Sloper in Lancaster W4863 of 101 Sqn. turned for home bombing Saarbrücken from 6,000 feet on dead reckoning.[55] Four minutes later a pathfinder aircraft (83 sqn. W4953) had strayed well south of track and was heavily engaged by flak near München at 01:05. This caused her to release her 4000lb. 'Cookie' and white flares, inflicting some damage. She then made haste to reach the target area and hopefully catch up with the tail end of the main stream of aircraft.

McCrae's Halifax DT690 of 51 sqn. which had already been troubled by fighter attack, now ran into much heavy flak south of Mannheim. A few miles further east the condition of the damaged engine worsened and started giving off lots of blue flames and was feathered. Progress had now became difficult and a railway line was bombed east of Mannheim from 7,000 feet. No results were seen. Turning onto a course for home, the aircraft passed south of Mannheim sometime after 01:00 hours as the raid there was in full progress. The pilot climbed to 11,000 feet and some cloud cover.[56]The aircraft was to see further action over France.

Halifax DT670 of 51 sqn. flown by Sgt. Inch had experienced an uneventful outbound journey until south of Mannheim where another aircraft was seen to be held in searchlights

[55] Given knowledge of the aircraft's airspeed, a forecast wind velocity and time on a particular bearing, the navigator could calculate the headings to fly and time to reach his objective.
[56] TNA UK AIR14/1442 K files 35 and 41

and was being heavily attacked by flak. About three minutes later DT670's rear gunner reported three searchlights searching for their own aircraft. The Halifax was not held, but almost immediately afterwards was peppered by heavy flak four times within a minute. Shells appeared to burst immediately below the aircraft, but no damage was reported. Five minutes later though the port-outer engine failed possibly due to being hit. Since the aircraft was responding well to the controls she continued on to the target. Sgt. Inch never suggested turning back.[57]

I will mention here two Wellington aircraft of the Mannheim force as they amply illustrate the flak danger in the area through which the Plzeň force was passing. The first was Wellington HE379 of 431 Sqn. skippered by Sgt. Sutterby. Things did not look good from the start, the bomb aimer forgot to fuse the bombs until the German frontier, the aircraft wouldn't climb, the Gee navigation system would not work and the whole crew seemed to have a premonition. As they neared the target at approximately 01:00, things seemed very quiet. Too quiet. There was no flak, no fighters, when the target was seen ahead. 'H' Harry hung back as two Halifaxes went in and the pilot decided to nip in between the cones of lights. At 12,500 feet they went in diving at 300 mph. The area between the cones was full of flak. After bombs away the Wellington set course for home but was hit twice and swung violently to port. The pilot controlled her and tried to feather the engine and use the fire extinguisher. This did not work and the port wing caught fire. The order to bale out was called and four of the crew got out. The bomb aimer W/O1 Rudd R.C.A.F. spilled his chute in the aircraft and was clutching it to his chest before he jumped. The pilot, Sgt. Sutterby baled out o.k. as did P.O. Patton, and Sgt. Cartwright. The rear gunner Sgt. Hadland was killed.[58]

The other Mannheim force Wellington worthy of mention was that of Sgt. Tomyn R.C.A.F. flying HE547 of 427 Sqn. The following incident again illustrates the danger of flak in the area of Mannheim.

Wireless operator/Air Gunner Sgt. Tony Johnson had been jamming the enemy fighter frequencies through the fighter belt.[59] A microphone was attached to the port engine and the Morse key held down transmitting engine noise over the enemy's radio frequencies.[60] Plenty of flak was observed. On the run in they opened the bomb doors but had to go around again, releasing the bombs on the second run. When leaving the target area, suddenly they were caught in what they thought was a master searchlight and then coned by others, filling the aircraft with light. Pilot Steve Tomyn took evasive action in a desperate attempt to avoid the lights, which he succeeded in doing. Shortly after this, a large explosion occurred on the port side close to the aircraft. She flipped onto her back and was sent screaming into spiral nose dive of some 10,000 ft. or more, vibrating badly. Tomyn halted the dive but they had lost the starboard engine with the other having problems too. The crew managed to bale out. The pilot sadly lost his life when the aircraft crashed at Kirf, several flak battery crews disputing who had shot down the Wellington.[61]

Back with the Plzeň force, at 01:10 hours yet another 51 squadron aircraft, Halifax DT671 found herself at 4,000 feet, south of München and a long way south of track. She was being stalked by a Junkers 88. The Halifax started a climbing turn to starboard followed by a

---

[57] TNA UK AIR14/1442 K36
[58] TNA UK
[59] The line of defensive night-fighter boxes, searchlight and flak positions.
[60] The codename for this equipment was Tinsel.
[61] Tony Johnson, phone interview with the author 25th November 2007

corkscrew manoeuvre as three searchlights on the ground indicated the track of the bomber. The rear gunner fired one long burst of two hundred rounds with the enemy closing from 200 yards to 150 yards, the enemy breaking off the attack on the port quarter down. Three minutes later the Halifax was coned in searchlights and dived a thousand feet in order to evade them. The rear gunner F/Sgt. Stacey R.C.A.F. had fired 500 rounds at the searchlights.[62]Whilst DT671 was fighting her way out of München airspace, Squadron Leader White's Lancaster (ED841) of 156 Pathfinder squadron, was engaged by flak in the Nürnberg area. Also at Nürnberg, on the way to the target, Lancaster ED379 (101 squadron) was hit by anti-aircraft fire at 3,000 feet. Wireless Operator Sgt. Lionel Green the only surviving crew member gave the following account;

I was in the Astro-dome[63] and witnessed the starboard outer engine burst into flames and the inside of the aircraft became like a firework display. The order to bale out was given by Aussy skipper Menzies and I made my way to the rear of the aircraft in a hurry, leaving by the rear entrance. The Lancaster crashed after releasing her bomb load. My chute had only been open a few seconds when the roaring aircraft struck the dry lakebed. [64]I was still aloft, when I felt the enormous blast which made me swing violently from side to side. With tracer bullets still screaming past me, I swung in a series of arcs toward the rooftops of Nürnberg. In the last pendulum swing I landed on a slate roof and the silken canopy draped over a chimneystack leaving me suspended down a wall. A hostile mob gathered below. Still more were coming from the shelters with revenge in mind after the full bomb load had been dropped in a desperate attempt to stay airborne. A youth reached up and tried to wrench me down, whereupon I released my harness and we both crashed to the floor. The youth then tried to throttle me. I threw the assailant off and stood with hands raised and experienced real fear. Again I fell to the ground, fists striking me.[65]

Police Commissar Georg Braun, when questioned after the war stated that, although the Luftwaffe personnel handled the crash, he was present at the scene shortly after it occurred. The remains of three or four bodies were found near the wall of the congress hall, on top of the hall and by the aircraft. The lake and congress hall in Dutzendteich were built by the Nazis as a showpiece and are situated near the infamous parade ground were the Nürnberg rallies were held.

The Luftwaffe informed Braun that the remains of the flyers would be buried in the south cemetery Nürnberg.[66] On the same night a parachutist was captured in Dutzendteich and was believed to have come from the same aircraft. One Max Fischer protected him from a hostile mob of German civilians. Fischer then took the parachutist to the local police station, where thankfully, it was the Luftwaffe and not the S.S. or the Gestapo, who finally took him into custody. The Luftwaffe in most cases did show reasonable respect to fellow airmen.

It must be mentioned here that the R.A.F. M.R.E.U named the man who rescued Green from the mob as Alfred Brunner in an investigation in 1947.[67] It is most likely though, that Green's account is the correct one. In the M.R.E.U report some inconsistencies occur in the information recorded. The name given by the captured airman was wrong, as was the intended target of the bomber. Perhaps Sgt. Green had given false information to his German

---

[62] AIR50/189 combat report TNA UK
[63] The Perspex Astro-dome on the Lancaster was on the roof of the aircraft at the back of the cockpit canopy
[64] B.B.C. People's War The Max Fischer Story by Lionel Green Article ID: A6448953 27 October 2005
[65] Ibid
[66] Later re-interred at Durnbach post war.
[67] Australian National Archives A705 166/39/59 File of Thomas Maxwell Taylor

54

captors. Green and Fischer, his rescuer, were able to meet in friendship after the war at the scene of the wartime drama. The Bavarian had placed an advertisement in an English paper asking to be contacted.

Only a few kilometres south of the crash at Dutzendteich, between 1941 and 1944, 1,631 Nürnberg Jews were taken from the Langwasser Pferdemarkt train station to concentration camps in the east. Only 72 survived.

The crash time for Lionel Green's Plzeň bound aircraft (ED379) at Dutzendteich, was given by a witness at 21:00 (in 1947) but this is impossible. The true time was probably around 01:00 hours. There was no time difference between German and British time at 16/17th April 1943. Britain was on Double British Summertime (GMT+2) the same as Middle European time, M.E.T. (summertime) in the relevant period from April 4th until August 15th.

Sgt. Green's brother L.A. Green had been shot down in a Wellington III of 9 squadron (X3358) on ops to Köln 22/23rd April 1942. They met in the same P.O.W. camp.

At 01:10 hours the 156 Sqn. crew of Lancaster W4851 witnessed an aircraft burning on the ground at Landau and at Bruchsal. Eight minutes later, an unknown aircraft was seen was seen by them to hit the ground and explode. Three New Zealanders in Lancaster W4851 (Kearns, Moller and Barclay) had done a first tour of operations on Wellingtons with 75 New Zealand squadron. Kearns the Pilot went on the complete a third tour with 617 (Dambusters) squadron.

Moller remembered his aircraft being forced down on the deck during a Hamburg raid in 1942. In this action Moller's crew shot up about seven lights and a gun battery, and nearly collided with some high-tension power lines. Kearns flew underneath the power lines skilfully lifting the nose of the aircraft to prevent the tall tail of the Wellington from snagging the wires![68]

---

[68] Night After Night, Max Lambert. Page 152

A Shaky do. The Plzen raid April 16/17th April 1943

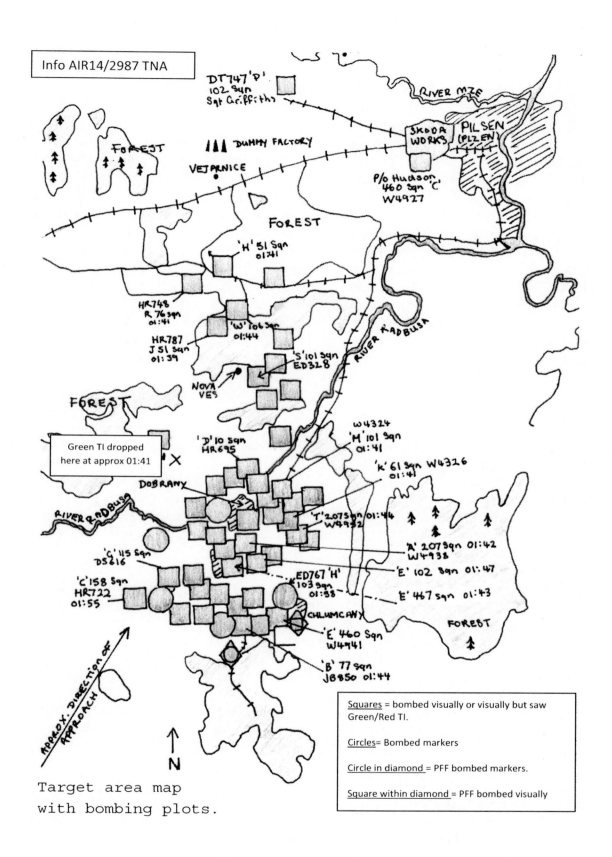

Target area map
with bombing plots.

A shaky do-The Skoda works raid April 16/17th 1943

Chapter Four
Target ahead

The attack on the Škoda works was timed for section one 01:28 to 01:53- 28 aircraft of the P.F.F. followed by section 2 at 01:30 to 01:50 -180 Lancasters of 1, 3 and 5 Groups and 122 Halifaxes of 4 and 6 Groups. No aircraft with incendiaries was to attack before 01:40 and all aircraft were to head for base at 02:19 hours. The attack was to be lead by eight 'Y' aircraft of the pathfinder force. These carried H2s ground looking radar, which picked up reflections particularly from rivers and lakes hopefully giving a more accurate target location. This equipment gave a low resolution image on a screen. Lakes and rivers gave the best reflections but false readings could also be obtained. The Germans often countered H2s by draining lakes and flooding areas which were previously dry.

Of the 'Y' aircraft two returned early, one 35 Sqn. Halifax (W7873) was lost to night fighter and two had equipment failure. Of the three with serviceable equipment, only one dropped illumination flares on H2s and dead reckoning in the target area. One dropped flares and target indicators visually. A single aircraft was using the equipment for training only.

The aiming point was supposed to be illuminated by white flares and green target indicators were to indicate the near edge of the target. At 01:30 hours the P.F.F. were to release white flares in a long stick from southwest to northeast. Green target indicators were to be dropped on the southwest edge of the target area if possible on the same run as the flare drop or on a second run. Backers up would then reinforce the marking. The main force was briefed to identify the aiming point by the light of the flares using the T. I.s as a guide.

Six Group were to bomb from around 10,000 feet and the rest as low as possible between 8,000-4,000 feet but not below 4,000. Instructions were given to avoid damage to the town of Plzeň.

At 01:12 hours P/O Horan's 156 Sqn. Lancaster ED822 saw a Junkers 88 but no combat ensued. Yellow pathfinder way markers were supposed to be dropped at about this time at position 'C' 48.55N-12.30E near Straubing on the Danube (Danau). These marked the sharp deviation in course from approximately 090° onto a roughly north easterly heading 030° for the run up to the target.

Five H2s equipped aircraft dropped flares on the supposed aiming point at 01:32-01:50 followed by 45 backers up commencing at 01:36 through to 02:03. 226 aircraft attacked between the planned period 01:30 and 02:10 and two aircraft attacked two minutes and 25 minutes late respectively. Of the 225 main force aircraft, 132 carried only high explosives, 93 aircraft carried only incendiaries.

Flight Sergeant Murray flying 460 Sqn. W4783 UV-G[69] for George was navigated by Clarrie Taylor. In his memoirs Taylor comments;

'On the way out-in and out of fog at very low altitude. On reaching the Danube, I estimated another ten minutes to go but as the bomb-aimer had been map reading throughout, the pilot accepted his position. A later plot indicated my position correct-on e.t.a. we were twenty-eight miles North West of the target.'

Arriving in the target area at 01:20 they circled for 25 minutes at 8,000ft, awaiting the pathfinder target indicators and saw none.[70] Probably Murray was over the true aiming point. He then left the area bound for his secondary target.

---

[69] 'G' for George completed 89 ops, survived the war & resides in the Australian War Museum, Canberra.

[70] Clarrie Taylor notes. Peter Dunn's 'oz at war' web site.

At 01:35 from 14,000 feet Halifax DT803 flown by Flight Lieutenant Cranswick of 35 P.F.F. sqn. dropped white illumination flares using H2s. A 10 squadron Halifax JB930 bombed visually using the light of the markers. Sgt. Glover and his crew received the attention of flak gunners who made three small hits in the port and starboard wings. Some fires were already seen on the ground. Soon HR691 of 10 Squadron bombed from 10,000 feet visually and with the aid of the flares. A P.F.F. aircraft, (W4953 of 83 sqn.) was now over the target area at 19,000 feet and the Captain believed some main force aircraft had bombed too early. There is evidence that several aircraft dropped in the area to the north of Nová Ves in woodland causing smoke to drift across the area. 156 squadron Lancaster ED715 skippered by Squadron Leader Duigan bombed the target at around 01:37 after having made four runs but didn't see his bombs burst due to the concentration of other bursts. He experienced moderate heavy and light flak and the attention of twelve tenacious searchlights. At approximately 01:39 hours Flt/Sgt Brigden's HR787 'J' of 51 squadron based at Snaith, bombed in woodland north of Dobřany (Wiesengrund to German speakers) causing smoke and fire as did several other aircraft. Brigden experienced medium flak but not very concentrated. This aircraft and crew were all lost on operations to Duisburg on 27th April, only ten days later.

At 01:40 hours, Flight Lieutenant Sale of 35 sqn. P.F.F. dropped a stick of white flares from 14,000 feet. Sale was well loved on the squadron and a man of extraordinary bravery as will be seen later in the book. As the flares went down Flt/Sgt. Bawden (Halifax JB874 76 sqn.) was arriving on target. By the light of the flares the bomb aimer Sgt. Musgrove saw rows and rows of sheds with railway lines running through them. After his bombs had gone he saw a vivid red flash and another gigantic flash when a hundred miles away. From 01:40 to 02:00 Cope on ED525 of 460 R.A.A.F. squadron circled and saw no flares, again he was possibly on the correct aiming point. He then headed west to a secondary target.

Eddy Hudson, also of 460 sqn. flying Lancaster W4927 'C' Charlie was being navigated by Ron Friend. Friend comments in his memoirs;

'The P.F.F was supposed to drop yellow T.I's at the last turn. I was surprised when on my E.T.A. at this point not a single T.I. was visible. I presumed my navigation was at fault and told Eddie to hold the course I had given him. About five minutes later our rear gunner reported T.I's being dropped to our rear.

Hudson had probably overshot the turning point at the Danau near Straubing and turned onto 350° to head roughly North to the target area. Friend continued…

'I was now sure my navigation was correct so ignored the markers, and had to dead reckon to a point ahead and from there give a course to the target. This required flying on against the stream [71] but due to superb piloting by Eddie and without having to alter the course I had given him we were able to drop our bombs on exact e.t.a. on buildings the bomb-aimer could see beneath us.'

They had arrived over what they thought was the Škoda works at 01:41 and saw one burst, probably a 4000lb 'Cookie' on a shed. It was thought that from inspection of the target photographs that Hudson had been the only aircraft of 327 to find the correct target and bomb it. However according to the Škoda works fire brigade records, even this aircraft had failed

---

[71] It is unlikely that a heading of 350° was against the stream when the main approach was on approx. 030°. It is *possible* that may have crossed the bomber steam at an acute angle after overshooting the turning point markers.

to hit the target and no high explosive bombs were reported being dropped on the works itself. Given that no other aircraft hit anywhere near the target and Hudson reported incendiaries on the ground and a shed these must have been somewhere other than the Škoda works despite the Operational Research Section plotting him on the aiming point. Consider Hudson's de-briefing comment;

"Long sheds seen in the light of P.F.F. reconnaissance flares. Green and one red T.I. marker seen to cascade in the target area after bombing. One burst of probable 4,000lb. seen on sheds. Saw numbers of incendiaries going down on a fairly concentrated area after bombing."

Sgt Griffiths flying Halifax 'P' (DT747) of 102 sqn was plotted the next nearest to the aiming point some three miles W.N.W. of the Škoda works between the river Mze and a railway track which ran into the west side of the works. One report stated that some flares were dropped near Křimice to the west of the true aiming point of the Škoda works.

Still at 01:41 ED369 of 460 sqn. flown by Sgt. Hewerdine and Lancaster W4324 of 101 sqn. skippered by Sgt. Magerum, identified what they thought was the target and bombed by the light of the P.F.F. flares, from 6,000 and 7,000 feet respectively. Sgt. Sanderson's crew (HR748 of 76 squadron) added to the smoke over the target when he dropped his load after identifying a loop in the river. The bombs dropped in the woods three miles to the North of NováVes. Their target photograph showed a bomb falling and a wood on fire. It was the wrong river, and it is possible he had mistaken a nearby railway line and a loop in a river for similar features at Plzeň He was five miles off target to the west south west of Plzeň

Aircraft were now arriving thick and fast over the area of Dobrany and 35 pathfinder squadron Halifax (DT803 'O') flown by Alec Cranswick, dropped the first long burning green target indicator on heading 028 magnetic from 14,000 feet at around 01:41. As he did so he observed many incendiaries dropping and one big explosion with a cascade of coloured lights and a pall of smoke. Within seconds after he turned away from the target, Cranswick was firmly coned by several searchlights - a perfect target for the flak gunners-for the next five minutes. Cranswick pulled every trick he knew to escape the glaring lights and flak which surrounded him![72]

At this time there was a thin layer of Strato-Cumulus at approximately 10,000 feet.
On the sixty-eight mile run up from the turning point on the Danube, scores of aircraft were on the approach to the target. Skipper of 44 squadron's 'J' Johnnie Sgt. J. Pennington, remarked about approaching the target on his 21st operation;

'We had the slip streams of other Lancasters all the way.'[73]

On the La Spezia raid on the 13th of April in Italy, which was the operation before the Škoda raid, Pennington's mid-upper gunner Bill Harrall remembers turning back after approximately two hours when the port-inner engine caught fire over France. Flames were streaming back well past his turret. They pressed on having feathered the propeller but the fire broke out again and the prop had unfeathered itself, forcing an early return. They were lucky not to attract night fighters with the bright flames. The fire eventually died out but caused quite a nervous trip back. The engineer dumped fuel to lighten the load and they made it back safely, landing at Tangmere on the south coast of England.

---

[72] Bomber Barons, Chaz Boyer. Permission for use given by Pen and Sword publishers.
[73] John Pennington 44 squadron pilot interview with Sunday Express, 18th April 1943

Four of the Rudge crew (W4845 Plzeň) in front of ED888 L-R Sgt Lancaster Nav, Sgt 'Jock' Baird Mid-Upper gunner, Sgt Greenwood W/op, Sgt Kilpatrick RAAF R/G ED888 'THE' Lancaster completed 140 operations; Photo Baird

Over the target at Plzeň, Bill would be trying his best not to stare at the fires on the ground as this would ruin his night vision and his chances of spotting an incoming fighter. On another occasion he remembered his skipper sending somebody back to check on him in his turret as he hadn't been answering the inter-com. In fact his oxygen tube had come out and he had passed out! It was also not uncommon for oxygen tubes to freeze up in the very low temperatures in the turret of a heavy bomber.

Pennington's flight engineer, Sgt Morrison carried a mascot onboard in the shape of a Golly doll. The said Golly was fastened to the escape hatch cover on the roof of the Lancaster behind the cockpit canopy. On the next op over Stettin, the aircraft was buffeted by flak and the hatch was blown off and disappeared below along with the mascot. John Pennington joked that perhaps he was taken prisoner of war!

Arriving in the Plzeň target area at 01:43, the Reynolds crew on 158 squadron Halifax HR735, had seen Yellow markers seen at last turning point but no timed run was made. White flares and green target indicators were seen. A Large 'factory' building with 'V' shaped glass roof sections and a furnace was seen. One H.E. (thought by the crew to have been amongst the first to fall) fell smack in the middle of the largest 'work-shops.' The roof was seen to cave in with a large red explosion. The skipper circled the target when the flares were dropped and waited until the high explosives went down. Their own incendiaries fell across what they thought was the 'centre workshop' and the aircraft was buffeted all the time by H.E. explosions. This was not surprising from an altitude of 3,000 feet!

The mid-upper gunner and bomb aimer would have had by far the 'best' overall view of the target and area. Seeing the flak rise up to meet them would be an awesome experience. It would appear to rise very slowly but then suddenly flash towards you at lightning speed.

At 01:43 and 7,000 feet 50 squadron Lancaster ED545 (based at Skellingthorpe) saw several 4,000 pounders bursting, she also dropped Czech nickels[74] in the area. At the same time Wing Commander Warner of 78 sqn. flying Halifax W7930, identified the target by large factory buildings and the cathedral. In fact the church Warner had seen was not in the

---

[74] Propaganda leaflets

square of Plzeň but Dobřany. This was the late Baroque church of St. Nicholas dating from around 1757, together with its neighbouring 45 metre high bell tower. The '*factory*' buildings he observed were partly concealed by smoke. Still at 00:43 Sgt. McCrossen in Lancaster ED810 of 50 squadron, bombed the outline of 'factory' buildings and observed what he thought to be dummy fires south west of the target.

At 01:44 hours P/O Herrin in Lancaster W4952 of 207 Sqn., bombed the target solely with incendiaries, making two runs. One small bomb container had hung up[75] and half of the Lancaster's port elevator was missing. The port fin and rudder was also holed and a ten inch square hole was suffered in the port main plane, due to light flak.

Also at this time Halifax JB850 (of 77 Sqn.) saw buildings with tall chimneys illuminated by incendiaries and high explosives throwing up debris. Still about one minute later HR752, a Halifax of 158 squadron which had orbited at the Danube awaiting the yellow markers until they were seen, now saw railway trucks on the ground in the target area. Sgt Shnier's Lancaster R5740 of 44 sqn. had no clear view of the target as it was obscured by cloud. She had her nose damaged by heavy flak over Nürnberg, the bomb aimer Sgt Wigley brought back a piece as a souvenir! Shnier was killed in action with 97 squadron on ops to Hamburg 29/30th July 1943. Sgt. Gibbons his flight engineer, rear gunner Knoesen (by then a Flt/Sgt.) and Sgt. Croft the mid-upper gunner also died.

At 01:45 hours 83 squadron P.F.F. Lancaster R5671 had a flap jack burst over the target probably due to flak and 50 squadron Lancasters, ED475 and ED828 dropped Czech nickels in the target area.[76] Pilot Officer Walter O'Toole a Navigator of 10 squadron was in Halifax HR695 'D' which bombed at 01:47 two miles north of Dobřany on the north side of the River Radbusa. He remembers;

'I remember this raid more clearly than most because of the discussion we had in the cockpit before we dropped our bombs. It was clear moonlight for most of the flight. It was a good night for Astro-navigation but also a good night for night fighters. On our final approach to the target the bomb-aimer called out that the pathfinders marker flares were falling directly ahead of us and quite close. As I had just got what I considered to be a very good Astro position 'fix' I was confident that the flares were some 15 miles south of the target. In the ensuing discussion the pilot and bomb aimer stressed that they had strict orders that we should bomb on the target marker flares only - there was no room for pilot discretion. We dropped our bombs from 4,000 feet and could clearly see what looked like a large cluster of factory buildings. On the return flight there was much fighter activity though we were not attacked directly.'

It is clear there was confusion about the various versions of what the instructions were regarding target acquisition. The above 10 squadron crew being convinced they were to bomb the markers whilst 102 Squadron Sgt. Hewlet's (Halifax JB894) Instructions to crews were to only take P.F.F. markers as guide and to remain free to make their own decision when bombing the target. Indeed in the official record of the raid, the official briefing stated just that.

Sgt. Pennington of 44 sqn. on ED611 described the deep orange glow and dense black smoke, which now covered the target area. Pennington and crew spent around ten minutes over the target having made two runs. He commented;

"Our bomb flashes illuminated factory chimneys, railway sidings and built up areas. Buildings showed up black and the streets white. There was a good concentration of fires

---

[75] A Hang up was a bomb or container which failed to release.
[76] Information/Propaganda leaflets

over the target when we first went in at 01:47. I did an orbit round the town while the bomb aimer picked out the works. "Then we went in and pranged it. There was a red blaze as our 4,000 pounder went down. It was followed by a couple of 1,000 pounders. We saw all our bombs burst and have no doubt that we hit our aiming point in the centre of a group of sheds. I could see far too many open bomb doors just above us."[77]

At 10,000 ft Flt/Lt. Allsebrook in 49 sqn Lancaster ED597 made his run up. At 01:47 he saw a green target indicator go down ahead of him, many 4,000lb cookies bursting and big columns of smoke and dust. At 01:48 Wing Commander Hope in Halifax HR720 (158 sqn) dropped his load of 450 x 4lb, 90x4lb X type and 24x30lb incendiaries. Only four operations later, Sgt. Ken Cottrell the wireless operator of this crew was shot down with a different crew and aircraft. He was downed on operations to Wuppertal 29th May, by night fighter ace Manfred Meurer. Cottrell was badly wounded on landing and broke an ankle and a leg. He was at first aided by Dutch civilians. He had prematurely finished his tour on his tenth operation and became a prisoner of war.

The target area was crowded with aircraft now and Flying Officer Pilgrim, captain of 'S for Sugar' of 44 squadron was over the target at 01:49 and stated in his report;

'We had bags of company all the way. I saw sticks of incendiaries criss-crossing the target like giant asterisks.'[78]

Squadron leader Peter Jennings, Captain of 'B for beer' Lancaster W4838, bombed from 8,000 feet at 01:50. He commented about the Plzeň raid on return to base;

'Frequently, I had to twist and dodge away from aircraft appearing to come directly at us. Once I saw a 4,000lb cookie drop only a yard or two ahead of our nose. We also saw the outlines of many Lancasters silhouetted against the mass of fires below us.'[79]

156 sqn. Lancaster ED822 had seen a night fighter at 01:12 but no action ensued. Over the target she made her way past approximately thirty searchlights and seven barrage balloons. Bombing by the light of the flares her crew saw no target indicators. There was a high risk of collision with other aircraft and the chances of bombs dropping on you from above were great. Tom Jackson of Six Group and 419 squadron (Halifax JB912) based at Middleton Saint George, saw a Lancaster approaching fast on the starboard side and below, he pulled back on the control column and his Halifax miraculously went over the oncoming Lancaster without mishap. Tom remembered the great feeling of elation when he realised he had avoided harm! His good fortune didn't last much longer though as he was on another operation to Stettin only a few days later on the 20/21st of April. This time on approach to the target he was intercepted by Hauptman Werner Hoffman of 4./NJG5. The aircraft came down 1.5 km east of Eggesin, south, south east of Uekermünde. Hoffman went on to score over 50 victories putting him in the top 20 German Night fighter aces. He survived the war. Tom was sent to Stalag Luft.III.

Sgt. Hutton the wireless operator on Lancaster W4366 (12 sqn.) was standing near the flare chute, as they approached the target, when he saw a big flash below the aircraft and felt it shudder, but could see no damage. They had been hit by flak, but managed to drop their bombs from 5,000 feet, and climbing to 10,000 feet, turned for home.

---

[77] Interview with Sunday Express, 18th April 1943
[78] Ibid
[79] Ibid

A Shaky do. The Plzen raid April 16/17th April 1943

Ian Duncan, a 419 squadron bomb aimer (Halifax W1271 VR-P) flying with New Zealand skipper Squadron Leader Clark, remembered;

'We almost boobed horribly as our DR Compass went u/s on the last leg and we continued merrily on until ETA and found nothing. Away in the distance we saw some flares and set course for them, sure enough it was the target. We bombed at 10,000ft and then turned for home. After leaving the target area we set course 268° true, supposedly going to the north of Nürnberg and Mannheim. We didn't observe any fighters, which was a good thing as we were on our own when we realized where we had gone wrong and turned north to get to the target area.

W1271's load was 1 x 2000lb HC, 2 x 1000lb RDX, 2 S.B.C. (90x4lb), 2 S.B.C. (8x30lb)+ one 250 gallon fuel overload tank located in the bomb bay.'[80]
The photo flash would be released first as the heavier bombs would fall past it. The flash would go off and hopefully light up the results for the camera. The switch numbers were repeated merely as a precaution in case activation did not take place the first time around. A stop peg usually delayed the dropping of part of the load, usually between incendiaries (small bomb containers). The C.S.B.S. (Course Setting Bombsight), being completely manual had a variety of height bars to correspond to various terminal velocities of the bombs. With the Mk XIV bomb sight terminal velocities were set in by use of a knob on the front panel of the computer box. See diagram below (not to scale) of Halifax W1271 VR-P's bomb bay.

Port Wing

15		
13	SBC	
11	SBC	

5		9	1000lb RDX	6
2		3		2000 1 H.C.	Nose
7		8	1000lb RDS	Photo 4 flash

Overload fuel tank occupying stations 5, 2 & 7

10	SBC
12	SBC
14	

Starboard Wing

---

[80] Ian Duncan 419 sqn bomb-aimer.

A Shaky do. The Plzen raid April 16/17th April 1943

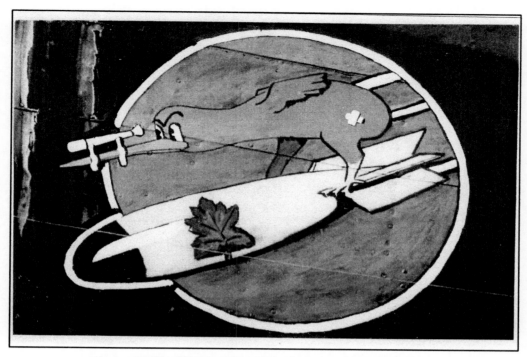

Nose art Halifax W1271 419 Squadron (Photo Duncan Bomb Aimer)

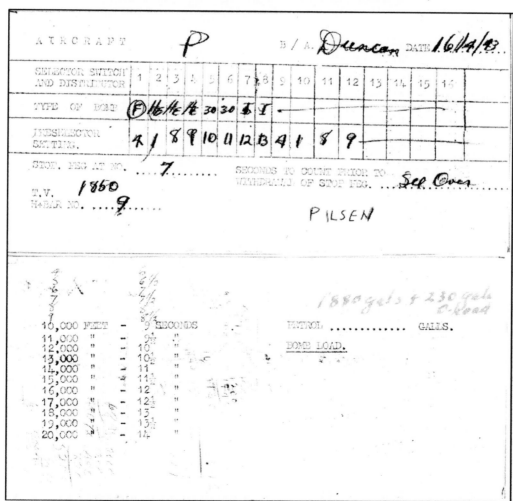

Bomb Aimer's selector slip Halifax W1271 419 Squadron (Duncan) Top of this form: the order of bomb release on the Plzen raid being stations, 4,1,8,9,10,11,12,13 with 1,2,3 being repeated on switches 9, 10,11,12. Bottom of form time to impact

A shaky do-The Skoda works raid 16/17th April 1943

AIR BOMBERS HAVE YOU ?

1. Cleaned the glass of the bomb sight.
2. Cleaned the perspex of the bombing window.
3. Tested the rigidity of the installation of the Bomb Sight.
4. Checked the presence and size of bubbles in the levels.
5. That the Bomb Sight Compass bowl is correctly illuminated.
6. Checked that the Navigator has an H L and L L Computor.
7. Checked the travel of the distributor arm.
8. Checked your oxygen and inter-comm.

Bomb aimer's check list found in log book of Frank Ward, KIA on ED711 460 Sqn.
(Image Bruce Hall)

Sgt Rudge and crew on Lancaster W4845 'Q' of 103 squadron arrived over the target area. He dropped his bombs from 7,000 feet at 01:57 hours.

Sgt. Jock Baird the mid-upper gunner recalled;

'We certainly found Plzeň and on the signal 'BOMBS GONE'! , a blue master searchlight caught onto us and another God knows how many searchlights coned us and the barrage of flak must have had us alone. We had much crumping of shell bursts around us and Den (the Pilot) once more threw us around the sky. We then received a mighty hit and I saw what I thought was smoke from the port outer. I warned Den who was very busy still coned. The flight engineer evidently realised it was petrol leaking and did the necessary transferring [of fuel]. All this happened in seconds and at the height of it I had the experience of flashes of my Mum, Dad and siblings. Apparently a few of us had similar happenings. Anyhow we got out of the cone and George Lancaster (the navigator) gave Den a course for home. Martin Middlebrook reckons the raid was unsuccessful. Well if we were not over Plzeň we certainly had a fiery welcome. We gunners were unable to douse any searchlights due to Den's gyrations, but thank God for Den! We saw plenty of fires and explosions under us in the target area but nothing compared to what lay ahead of us in the Battle of the Ruhr etc. It was only our third Operation.[81]

Baird also remembered;

---

[81] Correspondence between the author and Jock Baird 2007

A Shaky do. The Plzen raid April 16/17th April 1943

*Having returned from one operation to Nürnberg (10th August 1943) on which we took Wing Commander Slater as a second Dickie, the Winco said that our crew 'lacked animation.' Rudgie said to us, 'b***** the animation, we're going O.K. as we are!'*

Baird's squadron mates on Pettigrew's W4337 'R' were coned by approximately thirty searchlights and hit by flak almost on top of the target. A great deal of smoke haze and fire now covered the whole target area making observation much more difficult.

On board 9 squadron Lancaster ED654 'W' nicknamed 'Cutty Sark',[82] was bomb-aimer Ken Dagnall. In a letter to the author in 2006 he commented;

'The flight to Plzeň was uneventful-the odd ack-ack fire but not much else. The target was difficult to identify and I was not sure that the building I was aiming for was the target. It looked like it but in my uncertainty I made two dummy runs. As the smoke from the burning buildings was beginning to obliterate the target I dropped the bombs on the third run-at the time I was sure it was the Škoda works. The rest of the crew were as keen to leave Plzeň as I was. The long journey home was quite 'restful' we could see the odd plane going down but fortunately we were unscathed-hence I can write to you.'

At 01:48 a 101 sqn. Lanc. (ED835) flown by Wing Commander Reddick, complained that too much smoke caused by incendiaries made identifying the target impossible. S/Ldr. Gilpin (ED805 of 49 sqn.) also saw much smoke but made three runs and eventually dropped his weapons amongst a great concentration of fires and exploding 4000lb 'cookies.' The crew of Lancaster ED412 of 207 sqn. saw several large explosions when 35 miles away on her way home and P/O Thompson's Lancaster ED837 of 156 squadron saw a Bf110 fighter, which did not engage her.

About one minute later, Pilot Officer Byres'51 sqn. Halifax DT637 was caught in searchlights and broke free to make a second run only to be caught a second time but this time she released her weapons receiving some damage in the undercarriage doors.

Squadron Leader Lashbrook's Halifax HR663 (102 sqn.) having flown at about ten thousand feet, had seen one aircraft going down about half way out on the trip outbound. Now arriving over the target at about 01:50 they then dropped height to around 4,000 feet. bomb aimer Alfie Martin recalled;

'On the first run in we were unable to identify the factory so they circled and came in again on the same heading this time unleashing the load of all high explosive bombs. The defences were not very heavy but several bursts of flak came fairly close, you could hear them and they shook the aircraft.'[83]

Lashbrook's Halifax was a special reconnaissance Halifax that carried a special camera for photographing the bombing results. They had been over the target dropped their bombs, and then made a reverse run over the target with great risk of collision with on coming bombers. In correspondence with the author between 2003 and 2007 Squadron Leader Lashbrook commented;

'My briefing instructed me to make a reverse run over the target after I had dropped my bombs to take photographs of the damage etc. Looking back this was indeed a reckless if not

---

[82] So named after a Royal Navy vessel which rescued them when ditched 40 miles off the Scillies 29th Oct.42
[83] Author's phone interview with Alfie Martin October 2007

stupid idea, as there were scores of aircraft over the target at the time. Fortunately we did not have a collision, nor were we hit by bombs dropped by Lancasters from above. We certainly encountered plenty of slipstreams on the way back over the target area.'

Lashbrook was to have further troubles on the return leg of the flight.

Also at 01:50 35 sqn. Pathfinder Halifax DT801 dropped more target indicators on the existing markers and identified an airfield on the run up. 460 sqn. Lancaster W4941 skippered by Australian skipper Sgt. Fuhrman, considered the target 'well blitzed.'

At this time a pathfinder P/O Milton's Lancaster (R5622 83 squadron) was seen to be hit with flares igniting and coloured target indicators exploding in the sky. The Lancaster was claimed shot down by the crew of one of the small calibre 2.5cm Hotchkiss guns and fell out of the sky. The weapon used was probably a captured French weapon known to the Germans as a 2.5cm Pak 112(f). Squadron leader Gascoigne-Cecil (61 Squadron ED718) and Squadron Leader Duigan (156 squadron ED715) witnessed this event on their runs up.

One report from a witness on the ground, states that the aircraft lost altitude, descending in wide spirals turning south west and passing the blazing church tower. An unsubstantiated witness report claimed that the aircraft hit the tower but German damage reports make no mention of this, only fire damage. Photographs showed no damage caused by the crash of a heavy bomber. After flying past the church the Lancaster went on for 750 metres very low over the roofs of the houses to crash near Dobřany railway station. The fuselage was broken into two main sections but did not catch fire. Probably the weapons had already been released which would account for other aircraft witnessing TIs going off in the air and no fire on the ground. Witnesses stated the port wing was missing. The crew was buried hastily outside the cemetery walls. In 1946 they were exhumed later and re-buried at Prague war cemetery.[84] There were no survivors of this, the only aircraft to be shot down over the target area.

At 01:55 Halifax HR719 of 158 sqn. arrived having map read up to the target from yellow markers at the last turning point. She first did a circuit and approached from the east. Seeing a lake to north of target Sgt. Williamson and crew followed a railway in. Long buildings and smoking chimneys were identified. They approached at an indicated 240 M.P.H. at 7,000 feet and bombed just before the chimneys to allow for the unusual airspeed. The crew saw their own incendiaries burst on the ground and several large explosions on the run up. Sgt McQuaker the bomb aimer went on to complete a second tour with 644 squadron including S.O.E., D-Day and Arnhem glider towing ops. The pilot, Williamson was killed in a training accident at a Heavy Conversion Unit in November 1945.

At about the same time (01:55), the Blackhall crew of 408 squadron Halifax JB898 'Q', dropped their load comprising 4x1000lb explosives and 150x4lb, 30x4lb'X' type and 16x30lb incendiaries. They had found the target visually with a pinpoint and dropped on the fires in the bomb sight. This aircraft was to last only a few weeks more on operations when tasked to attack Dortmund. She was shot down on the 5th of May by night fighter ace Oblt. Lothar Linke of IV./NJG1. The aircraft crashed near Akkrum Holland. The burning plane carried a full load of incendiaries and was witnessed by a young Dutch boy, Albert Jeeninga, as it passed over the village. Thirty years later he contacted the surviving crew and their families and helped reconstruct events. Bob Blackhall and Ken Emmons were killed by cannon fire, and Albert Sutton's chute failed to open. They are buried at Akkrum. The other crew members just baled out successfully at about 3,000 feet. Oblt. Linke himself died one week later when he hit the tail of his plane bailing out over Issjelmaar. Of the crew that flew to Plzeň, Sgt. Blackhall R.C.A.F., Sgt Emmons R.C.A.F., and Sgt Sutton R.C.A.F., were

---

[84] Dr. Krátký, Škoda Museum

killed. Navigator Carl Norton, bomb aimer George Semper, and wireless operator Kenneth Godfrey, were taken prisoner of war. Through the efforts of Albert Jeeninga, an axe (see photo on page 37) dredged from the crash site by a local farmer in the seventies, was identified and presented to Ken Godfrey's son Steve. [85]

Meanwhile, Halifax DT791 of 10 sqn, was coned by searchlights and hit by flak in the target area, shrapnel was heard hitting the aircraft. This resulted in the loss of the port outer engine. Some Messerschmitt Bf110 and 210 fighters were seen but the flak although moderate compared to Happy Valley (the Ruhr), was the bigger threat.

Over the target, 467 sqn. Lancaster ED737 Flt/Sgt. W.L. Wilson had the top Perspex of the rear turret holed. Flying this night on main force, Sgt. Petrie-Andrews' 35 sqn. P.F.F. Halifax W7779, received holes in leading edge port wing and bomb doors; 83 sqn. Lancaster W4231 suffered flak damage to nose; and 10 sqn. Halifax JB930 suffered three small flak hits in both wings. 101 sqn. Lancaster ED775's mid-upper turret, intercom and flaps became unserviceable due to flak. 44 squadron Lancasters W4268 and W4949 received holes in the port wing and rudder respectively. Gilmour's 50 squadron[86] Lancaster made three runs encountering accurate heavy flak and searchlights sustaining damage to the port aileron. Even the smallest piece of shrapnel in the wrong place could have dire consequences, perhaps a cut control or hydraulic line or a leaking fuel tank.

Sgt. Petrie-Andrews and crew mentioned in the above paragraph were to have a busy year in 1943. On the next operation to Stettin they were outward bound at a thousand feet over Denmark when hit by a flak shell which exploded in the nose. In November of the same year they were again hit by flak on ops to Cannes and ditched in the Mediterranean, making it safely to Sardinia after three days in a dinghy. On another operation they found themselves in the unusual position of stalking a night fighter. They had moved up behind the unsuspecting enemy and gave him a few bursts at close range surely hitting the fighter. However the C/O didn't take kindly to the practice and had the incident struck from the record. Perhaps he didn't want to encourage the practice of Halifaxes chasing fighters!

At 01:58 as the last elements of the Plzeň force were arriving in the area, Pilot Officer Smuck's Halifax DT769 (408 squadron) having already had trouble with flak and fighters earlier in the Saarbrücken area, bombed from ten thousand feet and had the Astro hatch blown off due to flak.

At 01:59 hours Sgt Tolchard arrived over the target in 49 squadron Lancaster ED448 and bombed what he thought he had clearly identified as the Skoda works from 8,000 feet. Australian Flt/Sgt. Arnold had replaced his regular W/op Sgt. George. Tolchard had had a busy April when he was fired at by a Lancaster on the 3/4th April when on ops to Essen. Only ten days later, he was fired on again by coastal guns at Folkestone when on ops to Stuttgart on the 14th/15th of April! He completed his first tour and then a second tour with 83 squadron.

Wing Commander Gomm of 467 squadron grew up in Brazil and left aged 19 to join the R.A.F. in 1933. He flew Whitleys with 77 sqn and Beaufighters with 604 sqn. On the Škoda raid, flying Lancaster ED547 he arrived on target at 02:01 and bombed from 6,000 feet. He and his crew were coned by searchlights in the target area and twice more on the return trip. In his report to the Operations Research Section he commented that he thought the P.F.F flares had ignited too low and burned on the ground causing an effective smoke screen. Gomm's log book records;

---

[85] Steve Godfrey
[86] Possibly flying ED755. The ops records are indistinct.

A Shaky do. The Plzen raid April 16/17th April 1943

47th op Škoda works, too much smoke for accurate bombing. Coned three times, once by target and twice on way back-Low flying-forward escape hatch came off. Landed Boscombe. 8:45 hours [duration].[87]

A great deal of smoke from the target damage and woods to the north was another cause of the smoke mentioned by Gomm. Squadron Leader Campling D.F.C. stated that at 02:05 hours the target was completely covered by smoke. Campling and crew covered considerable distances at 100 feet and shot out some searchlights near Mannheim. At this same time ED706 of 57 squadron, dropped her bombs south east of München on a crossroads, being well south of track. Her port inner was unserviceable and she was well behind time.

As the last few aircraft dropped their loads, Sgt. Reid flying ED409 of 106 sqn. was convinced that a dummy target had been bombed. His photo was later plotted at 6.5 miles south of the correct aiming point. P/O Chopping on 50 squadron Lancaster ED468, made three circuits of the target area but saw two rows of regular red lights and concluded he was over dummy target and turned to bomb Nürnberg on the way back. Chopping had also been caught in searchlights and chased by a JU88 at one point.

The Plzeň force's early elements had long turned for home. The run back to the safety of home would be as long and costly in lives and machines as the run out. Many optimistic reports were to be filed upon return to base but most aircraft failed to locate the Škoda works at Plzeň and many bombed secondary objectives or targets of opportunity. A good many crews knew the markers were in the wrong place. Tom Wingham D.F.C. a bomb-aimer with 102 sqn. Commented,

'The Intelligence report in the squadron records bears no relationship to what we reported. It was a fairly clear night and we navigated on Astro-navigation to the target. Blackie (The Nav.) and I had every confidence in our Astro-navigation and at E.T.A. were surprised to see the PFF marking well to the south of us. Instructions to crews were to only take PFF as guide but to remain free to make own decision in bombing target. We flew south to investigate when I advised Dave (Pilot) that P.F.F. had made a boob and that Plzeň was further north. We debated whether to call up the rest of the squadron to advise them but decided against it.

We then turned north to search for the Škoda works and after some time, it was very dark, I identified a river similar to that at Plzeň where I aimed the bomb load, (4 x 1000lb & 1 x 500lb HE). Unfortunately, our photograph showed up as open fields about 5 miles south of the Škoda works, but I did not bomb the infirmary or whatever it was that the P.F.F. had marked. The raid was a cock-up, no more that up to half a dozen aircraft getting anywhere near Plzen.'[88]

Harry Hughes D.F.C., D.F.M., AE. navigator aboard Halifax W7920, also of 102 sqn. Stated;

'I was still new to operations (a sprog) and as a navigator the most important thing was to know where you were. I knew where I was because the bomb aimer gave me a pinpoint at the river Moselle. We were coned and hit by flak just after this near Saarbrücken and again suffered flak damage near Karlsruhe. Well, we carried on to our next turning point which was to the South of Plzeň but about 7 minutes before my E.T.A. the Pathfinder flares went down and bomb aimer Harry Hooper insisted that he could see the Škoda works so we bombed along with everyone else despite my protestations. We landed at Harwell we did not get back to base until 13:30 hours the following day having had to repair the flak holes in the ailerons and the tail plane.'

[87] Winco Gomm's log book AIR4/38 TNA U.K. Wing/Co Gomm D.S.O. D.F.C. was KIA 15/8/43
[88] correspondence/phone interview with the author 2006

A Shaky do. The Plzen raid April 16/17th April 1943

Navigator Harry Hughes finished his tour and after a period of instruction went off to 8 Group Pathfinders on 692 Squadron, which was part of the Light Night Striking Force. Among the targets were railway tunnels during the 'Battle of the Bulge' and the mining of the Kiel canal.

W7912 of 102 squadron (Flt/Sgt Quigley) strafed a goods train on her way out of the Plzeň target area. At the controls of Lancaster 'E' of 12 squadron was Flight Sergeant Head in the target area at an unknown time. The log book entry of his navigator Sgt. Joe Short recorded after this his third operation;

First low level night raid. Disappointing. Missed the target and bombed a railway junction. Shot up three trains. 14 S.B.C. 8 Hours 40 minutes [duration].[89]

One 77 squadron Halifax (DT796) crew captained by W.O. Pye R.A.A.F, bombed the target from 9,500 feet at an unknown time. This crew was to lose their pilot and Sgt. Wells, one of the gunners on the Duisburg operation on 26/27th April. Stewart, Atter and Gibbs were taken prisoner of war. The navigator, Stewart, was brutally murdered by Lux and Scharpwinkel after the Great Escape from Sagan in March 1944. He was cremated at Liegnitz.[90]

---

[89] Nav's flying log book Sgt. Joseph Short RAF Museum archives Hendon X001-6464/008
[90] http://www.elsham.pwp.blueyonder.co.uk/gt_esc/

A Shaky do. The Plzen raid April 16/17th April 1943

Rudges crew 103 sqn; L-R 'Dickie' A/B, Sgt Kilpatrick 'Killer' R/G, Sgt Robinson F/E, Sgt Baird 'Jock' M/U, Sgt Greenwood W/op, Sgt Lancaster Nav, Sgt Rudge Pilot.

(photos Baird)

Rudge's crew and Erks, in front of ED888 at Elsham Wolds, which became THE Lancaster with 140 ops. L-R Sgt Robinson F/E, Bob Draper (Rigger), Bert Booth (Fitter), Tom Gean (a/c hand), Sgt Greenwood W/op, Sgt Rudge (Pilot), Sgt Lancaster (Nav), Sgt Baird (M/U) Sgt Kilpatrick RAAF (R/G) On the Skoda raid they flew W4845 'Q'

A Shaky do-The Skoda works raid 16/17th April 1943

Above:The crew of 'Cutty Sark' ED654 WS-W 9 sqn. L-R 'Taffy, Sgt Dagnall, DFM, P/O McCubbin DFC, Sgt Sherry, Sgt Smith, Sgt Owen DFM   (Photo Dagnall)

The crew of 'Cutty Sark' ED654 WS- W   (photo Dagnall)

A Shaky do-The Skoda Works raid 16/17th April 1943

Crew of J-Johnny 44 sqn 16 April 1943 About to depart on the Skoda works raid. L-R Sgt Betts W/op RCAF, Sgt Homewood R/G, Sgt Harrall Mid-Upper, Sgt Hawkes B/A, Sgt Hewitt Nav, Sgt Morrison F/E, Sgt Pennington Pilot, Sgt Dowding Pilot-second dickie. (Photo Pennington)

A bomb-Aimer probably Sgt Wigley, shows off a piece of flak which came through the nose of Sgt Shnier's aircraft 17th April 1943 (Photo Pennington)

A shaky do-The Skoda works raid 16/17th April 1943

Above: Flt.Lt. Kearns' 156 sqn crew seen posing with a dinghy sponsored by a local school. Left to right: Honi Barclay RNZAF Nav, Sgt. 'Taffy' Evans F/E, Flt.Lt. Terry Kearns RNZAF Pilot, P/O Jack Moller RNZAF B/A, Jimmy Barnham RNZAF W/op, Max Dowman RNZAF M/U gnr, F/S Ken Krankshaw RNZAF Rear Gunner. (Photo Jack Moller.)

Robertson and crew with Panic II. ED499 WS-X The caption on the fuselage in Portuguese reads, 'God looks after drunks and children.' (Photo: Gordon Thorburn)

A Shaky do-The Skoda works raid 16/17th April 1943

**Francois Pilon Nav KIA Halifax BB343
408 Sqn on 3rd operation**
Photo Pilon

**Sgt Irving MacDonald Air Gunner KIA
Halifax BB343 408 Sqn on 2nd operation**
Photo MacLeod

Air Gunners course 36B Irving MacDonald is 4th from right
(Photo MacLeod)

All for one and one for all-The crew of 408 Sqn. Halifax BB343. Back row L-R Sgt MacDonald A/G, Sgt Fill F/E, Sgt Winter Wop/Ag, W/O Guay Capt, Front row L-R Sgt Gielty A/G, Sgt Haines B/A/Nav, Sgt Pilon Nav. (Photo Jean-Luc Pilon)

The monument at Lequielles St. Germain, paid for by local villagers in memory of the crew of Halifax BB343

A Shaky do-The Skoda works raid 16/17th April 1943

Crew of Halifax DT773 78 squadron

L-R Sgt Orr R/G, Sgt Hoare M/U, Sgt Slater F/E, F/L Dowse Capt., Sgt Langsford Wop/ag, Anon Nav, Sgt Thompson A/B

photo Langsford

A shaky do-The Plzen raid 16/17th April 1943

Halifax HR695 'D' 10 Squadron Melbourne; (Photo O'Toole)

Note the lack of front or mid-upper turret. Also note the ventral Perspex blister aft inline of sight with the rear door

A shaky-The Skoda works raid 16/17th April 1943

Crew of 10 Sqn.Halifax HR695

L-R Sgt Gladwell F/E, Sgt Pullen B/A, Sgt Gale W/op, Sgt Wade Capt, Sgt Hainsworth R/G, Sgt Beaton M/U, P/O O'Toole Nav. Photo O'Toole

36 Course 16 OTU Upper Heyford (photo Langsford)

Flansburgh-Washbourne - killed 11 Feb 43 with 102 Sqn, Thompson - killed 3rd Feb 43 with 102 Sqn, Moore - killed 1st Aug. 42 16 OTU. Elliot P.O.W. 23/09/1942 Ops to Flensburg. Elliot gained fame as a Shakespearian actor and film star. Langsford was shot down in DT773 of 78 sqn. on the Plzen raid 17th April 1943.

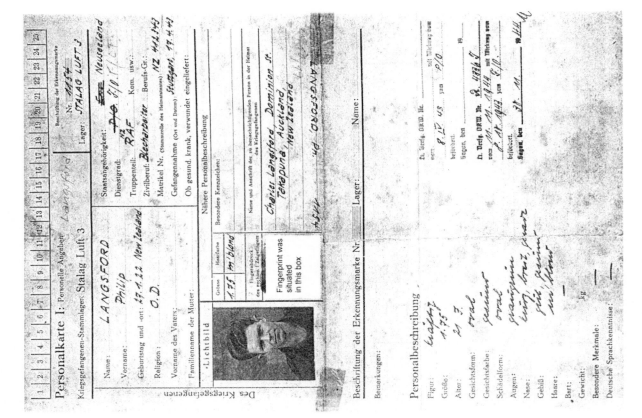

Left: Personalkarte of Phil Langsford RNZAF interned at Stalag Luft III. He remained there until the end of the war when he was force marched westward across Germany away from the oncoming Russian forces. He had been shot down in Halifax DT773 of 78 squadron based at Linton On Ouse near York.(Phil Langsford)

Above; Prisoners at Stalag Luft III pose for a photograph. (Photo: Ray Dennis 78 Sqn.)

A Shaky do-The Skoda works raid 16/17th April 1943

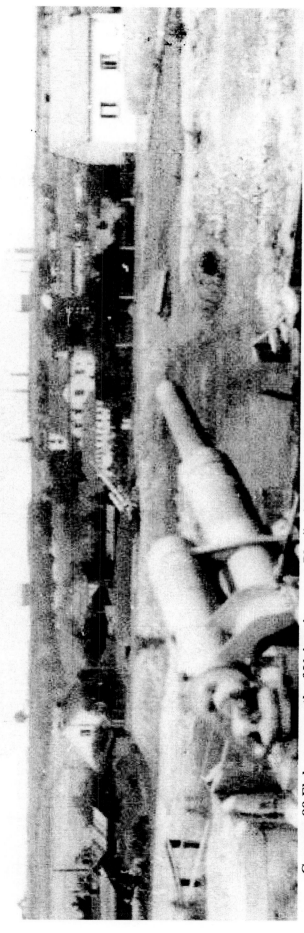

German 88 Flak guns south of Vejprnice, near Plzeň with dummy Skoda works on horizon. (Photo Krátký, Skoda Museum)

A shaky do-The Skoda works raid 16/17th April 1943

82

Main square Dobrany with bomb damaged to tower of St Nikolaus
(Kratký Škoda Museum)

Damaged houses, Hus St. not far from the military barracks
Dobrany (Kratky Skoda Museum)

Damaged houses in the vicinity of Dobrany main square
note church tower in background. (Kratký Škoda Museum)

A Shaky do-The Skoda works raid 16/17th April 1943

LOG BOOK PAGES (JOCK BAIRD)

START OF 1ST TOUR.   103 Squadron Elsham Wolds

Time carried forward :—   43.45   09.00

Date	Hour	Aircraft Type and No.	Pilot	Duty	REMARKS (including results of bombing, gunnery, exercises, etc.)	Day	Night
APRIL 1943.		Lancaster					
8.4.43	11.15	Q	Sgt Rudge	Mid-upper	Air firing Air Wallethorpe D.N.F.	1.40	
9.4.43	1130	Q	" "	" "	Cross Country Whitby-Kinnaird Head crossing pond (Atlantic) Bardsley Ile - Base.	8.40	
11.4.43	23.50	Q	"	1	(....... road) FRANKFURT S.W.II. 502 A/c 21 MISSING		7.1.
13-14.4.43	20.30	Q	"	2	(Operational) Spezia Italy 2 (overland flight) 1500 miles round trip 4 MISSING		9.4
14.							
14.4.43	17.40	Q	"		Westcott to base	1.00	
16.4.43	12.30	O	"		Base to Tangmere (with another crew)	1.50	
	16.40	O	"		Tangmere to base.	1.20	
17.4.43	21.10	W/4845 Q	"	3	MISSING 38. ✱ (Operational) Pilsen Skoda works 3		9.50
18.4.43	16.10	O	"		Shaky Kite CZECO-SLAVAKIA TRAVELLES Port outer petrol tank holed by flak NFT	-.45	
18.4.43	2.05	O			Turned back from Spezia slid eng U.S.		5.20
19	14.50	T	SGT PETTIGREW		Air to sea firing	1.00	
					TOTAL TIME ... 60.09		

Date	Hour	Aircraft Type and No.	Pilot	Duty	Remarks (including results of bombing, gunnery, exercises, etc.)	Flying Times Day	Night
					Time carried forward —	15:10	NIL.
APR. 2nd	21:00	Lanc IV	f/Lt BARRATT.	ENGINEER.	CIRCUITS AND LANDINGS.		1:30.
" 3rd	21:00	Lanc II Z	W/OR CHILTON	"	CIRCUITS AND LANDINGS.		:20.
" 3rd	23:00	Lanc II R	SGT. PLUM.	"	CROSS COUNTRY.		2:50.
" 4th	20:45	Lanc II F.	SGT PLUM	"	OPERATIONS – KIEL – 10×1000		5:45.
" 9th	10:45	Lanc II B	SGT PLUM.	"	AIR TEST – FIRING	1:15	
" 11th	21:08	Lanc II M	SGT. PLUM.	"	OPERATIONS – BORDEAUX – 6×1500' mines		6:10.
" 14th	22:02	Lanc II C	SGT PLUM.	"	OPERATIONS – STUTTGART – 80×18S		
				JETTISONED NEAR ARRAS RETURNED TO BASE		
				ON 3 ENGINES		3:45
" 16th	21:40	Lanc II G	SGT PLUM.	ENGINEER.	OPERATIONS – SKODA WORKS –		
				CZECHOSLOVAKIA	1×4000 – 4×1000 – 2×500 LBS.		
					AIRFIELD MACHINE-GUNND. 1×4000 – 6 C.ANS.		7:45
" 26th	01:20	Lanc II C	SGT PLUM.	ENGINEER.	OPERATIONS – DUISBURG		
" 28th	15:15	Lanc II c	SGT PLUM.	"	1×4000LBS –12 S.B.Cs OF 4 IB INCEND		3:45
" 29th	14:45	Lanc II C	SGT PLUM	ENGINEER	FORMATION FLYING	:45.	
" 29th	11:50	Lanc II m	P/c SIMS	PASSENGER.	TO BRISTOL	1:15	
"	18:30	"	"	"	FROM BRISTOL TO BASE	1:00	

	DAY	NIGHT	TOTAL
TOTAL FLYING TIME	19:25	31:50	51:15

TOTAL FLYING TIME	DAY	NIGHT	TOTAL
	15:10	15:10	
MARCH.	4:15		
APRIL.	4:15	31:50	36:05

TOTAL TIME — 19:25 | 31:50

FOR "G" IN FLIGHT

Log book C.F. Trott 115 squadron Flight engineer-Lancaster MKII DS616 G (Tony Trott)

A Shaky do–The Skoda works raid 16/17th April 1943

(PHOTO ROLFE)

Sgt D.H. Reid air gunner 51 Squadron Halifax HR784. Killed in action near Eppeville, Somme, 17th April 1943. Five aircraft from 51 squadron failed to return.

A Letter from 51 Sqn's. Commanding Officer, to Reid's parents 17th April. One of thirty six families who received a similar letter from the same officer. Only eleven of which were later to receive better news that their sons were evaders or POWs.

The graves of the crew of HR784 at the French Military cemetery, Maucourt, Somme.

A Shaky do-The Skoda works raid 16/17ᵗʰ April 1943

Chapter Five
Westbound

The return route from Plzeň (49.50N 05.50E-49.37N 02.05E-50.10N 01.30E) was to the north of Nürnberg roughly in the direction of Würzburg, Darmstadt, Trier and northern Luxembourg (position D), north of Sedan and back across France to the final turn north of Beauvais and re crossing the coast near Cayeux-sur-Mer. Certainly various other routes were taken, some favouring a route closer to the Belgian border country.

At 01:45 hours over the boundary of Mundelsheim a fighter shot down Halifax JB800 of 76 squadron. Lt. Heinz Bock of 7./NJG101 a night fighter training unit, claimed his first victory. Sgt. Wright, the skipper of the Halifax had struggled but failed to pull out of a steep dive trying to give his crew time to get out and knowing he would never make it out himself. The aircraft exploded a few seconds after Sgt. Read had baled out. The bomber crashed into the Hofkammerwald forest not far from the Reichsautobahn-Durchlass at Holzweiler Hof. The German soldiers of Schwäbisch-Hall recovered the remains of 3 or 5 very badly burned airmen. The remains were buried in a common grave on the 18th of April 1943 in the cemetery of the community of Mundelsheim. One crewmember (according to the statement of the mayor) parachuted safely, was captured and interrogated by members of the Luftwaffe in the town hall of the neighbouring community of Höpfigheim.

Exhumation of four corpses happened on the 9th and 10th of August 1948. The only I.D. tag found was that of the Wop/Ag Flying Officer J. F. Webb 49997.[91] Sgt. Read who had been taken prisoner of war was sadly later killed when strafed by allied aircraft on the 19th of April 1945 at Gresse. He was in a column of prisoners mistaken for enemy troops, when being force-marched by the Germans away from the advancing Russians.[92]

Lancaster ED427 of 49 squadron flown by Flying Officer Bone, was heading for home but strayed over the Mannheim defences and was downed by flak as she flew west at approximately 02:00 hours. She crashed in flames and exploded on contact with the ground at Laumersheim south of Dirmstein.[93] This aircraft was listed as lost without trace in many records but an investigation took place after the war and witness were interviewed by the R.A.F. M.R.E.U.[94] identifying the place of the crash. Sadly it wasn't so easy to do likewise with the crew, who are remembered on the Runneymede memorial in the U.K.

At 02:05 Squadron Leader Frank of 10 sqn. (Halifax HR697) dropped his bombs fifty two miles north east of Nürnberg having failed to release them over the primary target. Frank was a remarkable character having serving in the early days of the war on obsolete Fairey Battle aircraft over France in May 1940. After the war he commanded 83 squadron's Vulcan force in an outstanding career.

Many aircraft which had turned away from the Plzeň target area, having failed to locate the aiming point, now hit secondary targets. Flight Sergeant Cope and crew (Lancaster ED525 460 sqn.) bombed what they believed was Erlangen north of Nürnberg at 02:24. Flight Sergeant Moodie flying Lancaster W4330 of the same squadron dropped her load just south of Nürnberg a minute later, buckling the bomb doors as the weapons were released.

---

[91] Mundelsheim Historical Society
[92] RG24 Vol.28526 Library and archives Canada, File of Sgt. F.A. Robb
[93] Canadian National archives file of Sgt. Watt R.C.A.F. BG24 vol. 28904
[94] RAF Missing Research & Enquiry Unit.

87

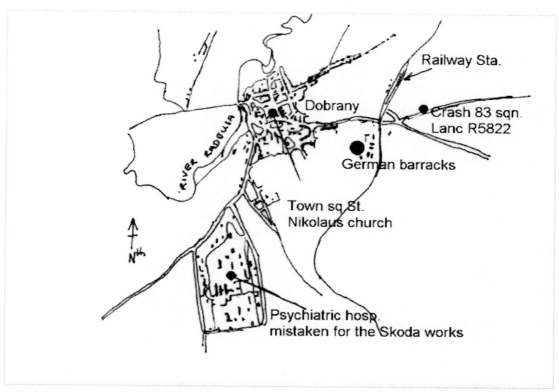

Dobřany nestled in a 'V' shape between the river Radbusa and a railway. Unfortunately the town mirrored all the key features of Plzeň leading the PFF and early main-force aircraft to believe they had found the Škoda works.

They also had a contact with a fighter at one point on the way out, the rear gunner claiming hits on the fuselage.

At Nürnberg DT791 of 10 squadron was coned by approximately 30 searchlights and again hit by flak already having lost an engine over the target. The captain F/L Wood dived to 5,000 feet and was then attacked by a fighter. The Canadian rear gunner Sgt. Frank Prebble gave successful evasive instructions to the pilot and the enemy was shaken off. During these manoeuvres approximately 200 gallons of fuel was lost but the engineer calculated that sufficient fuel was left to reach the English coast.[95]

At 02:32 an aircraft was shot down by night fighter at the hands of Lt. Herbert Jung of 12./NJG4 at Bechtolsheim, 15 miles (23km) north west of Worms. This was Halifax HR729 of 51 squadron based at Snaith. Only one crewmember, F/O Marriott baled out and was taken prisoner of war. He later attempted but failed to escape when on a forced journey from Statroda to Sagan in May 1943.

Also in the area at around the same time, Flying Officer Wilson's 57 squadron Lancaster (W4944) which dropped her bombs on the already well alight Mannheim, the other major target of the night.

Murray, skipper of W4783 'G' for George of 460 squadron dropped on Koblenz on his way back seeing large blasts from his own bombs. They were flying at around 6,000 feet and felt the blast of their own 4,000 pounder, which gave the aircraft a big jolt and blew off an escape hatch. Sgt. Walter Pridgeon on the aircraft as Second Dickey, was killed only four days later on the Stettin operation when captain of his own crew for the first time.

---

[95] Air 2/8780 TNA UK

A Shaky do. The Plzen raid April 16/17th April 1943

'G' for George was on her thirtieth operation and according to the memoirs of electrical fitter Charlie Catt, the ground crew awarded her an unofficial D.F.M. and painted another bomb symbol on her fuselage.[96]

Meanwhile, 460 sqn. Lancaster ED315, made her way back from being well south of track by dead reckoning from Augsburg/ München area to bomb Nürnberg. She had flown at very low level, 150-200 feet. F/O Pilgrim's 44 sqn. Lancaster (W4961) was also hit by flak near Augsburg when well south of the intended track.

At 02:55 the crew of Lancaster W4818 (460 sqn) observed Mannheim still burning as they passed on the return journey.

Incidences of 'friendly fire' or 'Blue on Blue' are not confined to the post world war two era. Flt/Sgt. McCormack's Halifax (HR712 102 sqn.) was fired at and hit between the starboard-inner and the main plane by a Lancaster aircraft when 40 miles North West of Mannheim. Outbound, Halifax HR773 on the Mannheim op reported a Wellington closing and when the Halifax evaded the Wellington followed. After being given a short burst the 'Wellington' turned away. Perhaps it was really a JU88 but the confusion in battle is well illustrated by these events!

Major Heinz Schnaufer, who ended the war as the top German night-fighter ace with 121 victories when interrogated at the end of the war by the British, told his questioners the following. On one occasion he saw two Lancasters shoot each other down as he was about to move in for the attack. He also said that on a bright moonlit night he could see approximately 25 bombers in the stream at any one time.[97] A night such as this.

On the way home 419 squadron Halifax W1271 flown by Sqn. Ldr. Clark took a bit of a beating over Mannheim. Bomb aimer Ian Duncan commented;

'As a result the starboard outer packed up. The starboard outer engine ran the generator which supplied the power for the primary navigating aid the "G", without it, it was a matter of relying on D.R. and antenna/radio aids on hand. And of course, the sextant to take star shots when the conditions were suitable for Astro-navigation. We managed to stagger home using radio aids and map reading and on to a point just south of Amiens on to the coast and turned onto 340° for home.'[98]

At 02:55 a combat ensued just east of the Rhein near Stockstadt Am Rhein involving Sgt. Dane's 78 squadron Halifax DT777[99] and a Junkers 88. Flying at 10,000 feet, the rear gunner Sgt. Webb saw the fighter going across the tail from port to starboard. The captain Sgt. Dane began a corkscrew to port. The enemy turned in from starboard and attempted to follow but Webb opened fire with a short burst at 330 yards range. Immediately the JU88 returned fire but missed the Halifax. As a deception the JU88 turned on navigation lights, turning one back off later. The rear gunner continued to fire until the enemy aircraft turned away with the port engine on fire. Sgt. Beatson observed the whole combat through the ventrally mounted Perspex observation blister. Both he and the bomb aimer, Sgt. Adams later saw the JU88 burst into flames well below them. Webb claimed the Ju88 shot down and had fired six hundred rounds in the process. The I.F.F. was set to 'special.'

Only a few minutes later at 03:01 another bomber fell victim to a night fighter. This time it was the 408 sqn. Halifax JB925, of Flight Lieutenant Hatle and crew. They were shot down by Uffz. Depperman of the 12th staffel of NJG4, and crashed in woodland between Nonnweiler and Bierfeld. Seven crew were found near the burned out wreckage and a further

[96] The Blue Emu, Charlie Catt
[97] AIR40/2422 ADT (K) report 337/1945 Interrogation of Major Heinz Schnaufer.TNA UK
[98] Ian Duncan, 419 sqn. bomb aimer.
[99] Combat report AIR50/195 TNA U.K.

body in a woodland clearing the next day. At the crash site one Sgt.'s mess card from R.A.F. Leeming was found. The dead included second dickey pilot O'Connell and an American air gunner, Sgt. Tschantre, serving in the R.C.A.F. His parents were from Thomasville, Georgia. Six French prisoners were ordered to bury the airmen. The grave bore a cross with the words;[100]

HIER RUHEN 8 KANADISCHE SOLDATEN DER ENGLISCHEN LUFTWAFFE GEF.

Hatle, the skipper of this crew along with Kapuscinski, Osmond, Richmond and Tschantre had all had a narrow escape in march 12/13th 1943 when they had been coned for a considerable time over the target and hit by flak on operations to Essen. When Halifax DT790 returned to base from that op, both port engines cut out, causing the aircraft to yaw violently and crash at 00:47 near the airfield. No injuries were reported. An aircraft accident report stated that the flight engineer mishandled the fuel systems causing the engines to quit. Despite the fact of fuel loss due to battle damage, the logbooks of Hatle and the Flight Engineer were endorsed rather harshly 'error of judgement!'[101]

Back with the Plzeň force at 03:07 Sgt. Ian Miller's Lancaster W4331 'R' of 460 squadron crashed after being seen by witnesses to be coming in very low already on fire after being hit by flak. She came down at Ludwigshafen-Oggersheim and exploded on impact at Am saumgraben. This was only their third operation having raided Frankfurt on the 10/11th of April and Stuttgart on the 14/15th. Some wreckage of the bomber was found in July 1999 after local fishermen drained a Lake called the Backstein-Weiher. The photograph shows the lake and the dinghy from the Lancaster.

Backstein-Weiher 17th April 1943 showing the dinghy of Lancaster W4331 (Photo Menges)

---

[100] RG24/Vol.27708 Library & Archives Canada. Dossier Hatle, Clifford Oscar J9407
[101] Library & Archives Canada. Dossier Hatle Clifford Oscar J9407

A Shaky do. The Plzen raid April 16/17th April 1943

Tail wheel of W4331 460 sqn. recovered from the wreckage of Lancaster W4331 (photo Menges)

Also at 03:07 Halifax HR659 was flying westward south of Bitburg and north of Trier and was pounced upon by a fighter flown by Feldwebel Paul Faden of 11./NJG4 at 4000 metres altitude. He had already shot down a Wellington returning from the Mannheim target at 01:51 hours. HR659 was his 3rd victory. Mortenson the pilot of the Halifax was killed, as was Pittman the mid-upper gunner.

Pilot Officer Ray Dennis the navigator noted in his war diary;

'On return journey from target just a few miles north of Trier two night fighters Me110s attacked setting the two port engines on fire and damaging the controls, with the result that we were forced to bale out. I landed safely on a grass slope at 03:15 on April the 17th 1943. Having done the necessary with the chute etc. I hid up in a wood until around six a.m. and came to the conclusion I had one of two alternatives, either to go through what appeared to be a small village or bye pass it which would mean I should have to pass very close to where the aircraft crashed. I chose the village and was almost through it when I was picked up by the goons and taken to a safe camp in the village, which I think was Bitburg. Another of the crew joined me here and later another three, the goons telling us that the other crew were killed. From Bitburg we went by truck to Trier and from there by train to Dulag Luft at Frankfurt. I Was at Dulag for just over a week including two days in the cooler before finally arriving at Stalag Luft III on April the 26th.'[102]

---

[102] Ray Dennis (78 Squadron) Memoires.

Ray Dennis was billeted in the famous hut 104 from which escape tunnel 'Harry' was started, and did good work diverting the German guards' attention away from the tunnelling activity.

The Bomber Command loss card states that a Me109 followed half a minute later by a ME110, shot down HR659 from 12,000 feet attacking from below. Both were seen before the attack. It incorrectly states that the attack was on the outward trip.

Another source states that the attacking aircraft was a Me210 and gives the following account;

F/Lt Mortenson, the pilot and Sgt. Pitman, the rear gunner were killed in the first burst of cannon fire from the fighter. In the second burst the intercom was knocked out so the crew could not speak to each other. The port wing was burning and the plane was going down. Jock Bell (flight engineer) left the plane with Lawson Minshaw, the air gunner on that night. They landed in an open field about one hundred yards apart.

Sgt Bell (flight engineer) had badly injured his leg on landing and Lawton Minshaw wrapped up his parachute, hid it and helped Bell to his feet. They started to move away from the area. They could hear dogs barking in the distance and the sound of vehicles moving so they decided to make themselves scarce. Bell was limping rather badly but they managed to make some distance keeping going until it got light and then they settled down in some woods, on the basis, that they would walk at night and lay low during the day. They had a compass, maps printed on silk handkerchief, and their emergency rations which they thought would last them for a short period. They decided to head for Luxembourg but after a couple of days Bell's leg was in a bad way, it had now turned black and he was having great difficulty moving.

Eventually they were taken in by the Germans and taken to Trier. Sgt. Bell had been put into a cart, as he now could not walk at all; Lawson had to walk behind it. They were placed in a cell and from there taken to an office and were ranted and raved at by a man who was the local Mayor. They didn't understand what he was saying and they were later returned to their cell. After a couple of hours they were collected by a Luftwaffe Officer and taken by truck to their next destination, a Luftwaffe Station. There they were put into a dormitory with a couple of guards. Later they were taken one a time to be interviewed and interrogated. The following day they were put on a train en route to Dulag Luft.[103]

The Plzeň force was still locked in attrition with the enemy as it fought its way back across Germany. At 03:08 F/L Pexton flying Halifax DT489 of 35 squadron, was hit by flak at 12,500 feet north of Mannheim. A petrol tank was hit and the Gee navigation system put out of action along with the wireless transmitter. An ammunition track to one of the turrets was also damaged.

At 03:12 another Halifax (DT561 51 sqn.) was brought down at Hadamar, Limburg with the loss of all the crew. She was the victim of a night fighter at 3600 metres altitude flown by Lt. Otto Blohm 10./NJG4. He had claimed his first victory. The Halifax Pilot, Sgt. Ernie Cox was one of five brothers. Two of these beside Ernie were also aircrew. Brother Steve Cox served in coastal command and earned the D.F.C. D.F.M. and M.I.D. Brother John served as a navigator on ferry command in the Middle East. Steve and John ended the war as Flight-Lieutenant and Squadron Leader respectively. Ernie's brother Kenneth wrote in 2007;

'A picture frame hung on the family wall over the years showing Ernie's photo, the King's letter and his war medals. Many years later, in 1987, I went to Hadamar and visited the town hall seeking information about the plane crash and the temporary burial of the seven

---

[103] Info provided by Steve Balance via Lawson Minshaw and Mary I. Haggarty. Edited slightly for clarity.

airmen in the cemetery there (They were later moved to Durnbach War Graves cemetery). The "mayor" was very helpful taking us round the town to both the place where the aircraft came down (describing how it came down in flames) and to the cemetery. Anyway, after we got back home the mayor wrote a nice letter with which he sent Ernie's 'dog-tag' (they'd been in his filing system all that time). I gave them to my sister who then had the picture frame in her house and she added the dog-tags alongside the medals.'

The wording of the King's letter is;

"The Queen and I offer you our heartfelt sympathy in your great sorrow. We pray that your country's gratitude for a life so nobly given in its service may bring you some measure of consolation."

Steve and Kenneth had plaque made and displayed in the memorial gardens to 51 Squadron at Pollington Airfield U.K. on a part of the old airfield. It shows all seven names of the crew.

At 03:10 a 467 sqn. Lancaster passed Mannheim and the Aussy skipper Flight Sergeant Parsons declared the results of that raid satisfactory. Stuttgart had still not declared the 'all clear.' They were right not to have done so.

A long way south of intended track and running late was Halifax DT773 of 78 squadron based At Linton-On-Ouse. She was attacked by night fighter to the south east of Stuttgart. The following chapter is devoted to these events.

Wurzburg radar which tracked the bombers for ground controlled interception by fighters.

A Shaky do - The Plzen raid April 16/17th April 1943

Chapter Six
Air battle over Stuttgart

On the night of April 16/17th 1943 looking up into the sky was a 16 year old German on fire watch called Heinz Bardua, himself later destined to be a veteran of Normandy and the Russian front. As he watched he witnessed two bombers shot down in the Stuttgart urban area. These were ED711 of 460 squadron R.A.A.F. mentioned earlier and Halifax DT773 of 78 Squadron R.A.F. Many years later after the war, Heinz was to track down most of the crew of DT773 and write their story. The Wireless operator on DT773 Phil Langsford has been a close friend of Heinz and has travelled from his home in New Zealand to meet him. For many years they have corresponded and encouraged each other in their shared Christian faith. Most of the information for this chapter came from a friend of the author, Mr Heinz Bardua. Heinz also wrote a book called Stuttgart Im Luftkrieg (Air war over Stuttgart).

Halifax DT773 of 78 squadron RAF, took off from Linton on Ouse at 21:00 hours it was to be her last operation. She was a Halifax Mark II special, which had had the mid-upper turret removed and the nose armament in order to give increased performance. The mid-upper gunner would take up a position on the floor of the aircraft looking aft through a Perspex blister for any fighters.

On the outward leg the aircraft was flying low enough to shoot out some searchlights which were indicating the track of the bomber stream to the fighters. The aircraft reached the target area a little late. Tom Slater the flight engineer remembered in a letter after the war to wireless operator/air gunner Phil Langsford,

'The night we went to Plzeň, I have always contended that that when we arrived at our plotted e.t.a. we were on target. There was no activity at that point but we saw flares and fires about five to six miles on our Starboard bow, we headed for these as it was obviously the Path-finders in action. I think we were probably there in which case our substitute navigator must have been good.'

Because of the changed run in to bomb where the Pathfinders had marked, DT773 was later than planned on target and thus became a straggler. In order to save fuel she was flown at reduced speed flying at around three to four thousand metres and well south of track. Being off track brought the aircraft over Stuttgart's defences. The wireless operator Langsford was busy jamming the radio frequencies of the night-fighter controllers with 'Tinsel' and had briefly unplugged his inter-com. Suddenly, they were attacked by a night-fighter at around 03:16 hours. The mid-upper gunner thought he saw the rear gunner return fire with several bursts from his four browning machine guns. The flight engineer thought that the fighter came from behind and raked the under side of the nose and wing with bullets. Several stray bullets penetrated the cockpit and within seconds the aircraft was on fire turning 180° to port and the pilot gave the order to bale out. The pilot and the flight engineer together tried to hold the aircraft in trim to allow the others to get out. The fuselage had now become engulfed in flames causing ammunition belts to explode and the Halifax was losing height.

The first crewman to bale out was the Sgt. Hoare (mid-upper gunner) who left the aircraft at about two thousand five hundred metres, saw factory roofs on his decent and heard a few shots fired which got his attention! Landing next to a canal he was partially dragged in by his parachute. No sooner had he landed than a mob crossed a bridge, came towards him and proceeded to kick him. At this point a soldier rescued him from the mob and took him to a guardroom where he was treated well. He was given a cigarette which he smoked. It wasn't until he finished it that he realised he had not smoked all his life! The soldiers gave up one of their beds and shared some rations with him. In the afternoon a truck came and took him to Nellingen airfield.

Second out was the bomb aimer, Sgt. Thompson, who had a very traumatic escape. He baled out through the forward hatch but it had closed on his legs and his parachute was damaged as it brushed against the tail fin of the aircraft. Upon landing with already injured legs he suffered a heavy landing and complex fractures. Help was at hand in the form of a German farming family who stopped the bleeding and took him to the farmhouse undoubtedly saving his life. Later German surgeons removed a leg and he was repatriated via Sweden in a prisoner exchange. After the war Thompson expressed his gratitude to Doctor Reinhold Maier who had treated him.

Canadian navigator Flight Sergeant Desjardins was third to exit the aircraft and did so from the rear main exit after walking over the wing spars and through a vale of flames. Wireless operator Phil Langsford went to check the forward hatch again hoping this would help the pilot escape, but the force of the slipstream had shut it again, one of the bomb-aimer's boots was still jammed in the door. Langsford then baled out. He reported;

'In leaving the aircraft I only remembered the cold blast of air and nothing of the descent. My chest parachute had hit me in the head before it opened and gave me a black eye. I crossed a terraced garden (which turned out to be a vineyard). The time was around 03:30 hours'

Langsford had landed 30 metres from some houses where he hid in some bushed until found by the German soldiers. They did not threaten him in any way but near the police station the crowd shouted, 'Crucify him!' In contrast, Langsford saw one young woman in a crowd. His eyes met hers, yet in them he saw only compassion and pity.

He was fed before being moved on. On the journey he saw a huge pile of corpses from the raid on Stuttgart on the night of the 14th/15th April. That night 619 people were killed including 257 French and 143 Russian prisoners. A bomb had scored a direct hit on an air raid shelter[104]

The flight engineer Sgt. Slater had been helping the pilot in spite of the burning wing tank. He told the pilot that all the crew in the nose had jumped. He then headed toward the rear main hatch, the floor gave way underfoot as it had been melted by the fire, but he made it out. It was clear to him that they had lost considerable height but he let himself fall sufficiently to clear the aircraft tail and pulled the release for his parachute. As he descended he heard machine gun fire and was concerned that the fighter may have re-attacked. He was fifth to leave the aircraft.

Sgt. Slater remembered'

'I landed quite heavily, crashing through vine support sticks in a vineyard. In order to move more freely we clipped on the lower part of the chute fairly loosely. In the sudden breaking of the fall as the parachute opened out, this loose belt caused severe bruising to the upper thigh and lower body. For this reason it was hard for me to walk. After landing I crept under a bush and after perhaps two hours I was discovered by some German soldiers.

The people nearby were shouting "strike him dead" no doubt due to their anger over the heavy raid on the city two days earlier.

---

[104] Bomber Command War diaries, Middlebrook/Everitt

A Shaky do. The Plzen raid April 16/17th April 1943

Slater continued;

They escorted me downhill along a rough path. On either side of the path were people who shouted and made a lot of noise and by whom I was slapped and punched. The soldiers brought me into a room, probably at a farm.'

The night fighter pilot, Lt. Josef Nabrich of III./NJG101, who had shot down the Halifax found Slater. He gave him a cigarette much to the disapproval of the S.S. soldiers present!

Still in the rear turret of the stricken bomber was Flying Officer Orr. Orr had his parachute stowed close to him near the rear turret, but as he heard the call to bale out and tried the doors, he found to his horror that they were jammed due to the damage from the fighter attack. In panic he twisted the handles off. Orr related after the war;

'In desperation I called over the intercom, Paddy, Paddy I can't get out! Paddy replied, "settle down. Try the hatchet! I can still fly this dragon." I tried the axe but it broke clean through and disappeared below. The doors remained jammed. Now I was in a complete state of panic as flames, sparks and glowing bits of metal from the burning wing flew past the side of the turret. The night fighter also began to fire again at short range. I turned the turret forwards. I begged Paddy not to abandon me. He replied "Try the doors with your shoulder; I will stay with you until you are out!" I did this and the doors flew open.'

Orr fell out of his turret but amazingly his flying boot caught in the structure and he was left hanging. He struggled against the powerful slipstream of the burning aircraft until completely exhausted. Looking forward again he noticed the port wing drop lower which then was corrected by flap, showing that the pilot was still in control. The fire now was much worse and Orr who was completely exhausted waited for the end. Suddenly the burning wing broke off sending the aircraft in to a spin. Round and round again it went until the centrifugal force catapulted him free. He survived to become a prisoner of war.

Patrick Dowse the pilot did not escape from the aircraft and his body was found on the ground and was probably thrown out of the aircraft during the explosion. The parachute had not opened and the buckle on the harness was found not properly latched. He had knowingly given his life for his friends, staying at the controls until it was too late for him to escape. The aircraft crashed in the drained lakebed of the Max Eyth See in the Hofen district of Stuttgart. He was originally buried in Steinhaldenfeld, but in 1948 re-buried at Durnbach war cemetery, Tegernsee.

When on operations to Genova on 7th/8th of November 1942 this crew were flying 78 squadron Halifax W1063. An engine failed when outbound to the target but the crew pressed on. After bombing the target, minus one engine it was impossible to gain enough height to re-cross the Alps and they attempted to reach Gibraltar. Dowse skilfully ditched the aircraft about 8 kilometres off the coast of Valencia. The crew were rescued and temporarily interned at Albacete in February of 1943. On two operations to Duisburg and Berlin on the 26th and 27th of March 1943, their aircraft was badly shot up. The Berlin op saw a propeller blade shot off by flak which flew through the side of the aircraft close to the wireless operator's and navigator's positions. The unbalanced and damaged propeller nearly vibrating the aircraft to pieces until it was feathered. This so unnerved the navigator that he was unable to continue on ops and was taken off the squadron.[105] He was replaced by the Canadian Desjardins.

---

[105] Max Lambert, Night after night (New Zealanders in Bomber Command).

A Shaky do - The Plzen raid April 16/17th April 1943

78 squadron bomb aimer Stan Hurrell commented on this incident;

'On that occasion the starboard inner engine had one of the three propeller blades sheared off at the spinner. The blade cut a slash through the fuselage from top to bottom. Looking at the aircraft back at Linton-on-Ouse the next day, I could have sworn the tip of the nose was bent to starboard in a most alarming manner. Having only just arrived at Linton my thoughts were, "What have we let ourselves in for?" In fact none of the crew was injured that night.
However, the interesting point is that within three weeks the aircraft was again ready for operational service and it was the squadron reserve aircraft on the 16th April. Paddy found a problem with the aircraft originally assigned to them that night so the crew went back to DT773. The work of the repair teams in those days was truly incredible!'

In the 1980s Heinz Bardua contacted all the surviving members of the crew of Halifax DT773 and put to together their story. A 12 year old school boy Rainer Moser found a piece of the tail fin of Halifax DT773 in 1943 and years later met up with Heinz Bardua. In January of 2001 Heinz and Rainer met with representatives of R.A.F. Bruggen. They handed over the piece of leading edge tail fin to the R.A.F. and the relic was transported back to England, where it now resides in the memorial room at R.A.F. Linton-on-Ouse, Yorkshire.

Stan Hurrell was himself shot down a few nights earlier whilst on operations to Frankfurt on 11th April. At 02:33 hours a fighter flown by Fw. Karl Gross of 8./NJG4, downed the Halifax. Again Stan Hurrell recalls;

'We never reached Frankfurt as a Me110 intercepted us near Metz. He attacked from below and we only saw him when it was too late. We had both our starboard engines knocked out and an unstoppable fire in the starboard wing. We were still carry our bomb load of H.E. and incendiaries and could not jettison them. DT775 came down beside the church in the village of Anoux near Briey. Our rear gunner was killed and our wireless op had a bullet wound but six of us got out in time. I have visited Briey and Anoux; the folk there were quite wonderful and I have made a few friends there for life.

Chapter Seven
Homeward bound

At 03:30 the all clear was sounded at Stuttgart and many bombers were now over France and Belgium on their long trip home. Many crewmen would now feel the need to take a dose of their Benzedrine or Wakey Wakey pills. Certainly battle weariness would be a constant companion.

Sgt. McCrae's Halifax DT690 which had already had a tough time with fighters and flak, was in the area of the Siegfried line heading west and caught by a blue (master) searchlight. Within forty seconds she was coned by about forty lights, the pilot put the aircraft into a dive as steep as he dared and tried a few slip turns, but evasive action was limited by the state of the aircraft. She had been in the lights for about two minutes and under fire from heavy flak for much of that time. Hits were sustained in two starboard fuel tanks and Sgt. Allerdice, the flight engineer, changed tanks from 1 and 4 to 5 and 6. The port inner was running roughly after a probable hit. An attempt was made to change tanks but the control wires had been severed. The engineer tried to feed the port engine from the starboard tanks but the cross balance pipe had been completely severed close to the fuselage on the port side, filling the well of the aircraft with petrol.

The aircraft would soon be without the use of the port engines and with rudder problems which made steering difficult but the aircraft was still under control. At some time around 03:00 the order to bale out was given. Sgt. Ings the bomb aimer released the pigeons and then left the aircraft along with Sgt. Davis the mid-upper gunner from the entrance hatch.

Ings was captured south of Perpignan on the 26th of April.[106] Sgt. Jones[107] the rear gunner jumped from his turret. The navigator (F/O Spencer), wireless operator (Flt/Sgt. Simpson),[108] flight engineer (Sgt. Allerdice) and pilot (Sgt. McRae) from the front hatch in that order. Allerdice jumped from about 10,000 feet, his chute opening at around 3,000 feet. He made a heavy landing in a field on the edge of a hole into which he rolled, banging his head on a rock. He was dazed due to this for some time. The bump on the head had made him act strangely looking for quite some time for his locker keys and the exact sum of 3/4d which had fallen from his pocket!

Rear gunner Sgt. Jones left his turret feet first with his helmet on, leaving it as late as possible to pull the rip-chord. His chute opened at about 3,000 feet. On his descent, Jones saw lights of an airfield flare path on the ground and at around three hundred feet a Heinkel 111 medium bomber came in to land immediately below him. A few seconds later he landed at about 03:25 on the eastern corner of the airfield at Laon-Athies, about 150 yards from the flare path, breaking two teeth. Just as he landed he saw four-engine bomber crash in flames about one and a half miles away. Jones then took out his compass and headed south to the village of Gizy. Whilst walking cautiously through the streets he saw a figure which turned out to be Alleridice. They hid in an old hay shed, tore off their badges and cut the tops off their flying books making them look like ordinary shoes. They ate some Horlicks tablets and also stole and ate some raw eggs. At 21:30 on the 17th of April they saw a farmer who offered to give them some clothes. But on watching the house they saw a man leave on a bicycle towards the German airfield. Allerdice and Jones left the village and walked to Liesse and found a porter but he was too afraid to help them. They then walked east along the Laon-Charleville railway and stayed in a wood shed until the 18th of April when a man brought them some food. Later, new helpers brought them railway tickets to Paris where they arrived

---

[106] Clutton-Brock, Sands of time.
[107] Escape report WO208 file 3114 report (-)1357 Sgt. Jones TNA UK
[108] Simpson was killed after the war in a flying accident when with 61 sqn. aboard Lincoln RF407

at 20:30 hrs. on the 19th then Bordeaux on the 20th. After an amazing evasion Jones and Allerdice[109] arrived in Gibraltar on the 14th/15th August and were both back in England a day later. Allerdice was on his 14th operation and Jones on his 13th. At one point during their escape they had found themselves standing in a train corridor for some time with some German soldiers!

Jones' and Allerdice's Halifax DT690 came down on the water at Missy les Pierrepont. Prior to the bale out a radio fix was attempted but the set was found to be unserviceable. The pilot then detonated the charges to destroy the I.F.F.[110] and Gee equipment, trimmed the aircraft and baled out last. He did not engage George as he wanted to be sure the fuel tanks would explode.

After he had left the aircraft he watched her fly normally for about two minutes after which she dived straight down and on hitting the ground exploded and burst into flames, the Germans believing all the crew to be killed. In fact they had all survived.

Hptm. Haesler of 1./NJG4 made a claim for a bomber at Missy though there was no mention of an attack by fighter in the crew's evasion reports or the aircraft loss reports K35 and 41. It is possible a fighter attacked after the crew had left the aircraft. After landing Allerdice heard Germans shouting in the distance and saw what he thought was a Stirling bomber pass over the airfield at about 500 feet, being heavily attacked by light flak and with at least one engine out of action. She was not seen to crash. An enemy aircraft was thought to have crashed in this area a little while after this, though no Luftwaffe losses were recorded in this area that could have accounted for this. Just after he landed at around 03:30 near the airfield at Laon-Athies, McRae[111] reported what he thought was a Wellington being attacked by a night fighter, bursts going into the tail end of the aircraft which caught fire immediately. The fire spread rapidly forward forwards until the tanks exploded, when the aircraft dived vertically and crashed in flames about four miles away. Probably though, this was actually Halifax DT575 which Sgt. Jones also witnessed crashing. It is unlikely that any Wellingtons were in this area from the Mannheim force at this late hour and in any case the author has documented all the Mannheim losses. None of them were in the Missy/Leon area at this time. The pilot McRae also evaded captivity. He was on his 18th operation, 7 of which had been with Coastal Command. The rest of the crew was taken prisoners of war.[112]

At 03:38 hours as witnessed by Sgt. Jones rear gunner of DT690, another Halifax this time DT575 MP-Y of 76 squadron based at Linton on Ouse, was shot down near Vesles-et - Caumont. She was seen to be well on fire and explode in the air. The debris was spread over a wide area. The author interviewed a resident of Vesles-et-Caumont, Mr. Tambouret in June 2005 and Michel Leprêtre a researcher in the region also interviewed him some time later.

M. Paul Tambouret stated: Towards 9h30-10h00 pm (time incorrect), *he saw a large plane in flames above his house (apparently flying west to east, but he did not know at what altitude). The plane exploded in the air and fell down in a field near Vesles-et-Caumont. The wreckage was widely dispersed. An engine was found in a field on the other side of the road. Debris then spread through fields towards the place of the crash. M. Tambouret was one of the first to arrive on the spot. He then saw the lifeless body of one of the members of crew that lay on the ground. His parachute had not opened. Then he approached the remains of the fuselage with other people and saw the charred bodies of the other members of the crew (an unknown number). At this moment, the plane had ceased to burn. The Germans then arrived (Probably from Marles) and all had to leave.*

---

[109] Escape report Sgt. Allerdice WO208 file 3114 report (-)1358
[110] Identification friend or foe equipment.
[111] Escape report McRae WO208 file 3114 report (-)1383 TNA UK
[112] Information re DT690 AIR14/1442 K31 & K36 TNA UK

One witness who lived in the area of Pierrepont at the time, a M. Burlot, confirmed that;

"the aircraft crashed in flames two Kilometres from Pierrepont on the way to Marle". The aircraft was shot down by a night fighter and that events happened so quickly no combat developed."

Two members of the crew baled out from the Halifax as it came down but, due to the proximity to the ground, their chutes failed to open (one was Jonasson). The other 5 died in the aircraft. French Gendarmerie secured the site, with the Germans arriving 12 hours later recovering all the bodies from within the immediate impact area. The bodies were buried by the Germans in Liesse cemetery and exhumed by the US Army's 605th Quarter Master Grave Registration Unit after the war. Only Jonasson was identifiable at that time (due to his ID disks being found). The bodies were reburied.[113]

17 yrs old Sgt Leonard Jonasson RCAF 76 sqn (Photo Chuck Jonasson)

It is possible to accurately pinpoint the time of this crash at after 03:25 as witnessed by Sgt. Jones of DT690, the time given by the gendarmes at around 04:00 and the claim of fighter pilot Uffz. Thiell of 9./NJG4 at 03:38 south of Marle which fits the location of Vesles-et-

[113] Details from R180403 Sgt Jonasson L.N file Canadian National Archives.

A Shaky do. The Plzen raid April 16/17th April 1943

Caumont. Local people also told Sgt. Jones that the aircraft he witnessed crashing carried the letters MP-I. It is likely that Jones misunderstood the pronunciation of the letter Y (i grec pronounced *ee grek* in French), as an 'I'. The squadron code letters of DT575 being MP-Y. The time was the same in England and France this night. Only two aircraft crashed near this place on 16/17th April 1943. Three other 76 Sqn. aircraft crashed, one near Mundelsheim (JB800), one (DK165) near Lachen and Speyerdorf and one in France at Goyencourt (JB870 Mannheim operation.) borrowed from 76 Sqn. by 78 Sqn.

Possibly the youngest airman killed on operations with Bomber Command was Leonard Jonasson, a 17 year old Canadian mid-upper gunner from Winnipeg (Halifax DT575 76 Sqn.) The young man had altered his birth certificate in 1942, making himself a few years older than he really was and enlisted in the Royal Canadian Air Force. When his mother threatened to turn him in and get him discharged, she was forced to change her mind when Leonard told her that he would go elsewhere and enlist under an assumed identity and that she risked not hearing from him. He was sixteen. Leonard was killed in action on only his third operation. He and his crew rest in the cemetery at Liesse.

Gilmour's 50 Sqn. Lancaster also over the department of the Aisne, made a low level return over France and shot up several railway engines and the airfield at Laon-Athies. Sgt. Plum's radial engine MkII Lancaster (DS616 'G') of 115 Sqn. also shot up an airfield.[114] For some considerable distance Sgt. Shearman's 44 squadron (Lancaster W4949) crew had flown at roof top level on their return journey. His gunners raked the barracks of a German airfield with machine gun fire, their bullets hitting the windows.[115]

Lancaster W4366 (12 Sqn.) when homeward bound, had the oil pressure in the starboard outer engine drop and soon fail altogether. It would not feather completely, was still wind-milling[116] and soon caught fire. The graviner extinguisher system was used and put the fire out. A restart was attempted but this brought only flames. At 03:41 the skipper Sgt. Mizon gave the order *standby* to bale out, and discovered at 03:50 that the rear gunner (Sgt. Rudkin), the mid-upper gunner (Sgt. McKay) and the wireless operator (Sgt. Hutton), were missing. They had baled out![117] Again feathering was attempted but failed. The engine burned out at 04:06 but the Lancaster continued on with three engines.

In the area of Darmstadt at 03:45 hours, flying at 4,000 feet with the setting moon in front three quarters full, was Lancaster ED396 of 103 squadron. Flown by Canadian P/O Ewer, the Lanc. was weaving through searchlights, when the rear gunner (Sgt. Lee) sighted an ME210 fighter 400 yards astern and slightly below. He opened fire firing 100 rounds and hitting the enemy. Simultaneously he gave instructions to the pilot to make a diving turn to port. The fighter returned fire, his cannon shells damaging the starboard inner radiator and a blade of the same propeller. The starboard main-plane, flaps, a tyre and the bomb doors were also hit. As the Lancaster made the diving turn to port the fighter broke away exposing his belly at 300 yards climbing on the starboard quarter. The rear gunner gave him a burst of 200 rounds, which were seen to hit the underside of the ME210. The gunner claimed the fighter as damaged. Searchlights had been co-operating with the fighters.

Halifax DT670 of 51 squadron having been previously hit four times by flak south of Mannheim, and dropped her weapons on the green markers in the target area. She had turned for home and all had gone well until making a last alteration of course before the French coast. The Pilot had been weaving continuously through the fighter belt and at 03:50 hours the aircraft was just west of Châlons-sur-Marne. Flying officer Clements the bomb aimer noticed something happening and remarked, "hello what's happening to starboard?"

---

[114] Log book entry Sgt. C.F. Trott Flight Engineer (Tony Trott)
[115] Manchester Guardian 18th April 1943
[116] Wind milling of an unpowered propeller caused excessive drag.
[117] WO208/file 3314 reports 1322 & 1323 TNA UK

Immediately afterwards there were at least three explosions witnessed by navigator Sgt. Riley who saw flashes in the bomb aimer's compartment. This was probably cannon shells going off. One of the starboard engines had stopped. This must have been the inner one as the Gee set was still working. Riley had just been taking a Gee fix to plot their position and had turned to see Flt.Sgt. Lancaster, their Australian wireless operator with his parachute on, the escape hatch half open and his legs dangling from it. Lancaster asked his navigator if he was going to jump. The navigator first checked with the skipper over the inter-com, asking if he could hold the plane. Sgt Inch replied "no, no, get out, get out!" The aircraft was now weaving violently. Riley motioned to Sgt. Lancaster to jump which he did, apparently getting clear well. The aircraft was now down to seven thousand feet, in a slight dive and still weaving. Sgt. Riley baled out not seeing any other parachutes as he descended. He landed in wooded country east of Chaintrix, about 150 yards away from the aircraft wreckage, which was burning furiously. He tried to approach it but then heard a dog barking and a man speaking and did not make his presence known.[118] The aircraft had been shot down by Oblt. Hans Autenrieth of 6./NJG4, crashing between Pocancy and Chaintrix. Sgt. Riley successfully evaded capture via Spain, sailing on the SS "Esneh" from Seville to Gibraltar 11th-13th of August 1943. Sgt. Dards was taken prisoner of war. Flt/Sgt. Lancaster was seriously injured and Sgt. Dards went with him to hospital, where Lancaster died soon after arrival. Sgt. Inch (Pilot), Hayden (Flt./Eng.), Clements (bomb aimer) and Mumme (rear gunner) were found dead in the aircraft wreckage.[119]

Sgt. Lancaster had been previously injured in a crash when at 15 O.T.U. in on a training flight in Wellington HE102 which stalled on take off, crash landed and caught fire on 11th September 1942.

At 03:52 hours west of Charlesvilles-Mézières (near Sedan) at 13,500 feet, another Halifax of 51 squadron (HR787) flown by Flt/Sgt. Brigden, made contact with a night fighter. The Halifax was on a heading 271° magnetic, when a Ju88 with four cannons in the nose was spotted on the starboard quarter at 200 feet below at a range of only fifty yards. The Ju88 opened fire with a three-second burst and the Halifax made a climbing turn to starboard. The Australian rear gunner Sgt. Green fired one long burst experiencing two stoppages, one in the bottom left-hand gun and one in the top left with faulty ammunition. He claimed hits on the Ju88 with no damage to the Halifax. The fighter broke away from the port quarter level. In this action, red track marker flares had been used by the enemy to show the heading of the bombers.

At approximately 04:00 hours, just after having made the final turn for the French coast and only a few minutes flying time from it, Lancaster ED780 of 467 squadron came down at La Haie Mouret close to Thieulloy l'Abbaye to the west of Amiens. All the crew's bodies were found including one in the aircraft.[120] There were no bombs on board. The aircraft was thought to have been hit by flak but this is unproven. No night fighter claims were registered that could have been connected with this, the squadron's first operational loss. The seven crew included an Australian skipper and mid-upper gunner and a New Zealand wireless operator. All the crew rest in the churchyard at Poix-de-la-Somme. (Now Poix de Picardie).

---

[118] Escape report of Sgt. Riley WO208/3314 TNA U.K.
[119] National Archives of Australia: A705,163/136/198
[120] Errol Martin author of 'For Your Tomorrow'

Sgt. Martin ED780 467 Sqn.

(photos Brad Martin)

Sgt. Martin F/E 467 Sqn. ED780 K.I.A.

A Shaky do. The Plzen raid April 16/17th April 1943

Chapter Eight
Six minutes

At around 04:00 hours on the morning of April 17th 1943 a few aircraft were heading west across the Ardennes area when the 1st night fighter group of NJG4 based at Florennes in Belgium, picked up three aircraft of the Plzeň force. The first of these was W4317 QR-R, a Lancaster of 61 squadron based at Syerston in Nottinghamshire. At the controls was William MacFarlane probably on his 29th operation, one short of a full tour of 30 ops. The Wireless operator Flight sergeant J. Edwards was on his second tour and had completed 50 or more operations earning a Distinguished Flying Medal. Unusually Sgt. Peter Keay, the flight engineer was an Australian on an otherwise all British crew. The crew were P/O Macfarlane (captain); Sgt. Keay R.A.A.F. (flight engineer); F/O Williams (navigator); Sgt. Dawson (bomb aimer); F/S Edwards D.F.M. (wireless operator-air gunner); Sgt. Rees (mid-upper gunner); Sgt. Holdsworth (rear gunner); Sgt. Davidson (navigator-under training).

According to Belgian researcher and Givry resident M. Penant he viewed a document regarding a signal sent back by W4317 at around 01:00[121] when over Bavaria. The signal told of three airmen who had been grievously wounded earlier, possibly by flak. These were the flight engineer Sgt. Keay, The navigator Williams and the under training navigator, Davidson.[122] Sadly these airmen were said to have now died of their wounds. The author had not been able to re-locate the signal which M. Penant saw but has no reason to doubt his research. At 01:00 they would already have been in the area of the final turning point for the run up to the target and presumably Macfarlane deemed it safer to remain with the main stream of aircraft despite having wounded aboard. Certainly W4317 was heading for home with at least one aircraft which had been to the target area, which was (Halifax HR663 of 102 Squadron) flown by Sqn. Leader Lashbrook.

At 2,400 metres on a westerly heading Lashbrook saw tracer rounds indicating fighter activity and an aircraft already on fire. He warned his own crew to keep a look out, as he witnessed an attack on Lancaster W4317 at 04:02. The attacking fighter, flown by Oblt. Rudolf Altendorf of 2./NJG4, made two attacks. One of these (probably the second) was seen by a Belgian resistance worker Achille Jaupart who was awoken by the roar of aircraft engines. He commented;

'I was awakened by the roaring of an engine which seemed to run badly. I jumped out of my bed and went to the window of my room. I thought that it was an allied plane searching for a place to land. In my garden, I took my bicycle to go as fast as possible and help the crew after the landing of the plane. (M. Jaupart thought the aircraft might have a chance of landing in the fields). From my garden, I saw the plane turning around and around between Givry and Harmignies[123]

Suddenly a German night fighter appeared and shot the bomber. I was angry with myself at not being able to help in any way.

The German pilot came to the crash site the day after at 09h45 and was congratulated by other Germans who had come from Chièvres.

---

[121] M. Penant stated in his article '23:00 heur Anglais' but the hour must have been around 1:00 over Bavaria.
[122] The three named are indicated on the headstones as K.I.A. 16th April all others noted as the 17th April 1943.
[123] Philipe Savé

On the ground debris, was spread all around the impact area. I found an identity tag with the name of Sgt. Davidson, William, a piece of burned uniform with a plate and the number A.M. 539568.'

Achille Jaupart worked as an Intelligence agent. He also helped U.S. and R.A.F. lost airmen. His escape line was 'contaminated' by Jules Renuart and Marie Simoens, two Belgian Gestapo Agents. Achille was arrested on January 15th 1944 and sent to jail in Germany. He survived and made it back to Givry after the war ended.

       M. Penant reported the Lancaster's wing tanks blazing like a torch. The aircraft circled around the village of Givry passing over several villages, and crashed on land farmed by M. Maurice Rosart south of Givry.[124]The Lancaster made a large crater some 20 metres in diameter and 3 to 4 metres deep, debris being spread over a wide area. It was a sad end to an experienced Lancaster crew who must have been eagerly anticipating the end of their tour of thirty operations. This was Altendorf's 12th or 13th *confirmed* victory and he visited the site of the crash, which was still smoking the next day. He was an experienced pilot and had flown Bf110 Zerstorers with IV./LG(Z)1 in the Battle of Britain with his bordfunker Uffz.Arndt. His unit took heavy losses, but Altendorf scored some victories. Later he served with NJG3, 4, and 12./NJG5, then Stb./NJG5 finishing the war at the rank of Hauptman with 29 confirmed and unconfirmed victories.

       On the 18th of April M. Pennick, the local priest announced a memorial service for the crew 'fallen on our land' with the schools present. However the Gestapo heard about this and arrested M. Pennick and M. Doriaux who were taken to Mons and later tried at Charleroi. After this both men were taken to the citadel at Huy where they stayed until August.

       M. Penant a citizen of Givry today wrote to end his article about the crew;

*'William, Donald, John, Cyril, Peter, Jack and Edward ont donné leur 20 ans sur notre sol pour notre liberté (*they gave their 20 years on our land for our freedom)...REMEMBER!'

Dawson the bomb aimer had completed 28 ops, two short of a full tour of 30. These were not without drama. On only their second operation most of the crew had crash-landed at Bodney airfield, Norfolk, after returning from operations to Mannheim on the night of 6/7th December 1942. They suffered only slight injuries. The rear gunner that night, a Canadian named Glinz, was later to give his life with 617 sqn in Barlow's Lancaster flying operation 'Chastise' the famous dams raid. The whole of Barlow's crew were originally from 61 squadron.

       On the previous operation to Stuttgart on the 14th of April, the Macfarlane crew was coned by floodlights over the target and over France, the gunners shooting out a searchlight. Flight Sergeant Edwards the wireless operator/air gunner had completed 52 sorties when he earned the Distinguished Flying Medal gazetted on the 25th March 1943. The citation reads as follows;

This airman has completed numerous operational sorties over very heavily defended targets in Germany including Berlin, Hamburg, Cologne and Essen. Both as air gunner and wireless operator, he has never failed to complete his duties in a conspicuously successful manner and his courage and coolness at all times, especially when under fire, have been an inspiration to his crew.

---

[124]Conversation with the author in 2004/5 and Article by Reynald Penant, Les Livret Givryens No.12 June 1995

A Shaky do. The Plzen raid April 16/17th April 1943

German document showing night fighter claims for 16/17th April 1943. The annotation in pencil re Lancaster W4317 reads; Lancaster 17.4.43 04:00 1km S.E. Givry Strasse Mons-Beaumont Belgien (Régis Decobeck)

```
                        - 2 -


     IV./N.J.G.4 : Hptm.   Wohlers    - Ofw.   Kleilein
                   Hptm.   Floitgraf  - Fw.    Kessel
                   Lt.     Hadeball   - Uffz.  Volly

   4 wahrscheinliche Abschüsse :

     II./N.J.G.4 : Lt.     Braude     - Uffz.  Hennig
     III./N.J.G.4 : Uffz.  Thiele     - Uffz.  Brinkmann
     IV./N.J.G.4 : Ofw.    Benner     - Uffz.  Schramm
                   Fw.     Teden      - Uffz.  List

   Nacht von 16./17. 4. 1943 :

   34 sichere Abschüsse :

     I./N.J.G.4 : Hptm.   Herget     - Fw.    Lisbherr
                                     - Oblt.  Raith      2 Absch.
                  Oblt.   Altendorf  - Uffz.  Arndt
                  Oblt.   Meister    - Uffz.  Forke
                  Hptm.   Häsler     - Fw.    Heinz
                  Lt.     Pietrek    - Fw.    Bauchens
                  Ofw.    Rahner     - Fw.    Kühn
                  Ofw.    Brandstätter - Fw.  Kelbing
    II./N.J.G.4 : Hptm.   Materne    - Uffz.  Krüger
                  Oblt.   Autenrieth - Uffz.  Adam
                  Oblt.   Tober      - Lt.    Laumanns
                  Lt.     Schäffer   - Uffz.  Ertl
   III./N.J.G.4 : Major   Holler     - Fw.    Gotha
                  Hptm.   Knop       - Fw.    Stein      2 Absch.
                  Oblt.   Fladrich   - Uffz.  Bess
                  Oblt.   Bergmann   - Uffz.  Hauthal    4 Absch.
                                     - Obgefr. Pritsch
                  Ofw.    Macke      - Fw.    Mabon
                  Ofw.    Karsten    - Uffz.  Surböck
                  Uffz.   Thiele     - Uffz.  Brinkmann
                  Ofw.    Kollak     - Fw.    Hermann
    IV./N.J.G.4 : Hptm.   Wohlers    - Ofw.   Kleilein
                  Oblt.   Friedrich  - Ofw.   Giessen
                  Lt.     Hadeball   - Uffz.  Volly      2 Absch.
                  Lt.     Jung       - Uffz.  Schmid
                  Lt.     Blohm      - Uffz.  Scholz
                  Ofw.    Lerner     - Uffz.  Schramm
                  Fw.     Paden      - Uffz.  List       2 Absch.
                  Uffz.   Deppermann - Uffz.  Reichenberger
                                                         - 3 -
```

A Shaky do-The Skoda works raid 16/17th April 1943

The regular MacFarlane crew of Lancaster W4317
L-R Holdsworth, MacFarlane? Dawson, Keay, Edwards, (Rees & Williams unknown)

The Pilot Macfarlane had been engaged to be married as was the bomb aimer William Dawson and Holdsworth one of the gunners. The Australian flight engineer, Peter Keay, had a sweetheart who would have also felt the loss deeply. Flt/Sgt Dawson[125] and his Father were Methodist lay preachers. With this in mind one resident of their home village, Sedbergh, after this sad loss asked Dawson's Father a question. "You'll have trouble preaching about the love of God now won't you Mr. Dawson?" To which he replied, "It wasn't the love of God that killed my son it was the folly of men!"

In 1946 the R.A.F. missing research and enquiry unit, sent a team to investigate the crash at Givry. Local witnesses stated that they saw four coffins but the Germans did not allow them near the crash. M. Maurice Rosart who farmed the land on which the aircraft came down stated that the Germans had salvaged the wreckage. He was present when a German soldier was prodding the ground and heard him say there were two Tommies left in the nose of the aircraft. Arrangements were made to salvage the remaining wreckage. The M.R.E.U. also questioned M. Brasseur, a commandant of the gendarmerie who said he was on the scene of the crash soon after it occurred and found a parachute fully opened on the ground. He produced a witness a Monsieur Joseph Lecocq of Givry who said that he was resistance worker at the time of the crash. He claimed he was on the spot three to five minutes after the crash and had been living in a cabin nearby. He stated that he found an airman from the crash alive. This airman could not speak French. Lecocq thought that the man's name was Willy and indicated nine persons[126] aboard the aircraft. He said that he passed the airman to another resistance worker called Monsieur Capenaire of Grand Reng the same night. However when the R.A.F. missing research and enquiry unit visited Madame

---

[125] Dawson was a Sgt. on the ops records but Flt. Sgt. On the burial records.
[126] Only 8 crew were actually onboard.

Capenaire, they found that her husband had been shot by the Germans in 1944. The contact to which Capenaire passed evaders was also shot.

This incident is mentioned for the record as no survivors escaped from the crash and all remains were subsequently identified. Also both crewmen with the name William, Macfarlane the pilot and the bomb aimer, were well educated and more than likely spoke French. Dawson the bomb aimer certainly did.

Some years ago a relative of Sgt Keay flight engineer on W4317 went to visit the grave of her brother and was taken there some distance by a local taxi driver. The driver asked what the purpose of her visit was. When she told him, he refused to accept payment for the journey. Such was his gratitude for the price paid for his freedom.

Having experienced some flak and searchlights near Frankfurt, Squadron Leader Lashbrook on Halifax HR663 was above the French Belgian border. Three minutes after Lashbrook saw W4317 being attacked, he saw another going down in flames on the port side. This was Halifax DT752 of 408 squadron, flown by Flying officer Sergeant R.C.A.F. She crashed near Nassogne, Luxembourg just after 04:08 hours. The mid-upper gunner Sgt. Kwasney, was an American serving with the R.C.A.F. The victor this time was Ludwig Meister of the 1st Group NJG4.

When Lashbrook had given the order to keep a look out for fighters, no sooner than he had uttered these words they themselves were hit by bullets at 04:06 hours. The fighter was not seen but appeared to be attacking from astern and below on the port quarter. The pilot put the Halifax into a steep dive to port; the aircraft already had a fierce fire between the port inner and the fuselage. The aircraft was full of the smell of cordite and the inter-com had been destroyed. The extinguishers were not used due to the fire already being beyond control as they plummeted to around 6,000 feet. The pilot found it impossible to pull out of the dive nor could he throttle back the engines as the control rods were lose and probably severed.

Bomb aimer Alfie Martin recalls the same events;

*'The weather had been clear but around one hour from bombing we came into some cloud which caused icing on the wings, so we climbed to 14,000 feet to clear it. Once clear we descended to around 10,000 feet in clear conditions. It was almost a full moon and was quiet for a while then we saw some aircraft being shot down. The skipper told the rear gunner to keep an eye out as we continued a gentle weave for about two minutes, until suddenly there was a loud swishing sound as bullets ripped into the fuselage. The skipper called over the inter-com, "is anyone hurt," I replied O.K. skip, then the Navigator likewise. Then Willie the rear gunner said, "I didn't see the blighter." The skipper then said "I'm going into a deep turn, keep your eyes peeled in case they come in again." After a fraction of a second he said "the port inner is on fire", I looked out and saw blue flames all around the engine and back over the wing for about six feet. The flames were blue in the slipstream just like a blow torch looking anything but healthy. The order to bale out was then given. I attached my chute to my harness and went to open the hatch. I opened it but the slipstream caused it to jam edgeways in the opening. Frantically I tried to kick it clear. The skipper said, "bale out for ****** sake before the wing blows off!" I disconnected my oxygen and inter-com and the next thing I knew was falling through space........My first impression was a fleeting glimpse of the black tail against the starry sky.*[127]

The pilot baled out of the aircraft last, and caught his harness on the trim indicator and his inter-com lead on the control column, desperately trying to fight the centrifugal forces,

[127] From Alfie Martin's book 'Bale out' published by Colourpoint books Newtownards Northern Ireland.

A Shaky do. The Plzen raid April 16/17th April 1943

108

finally got free at a thousand feet or less with the Halifax spinning out of control. He managed to lean out of the hatch far enough to pull the cord and spill the chute out into the slipstream, and out he went! Seconds after he landed, he hit his head on something and thought, 'well that's finished you anyway!' He saw the aircraft crash and explode about 100 yards away on farm land close to the Chemin Mont Bliart and just to the east of Eppe Sauvage. He had *just* made it! So ended his 36th operation but it was not an end of his adventures.

Bolton the navigator and Martin (bomb aimer) had baled out before Sgt. Laws (w/op) who on his descent saw the aircraft break in two and fall in flames to the ground. He landed in a wood north of Montbliart and buried his chute before heading south. At nightfall on the 17th of April, Laws passed through Seloignes and Villiers La tours then La Taillettes on the 18th. At midnight on the 18th/19th he crossed the frontier into France north of Watigny reaching Fligny about 14:00 hours and then on to Auge. Here he sheltered in a home until on the 4th of May he was taken in a car to an unknown village where he met up with Group Captain Whitley. Whitley had been shot down by a night fighter whilst flying as second pilot on the night of the 10/11th April (ops to Frankfurt). His aircraft had crashed near Hirson. The remainder of this evasion by Laws and Whitley is documented in the book 'Escape or die' by Paul Brickhill. Whitley was station commander at Linton-On-Ouse at the time and went on to serve as A.O.C. 4 Group in 1945, A.O.C. of 8 Group (PFF) eventually becoming Air Marshal, and Inspector-General of the RAF. He died in 1997, aged ninety-two, the last surviving wartime R.A.F. bomber group commander.

Sgt Neil, the mid-upper gunner landed near Eppe Sauvage and had been found by a farmer near the crash site. He was taken into a house where a doctor was found to tend his wounds sustained during the fighter attack. The Germans picked him up and he spent the rest of the war as a p.o.w. The rear gunner Williams was killed in the aircraft and rests in Maubeuge centre cemetery. Bomb aimer F/O Alfie Martin, on his descent was feeling thankful to be alive as he looked around for signs of other parachutes, but all he could see over his shoulder was the aircraft burning on the ground. He looked at his watch in the moonlight was about 04:05 He landed heavily just missing a barbed wire fence, half a mile due east of Eppe Sauvage on the edge of the Forêt de Trelon. Alfie evaded via Sivry, Solre le Chateau and Liessies arriving at Sains (Du Nord) near Avesnes, where he remained until the 26th. The resistance organised his escape from there to Lille by train and then on to a safe house in Arras where he was joined by an American 8th Air Force B-17 'Flying Fortress' crewman, called Doug Hoehn. Then the evaders were moved to Paris and then Bordeaux and safety via Spain. Flight Sgt. Knight the flight engineer was taken p.o.w.

The skipper Lashbrook, evaded via Momigmes, Hirson, Bucilly and Montcornet fortuitously meeting Martin on a station platform in Paris avoiding any appearance of knowing each other. He then joined the others on the train. Using the Comèt escape network, he eventually reached Spain and departed from Gibraltar on 21st of June. Flt/Sgt Knight (flight engineer) was captured in Paris on 18th of September 1943.[128]

Wally Lashbrook re-visited the site of his crash in 2003 and was presented with a small piece of the aircraft the farmer. This is now in the Eden Camp museum in Yorkshire.

On one occasion, probably the night of the Plzeň raid, many 102 squadron pilots were very concerned about the all up weight of the aircraft with the extra fuel and were worried about taking off. 'C' flight-commander Lashbrook promptly had 'Q' Queenie (notorious for her poor performance) loaded up to the hilt and then proceeded to take off on the shortest runway, which had a nice hill directly in line. There were no more concerns expressed.[129]

---

[128] Footprints in the Sands of time, Clutton-Brock
[129] Yorkshire Air Museum archives, Elvington 102 Sqn. Files.

A Shaky do. The Plzen raid April 16/17th April 1943

Chapter Nine

The Aisne and the Somme

After being it by flak over Stuttgart, Sgt. Bill Steel R.N.Z.A.F. and Lancaster ED528 'Z' of 103 squadron, landed back at Elsham Wolds at 03:40 having narrowly escaped being guests of the Third Reich, they counted thirteen substantial flak holes in 'Z' for Zebra. At 04:23 50 squadron Lancaster ED800 flown by Sgt. J.G. Duncan, was heading for home over the Belgian/French border area when pounced upon by the Kommandeur of I./NJG4 Wilhelm Herget at 2,500 metres. Roger Anthoine, a witness, went out the next day to the place were the aircraft had crashed. It was located in the 'Bois de Rosette' at Yves-Gomezée. Antoine commented;

"I arrived with my bicycle at a huge crater in the forest. The area was guarded, but I was able to have a look and they even allowed me to take photographs. The bomber must have gone straight into the ground. I looked around. Not one tree was hit, but there were four craters from the engines and one big hole in the middle filled with water and oil, where the fuselage went in. Not one piece could be found which identified the aircraft, and what about the crew?" [130]

After the war a road was named Chemins des sept sergents (Way of the seven sergeants) in memory of the crew. Later after the war a carburettor with a serial number was found by an R.A.F. recovery unit and it was possible to identify the aircraft as ED800. (See Appendix)

Still in the four o'clock hour, many aircraft of the Plzeň force were making their way across the region of the Aisne and the Somme, the scene of so much loss of life during the First World War. Many aircraft were making a low level return.

At 04:36 a Halifax of fifty-one squadron (HR784) was approaching the town of Ham (Dept. of the Somme) when seen by a night fighter flown by Hauptman Hans-Karl Kamp and shot down in flames. The aircraft broke up into three major portions and came down over the communes of Eppeville and St. Sulpice. The navigator, Warrant Officer Keirnan D.F.M. was the only member of the crew to survive, albeit with a broken bone in the groin, probably his hip bone. After treatment by Dr. Auguste Puche of Ham, he was removed in a German ambulance and then later held at Stalag Luft VI and 357. A letter received by the R.C.A.F. HQ in Ottawa paraphrases a report made by W/O Keirnan on the 23rd Oct 1944 (P.O.W. Number 14, Stalag Luft VI). It states that 'Stewart was killed outright by machine gun fire from the enemy aircraft.' This was told to him by wireless operator Axtell before they decided to abandon the aircraft.[131] Four bodies were found soon after the crash, another body on the marshes on the 18th and a further body on the 22nd. A letter on file from a Lt. Col. in the 21st Army Group dated 1946, forwarded the following items found in the crashed aircraft at the time by M. Paul Martineu: 1316069 Reid's identity discs, Stewart's service and pay book, address book, bomb-aimer's selector switch list and order of leaving aircraft emergency plan.

Arrangements were being made to bury the first four bodies in the communal cemetery but as soon as it became known to the Germans that a 'sympathetic demonstration' was to be made by the people of Ham, they placed the coffins in a wagon and took them away. Supposedly to Lihons. The Germans salvaged all the wreckage. After the war an R.A.F

---

[130] Wim Govaerts Belgie in Oorlog 36 Lancaster verliezen in Belgie 1941-1945
[131] File of Ronald Henry Stewart Canadian National Archives 24 vol.28736 page 2

M.R.E. unit investigated and found no graves at Lihons, instead the crew's graves were to be found at Maucourt French military cemetery where they remain to this day.

William Reid Keirnan the navigator was a long serving airman who had joined up in 1935 and was awarded the D.F.M. in 1940 during his first tour of operations. The citation reads;

This NCO observer has now completed 24 sorties. His high standard of efficiency in navigation and bombing has considerably enhanced the good work done by his crew. He has always shown a high standard of zeal and courage and sets a good example to his juniors. 19/6/1940[132]

I mention here another aircraft returning from the Mannheim target due to its crash location being so close in proximity to that of Halifax HR784. Only 13 miles (20 Km) from Eppeville and approximately two hours earlier a Halifax aircraft had crashed only a few miles to the west at Goyencourt at 02:15. This was Halifax JB870 of 76 squadron, borrowed by 78 squadron. The aircraft was due to cross the French coast at St. Valery-en-Caux at 02:37 hours. This was only 90 miles/149k to go and approximately half an hour's flying time. Linton-On-Ouse's Station record book states that 76 and 78 squadron were to cross the coast at St. Valery-en-Caux rather than Cayeux.[133]

Eyewitness reports state;[134]

The aircraft was flying in an east-west direction when it was seen to be on fire. Having flown over the village of Roye, at about 300 metres, the fuel tanks exploded. The wreckage from the plane was scattered to the west of Roye and covered an area of 250 metres in diameter. The bodies of the seven members of the crew were recovered. A few moments before the explosion, the plane shed its incendiary bombs. One came to rest on the bed of a couple, who were lying in it, and burst into flames. Because it fell between the two of them, it caused no injuries, but destroyed the bedding and other effects. Another one fell in the children's bedroom but did not explode. Six other bombs fell in the farmyard and two others on the road where they ignited without causing any damage or injuring anyone. The wreckage of the plane was scattered over a wide area. The aircraft crashed at Goyencourt, several witnesses reported at exactly 02:15 hours.

This matches almost exactly a claim for a victory west of Ham by Helmut Bergmann at 02:19 hrs.

The rear gunner on this Halifax aircraft was Sergeant David Aubrey Watkins; he was on only his third operation. I include here some poignant words written by the 20-year-old gunner in a letter to relatives on the 11th April;

'I did my first Op a fortnight [two weeks] ago. You do a few every week. Well I thought I would be scared, but you have so much to do that you haven't time to be, and the flak seems to climb so slowly that you would hardly think it could hurt you. The only time I can say I nearly swallowed my tonsils was when I saw a Jerry fighter, but I think he must have been scared away. I've got my tonsils back now though thanks.'

---

[132] DFM Register WW2 Ian Tavender
[133] Linton On Ouse station record book TNA UK ref AIR28/487
[134] Archives départementales de la Somme Côte 26W804

A Shaky do. The Plzen raid April 16/17th April 1943

David Aubrey Watkins died on the 17th of April. 'So costly a sacrifice upon the altar of freedom.'

Shortly after HR784 had been brought down at Eppeville, a Six Group Halifax aircraft of 408 squadron, (BB343) was shot down in flames by Ofw. Adolf Brandstetter of 1./NJG 4 and his bordfunker Fw. Helbing at a height 2,200 metres at 04.37 hours. The Halifax crashed on the territory of the commune of Lesquielles in a meadow called Le Calvaire-St-Germain the fire was so fierce it was impossible to approach the aircraft, indeed it was still burning at 07:00 hours.

In 1951 a letter was written by the skipper Jacques Guay's brother Edgar to Sr. St Irénée, a relative of François Rolland's. He states that *"In the eyes of the population of Lesquielles who watched the aerial combat in all its ferocity and greatness, our aviators are heroes because they spared the village a tragedy. They managed, at the expense of great energy, to yank the aircraft from the valley where it had been flying in circles, to hit the ground outside the village."* The villagers collected enough funds to erect a memorial to the crew, which stands today by the roadside at Lesquielles. It reads;

EN SOUVENIR
DES AVIATEURS CANADIENS
ET BRITANNIQUES
TOMBES GLORIEUSEMENT
LE 17 AVRIL 1943
LES HABITANTS RECONNASSANTS

The Pilot W/O Joseph Jacques Alfred Guay had flown 14 successful operational sorties and air gunner Sgt. Irving MacDonald who had only been on two sorties. The rest of the crew had done three operations each. An inscription on the back of a family photograph of this crew read, 'All for one and one for all.' These novice crews were known as sprogs and the loss rate was very high indeed amongst them.

At approximately 04:30 hours a pathfinder aircraft of 83 squadron, (R5484) was making her way towards the final turning point toward the channel coast. She had made her way the target without too much drama except for the very bright moonlight, which was casting shadows making her presence known all too well to the enemy. After three runs the Lancaster dropped her bombs from 6,000 feet and then turned away keeping low for half an hour. In the Mannheim area they saw the city taking a beating when suddenly they were coned by a battery of searchlights and were forced to roof top height to try and evade the lights. They were hit several times by flak and lost an engine. Charlie Hobbs the rear gunner fired his guns to try and knock out the searchlights. Ten minutes later they lost another engine on the starboard side, which caught fire. The engine was feathered and the fire put out. They flew on with the two serviceable engines and were well into France then a third engine cut out and the decision to bale out was taken. As the intercom was out of action the navigator went back to warn the tail gunner. The mid-upper gunner had been hit and couldn't bale out. As Hobbs went forward they were hit by cannon shells from a fighter at 04:45 just east of Pontavert. He went to see if the fires could be put out, but they could not. Just then the fighter came in a second time and shot the controls out of Nichol's hands and the nose went up and then straight down. The brave Canadian was dead. The rear gunner had been badly scratched up with pieces of shrapnel. He had come to when on the ground and was glad to find some of his crew had survived and gathered inside a house, albeit with plenty of broken bones. They had crashed onto some buildings not far from the centre of Pontavert which is approximately 14 miles (22km) south east of Laon. Soon the Germans arrived and the crew was taken prisoner of war. Lewis the American bomb aimer was not present but was also captured and taken prisoner of war. The crew at Pontavert was visited by the Luftwaffe pilot who had shot them down. This was Ofw. Kurt Karsten of 7./NJG4 who had scored his fourth victory. He asked Charlie 'why he hadn't used his guns.'[135]

---

[135] Info from Gordon Hobbs and '*Past Tense* Charlie's story' General Store Publishing house

A Shaky do. The Plzen raid April 16/17th April 1943

Wickenby airfield Lincolnshire in 2007: Below, the monument which stands at the gate.

A Shaky do-The Skoda works raid 16/17th April 1943

L-R back row: Holton, Bayne, James, Tyler, Stephens, Grimes, Garbett
Ground Crew, Left to right front row: Des Richards,electrics; Stan Walford, rigger;
unknown; Nobby Hall, the engine man

Photos Chris James

L-R back row: Sgt Earle Holton, Sgt George Tyler, Flt.Sgt Sid Grimes, F/Lt Steve
Stephens, F/O Bruce Bayne, Front Left: Sgt Bill Garbett, P/O Ron (Taff) James

A Shaky do-The Skoda works raid 16/17th April 1943

**Sqn/Ldr. Lashbrook MBE DFC AFC DFM MID (left) with his bomb aimer
Alfie Martin DFC at a Paris reunion. Both successfully evaded when shot down
in Halifax HR663 of 102 squadron (Photo Martin)**

A shaky do-The Skoda works raid April 16/17th 1943

Chapter Ten
Last but not least

At some time between 04:00 and 05:00 on the morning of the 17th of April 1943 a 49 squadron Lancaster Mk.III ED441, approached Camon on the east side of Amiens. Undoubtedly suffering from damage, the aircraft Captained by Sgt. Penry, tried to crash land and one wing collided with a hangar near Rue Roger Solangro. Despite the impact the Lancaster did not catch fire but broke into several pieces, with the rear part of the aircraft standing vertically and fuel leaked from the tanks for days. The crew were killed with the exception of two which early witnesses said, were badly wounded. A resident of Camon at the time M. Vincent Herricote tried to help, giving them something to drink. Many villagers gathered to see the wreck. When the guard was gone many took souvenirs and some brought containers to collect the escaping fuel which of course was hard to obtain in time of war. The wreckage remained for several days before the Germans lifted it but not before someone stole the tail wheel right from under the guard's nose.[136] Sadly one of the survivors died and Sgt. Kerr the rear gunner was taken prisoner of war.

Another two Lancasters, both of 156 pathfinder squadron were lost at unknown times. On the return journey Lancaster W4854 was hit by flak from the Reims-Courcy airfield, caught fire and crashed just to the North West of the village of Brimont. The crew all died in the crash and were buried with full military honours by the Germans.[137] Sergeant Bordycott, D.F.C., D.F.M. and P/O Smith D.F.M. had already completed a tour of operations with 150 Squadron.[138] The flight engineer Sgt. Brougham-Faddy was only eighteen years old, one of the youngest airmen to be killed in the service of Bomber Command.

The other 156 squadron aircraft lost to an unknown cause was W4930 flown by the crew of Sgt. Gonce and crew. The rear gunner on this aircraft was Sgt. Louie Elmo Corley R.C.A.F., an American from Houston Texas. The aircraft crashed at Aigny (Marne). Six of the crew were buried at the east cemetery Châlons-sur-Marne. Sgt. Dean was buried at Condé-sur-Marne.[139]

Having for some unknown reason taken an alternative route back over the Köln area, Lancaster ED651 of 467 squadron was attacked by enemy night-fighter, after being coned when flying on the deck (very low level). The attack set the port inner wing on fire and centre section of the fuselage. The controls were partly damaged and with the aircraft well on fire the pilot ordered his crew to crash positions **and** carried out a crash landing. The two gunners Sgt. Dunn and Sgt. Bannatyne R.A.F. were thought to have been killed by the fighter's attack. The flight engineer, Sgt. Pallender was killed in the landing. Wireless operator Sgt. Goode, died of burns in hospital two days later. Stitt the navigator and Boswell the bomb-aimer each broke a leg. Stitt had a leg amputated later on and was repatriated. Wilson, the pilot woke up in a Köln hospital with fractured vertebrae.[140]He had completed ten operations.

When crossing the French coast homeward bound; 103 squadron Lancaster (W4901) shot up coastal batteries and Sgt. Frank Heavery's 467 squadron Lancaster (ED772) was trouble by flak. [141] They had a very close call when they were making a low flying return at 500 ft. As the aircraft approached the coastline Sergeant Nick Murray had been manning the front turret

---

[136] Camon Magazine Bulletin Municipal 15th June 2000 No.6
[137] Jonathan Webb 2002
[138] Chorley Bomber command losses 1943
[139] Ibid
[140] Australian National Archives. A9301/408545 and A705/166/43/148
[141] Syd Knott 467 sqn.

and was asked to climb down into the bomb aimer's position and look out for a pin-point. Navigator Eddie Foster gives his account;

'As we approached the coast-line Nick had been manning the front turret and, thinking it would be advisable to get an accurate fix if possible on crossing, I asked him to climb down into the nose and look out for a pin-point. This he did but before he had time to unplug his intercom lead, an enemy shell passed through the Perspex turret he had just vacated. It was surely our lucky night as it failed to explode. The immediate effect was that a howling and arctic gale roared through the Lancaster and removed my log, charts and maps like a whirlwind in the direction of the rear gunner. More importantly, the terrific thump up front which seemed to have come from the pilot's position had wrecked the communication system and, without Frank's charming Cotswold voice to reassure us, we were hurtling nose down towards the sea. At that moment I knew we were about to die and felt no fear at all. I have since learnt that this was a common experience of many a flyer in such a fraught situation but I still remember wondering who would have the unenviable task of breaking the news to Mary, my wife, and how she would cope with the shock.

It then occurred to me that, from 500 feet and at the angle at which we had been diving, we should have been nearing the bottom of the ocean by now. We appeared to have levelled off and, pulling back the black-out curtain, I noticed that the sea was racing by just a few feet below us. The frustrated German firing squad were still doing their damdest to down us but were unable to depress their weapon sufficiently and their erratic fire was passing well overhead. The Skipper seemed to have survived the trouble up front and, as I emerged alongside him, he dumb-founded me by sticking his tongue out and giving me an energetic and cheery R.A.F. version of Churchill's famous 'V' sign. That was the calibre of a 20 year-old that I was lucky enough to be going to war with. I realized that for the moment we had by-passed the Pearly Gates, my hands began to shake so that a simple manipulation of the Dalton computer became a difficult task. Eventually I did manage it and, without the benefit of the intercom, had to go forward and set the new course on Frank's compass before shouting in his ear the reason for the change of plan. Nick, who was still in his position in the bomb-bay[142] was looking very grim I noticed. His appearance, of course, was not improved by the fact that the hydraulic pipe above his head had shattered and the green oil that engulfed him had made him look even more like an authentic Irish Leprechaun.[143]

During this episode the rear gunner Syd Knott had fired 300 rounds at the ground defences to keep their heads down. In about forty minutes they would touch down at Boscombe down, having been diverted there along with the rest of the squadron.

103 squadron Lancaster ED727 'H' flown by Sgt Alan Egan and crew, had had quite a bit of attention from light flak put up from the airfields they over flew and also sustained a hole through the starboard wing at the French coast. This crew with the exception of the flight engineer was shot down on operations to Gelsenkirchen on the 25/26th June in Lancaster ED528. Flt./Sgt Egan, Sgt Johnston and Flt./Sgt Miller R.A.A.F. were taken prisoner of war. Flt.Sgt. Elliot and Sgts. Brown, Horrell and Britton were killed. (See Appendix)

At around 04:00 Flying Officer Elderfield's 50 sqn. Lancaster ED784 'N' was forced to ditch some 5 miles off the French coast near Berck-Sur-Mer. The pilot Elderfield, second pilot Cotter, and Hinchcliffe the bomb-aimer were drowned. The rest of the crew reached the

---

[142] More than likely the bomb aimer's position in the nose of the aircraft.

[143] Foster-Navigator 467 sqn. http://www.467463raafsquadrons.com/Pages/TrueTales/eddiefosterstory.htm

A Shaky do. The Plzen raid April 16/17th April 1943

dinghy which was damaged and unable to take all the crew. [144]Elderfield had last been seen swimming strongly for the French coast to try and summon assistance. The rest of the crew was picked up by Motor Torpedo boat at 02:00 hours on the 18th of April after having been adrift for twenty-two hours.

Many more aircraft were now approaching the welcome coast of England. Fuel was for many now very low and battle damage common place. Even after as many as ten hours in the air, mostly over enemy territory, the risk of attack was still great for tired crews. Night fighters and flak concentrations were still looking for easy prey. Many gunners aboard the Plzeň aircraft would be experiencing heavy eyelids, making it ever more difficult to discern the difference between a speck of dirt on the Perspex or stalking fighter below and behind. Risk of collision with the many friendly aircraft was also present. Navigation lights were to be switched on below 5,000 ft. within 50 miles of base and resin lights on above 8000 ft. over England.

At 04:17 when approaching the English coast Lancaster ED412 Q-Queenie had to take violent evasive action to avoid an unknown aircraft and was unable to find the coast and after homing in on radio beacons managed to land at Tangmere at 05:45 having been diverted. She had been airborne for 8 hours 25 minutes.[145]

At 05:20 a pathfinder Lancaster W4844 jettisoned some target indicators in the channel six miles south of Dungeness, the photoflash failing to release. Very soon after this a struggling Halifax of 10 squadron (DT791) approached the English coast having already lost the port-outer engine over the target and the port-inner to a night fighter[146] on the return leg. They were again hit by heavy and light flak on crossing the French coast and yet again by flak ships five minutes later.[147] The stricken bomber passed over the town of Lewes from south to north-west at very low altitude with one of the crew shining a torch on the ground and landing lights on as they looked for a landing place. When the aircraft crash landed near Offam road on the Landport estate allotments, it caught fire but the police and fire services were soon on the scene and quickly had the fire under control. The crew were lying on the bank, seven of whom were injured. The pilot 'Timber' Wood however appeared to be uninjured. All the crew were taken to hospital and were assisted by the 3rd Canadian Anti-Aircraft unit who were on duty only a couple of hundred yards away from the crash site. Assistance was also given by people from nearby houses.

The second Pilot, Rooney (1658 C.U.) received a knock around the eye and was unconscious for three days. Stepney the bomb aimer was later killed in action with 35 P.F.F. squadron on ops to Mannheim on the 18th of November 1943. Rooney recovered and went on to do 9 operations with 102 squadron and 30 operations with 640 squadron where he was renowned for being a 'press on Aussy Skipper' by his crew. He flew some 200 operational hours and earned a D.F.C. for an operation on Nürnberg. In August 1944 upon leaving the target his aircraft was hit by flak. With one engine out of action and the controls damaged, he continued on and was attacked twice by night fighters causing the rear turret and inter-com to

---

[144] The Second World War Experience Centre also AIR27/487 TNA UK.
[145] Sgt. 'Lucky' Pegrum's log gives the aircraft as ED498 but he stated in 2007 that ED412 was correct.
[146] TNA UK AIR2/8780 D.F.C. citation Prebble R.C.A.F./Rooney
[147] Chorley Bomber Command Losses 1943

fail. The crew communicated by other means and evaded the fighters. Flt/Lt. Rooney flew the aircraft back to base and landed safely.

Sgt Rooney 1658 CU Halifax DT791, & 640 sqn. He survived the war (Rooney Family)

At 05:30 51 squadron Halifax DT628 'B' touched down at Tangmere on two engines. 05:33 hours saw Lancaster W4844 of 460 squadron, land at Manston being short of fuel having turned back from the Regensburg area due to navigational difficulties. As mentioned earlier 207 squadron Lancaster ED412 landed at Tangmere at 05:45 after eight hours twenty-five minutes in the air. The aircraft had been badly holed by flak. 05:59 hours saw the return of P/O Collins who landed 57 sqn. Lancaster ED308 at Beaulieu due to feared fuel shortage. They had brought back a full load of 1,260 4lb incendiaries.

At 05:59 hours the 467 squadron Lancaster of the Heavery crew (ED772) arrived on the circuit at Boscombe Down and joined the many aircraft of 5 Group who were orbiting the airfield. Navigator Eddie Foster commented;

There was still some time to go before daybreak as we arrived on the circuit at Boscombe Down, and joined the many Lancasters of 5 Group which were orbiting the airfield. Our particular predicament was that with the wrecked R/T we had no means of contacting the Flying Control and with the fuel supply giving some anxiety, the skipper tried 3 or 4 times to gate crash the proceedings only to be confronted on each approach by an angry red Very cartridge. Finally as dawn was breaking over this unique grassy airfield, some alert controller noticed that the ' rogue ' Lancaster (who was due for a rollicking[148] on landing) had a re-arranged front end and might well also have a few re-arranged bodies on board. We were given some priority and returned to earth with a feeling of gratitude that many a member of aircrew came to know but few could put adequately into words.

The crew tried to grab an hour or two's sleep in a Mess chair or on the carpet. The bomb-aimer was still in some state of shock after they had landed after his very close call. That morning the crew left their Lancaster for some restoration work and scrounged lifts back to Bottesford in other aircraft.[149]

At 06:00 Halifax HR791 landed at Harwell but struck a tree on landing. The crew was uninjured but the aircraft was badly damaged. According the air ministry form 1180, the aircraft stuck some trees on approach and the pilot failed to get Q.F.E.[150] The pilot stuck a tree with the altimeter reading 6-700 Millibars. No glide path indicator was seen. The Air Officer Commanding stated that the glide path indicator was definitely working and the F/O Dawes' logbook was endorsed…'**carelessness**.' It had been a long trip, the crew having been in the air for eight hours forty five minutes, touching down at around dawn. At 06:15 hours Halifax HR695 'D' of ten squadron landed at Harwell after nine and a half hours in the air, being diverted due to weather conditions at their base, near York. The aircraft flew back to Melbourne during the afternoon of the 17th of April.

At 06:29 Australian skipper Sgt. Mizon and his 12 squadron Lancaster (W4366), called up the '*Darkie.*' This was a radio locator/homing (low frequency) device to get a triangulated position and vector to the base that responded to the emergency. They landed at Ford in Sussex after nine hours and five minutes flying. The aircraft had an engine failure and fire in the port-outer. The Air Officer Commanding judged that the pilot was not at fault as he had landed as soon as possible to save the engine. It will be remembered that the rear gunner (Sgt Rudkin), the mid-upper gunner (Sgt. McKay) and the wireless operator (Sgt. Hutton) had baled out mistakenly at 03:41. They had not heard the command revoking the previous 'prepare to bale out' order, due to a break in the inter-com. Rudkin and Hutton landed within a quarter mile of each other at Selagne, near the Belgium-Luxembourg border. Hutton was hanging with his chute snagged in a tree until Rudkin came to the rescue and freed him using his own parachute as an aid. Sgt. McKay broke a leg on landing and was taken prisoner of war.[151] Sgt. Rudkin and Sgt. Hutton evaded captivity arriving at Gibraltar on 17th of July and back in Liverpool on the 24th of July 1943. At one stage a resistance worker had taken them to the village of Musson. They were sheltered there by the courageous Priest, Father Goffinet. Goffinet was later betrayed and this extremely brave man was sent to Buchenwald concentration camp. He did not survive.

At 06:30 Halifax JB782 flown by F/O Kelly landed at a minor airfield in Wiltshire called New Zealand farm after nine hours and forty-five minutes in the air. A long haul!

Lancaster W4952 skippered by Pilot Officer Herrin landed at Tangmere at about the same time, after 8 hours 50 minutes in the air. There were some repairs to be made to the battle damaged aircraft so according to Sgt. Male's log book he hitched a ride aboard ED692 Sgt. Stubbs' aircraft back to Langar the next day.[152] Jack 'Lucky' Pegrum the wireless op on Sgt. Stephen's crew (ED412) used to play darts in the local pub with Sgt. Payton the W/op on Herrin's crew. Payton had owed 'Lucky' £5. He never did get his fiver back as all of Herrin's crew including Payton and Male were lost on ops to Mulheim on the 22nd/23rd June 1943.

---

[148] A reprimand.
[149] Eddie Foster Navigator 467 sqn. http://www.467463raafsquadrons.com/Pages/TrueTales/eddiefosterstory.htm
[150] Barometric pressure at airfield elevation
[151] Luft1, 6 and 4? Clutton-Brock
[152] Sgt Male service number 1315318, log book R.A.F. Museum Archives Hendon MF10089/8 Microfilm

Male was 19 years old at the time of his death. The bomb aimer on the same crew was George Kleinberg a Jewish Belgian, born in Antwerpen/Anvers. Being a Jew, it must have taken great courage to fly on ops over Germany for Kleinberg, but also he must have had more motivation than most.

At 06:37 hours, Halifax JB850 of 77 sqn based at Elvington, landed with engine trouble at Harwell and at 06:45 Lancaster ED413 of 57 squadron skippered by Sgt. Allwright had a tail heavy landing and the rear fuselage was found to have been strained. The officer commanding determined that the landing had not been unduly heavy and that the fuselage had probably already been strained.

At 06:40 hours 12 squadron Lancaster W4380'E' landed after 8 hours 40 minutes in the air. The skipper Flight Sergeant Head had brought them back in one piece. Navigator Sgt. Short's flying log book showed his 19th operation completed.[153]

Aircraft were now touching down all over southern England and at Tangmere at 06:53 hours, 103 sqn Lancaster (W4337) landed with flak damage. Sgt Lane the wop/ag received shrapnel wounds to the face and rear gunner Sgt. Woolard, a lacerated wound of the right foot. The aircraft was badly hit by flak in the target area. Both airmen were treated at R.A.F. Tangmere and admitted to the Royal West Sussex Hospital Chichester. Sgt. Woolard was placed on the S.I. list.

At 06:53 hours Sgt Griffiths (DT747 102 sqn) and crew touched down with the port inner just having failed. One of the last aircraft to touch down was 51 squadron Halifax HR790 'C' just after 07:00 hours. Sgt. Stringer's (mid-upper gunner) log book recorded a weary 10 hours 40 minutes in the air. It was his first operational raid. Stringer did one more low level operation to Stettin two days later with 9 hours 5 minutes airborne.[154] He and five of the same crew lost their lives on the same aircraft on operations to Bochum on the 14th of May. He had not survived three raids. Such was the grievous lost rate of Bomber Command crews in 1943.

Many aircraft landed at the following alternative fields due to shortage of fuel and also due to weather conditions at their home bases; Abingdon; Beaulieu; Boscombe Down; Castle Donnington; Chipping Warden; Colerne, Wilts; Enstone; Ford; Gatwick; Harwell; Hawkinge; New Zealand Farm, Wilts; Manston; Newmarket; Pershore; Stanton Harcourt; Tangmere; Waddington; West Malling; and Wittering.

---

[153] Sgt. Short's Flying log book, R.A.F. Museum Archives Hendon.X001-6464/008 Microfilm
[154] R.A.F. Museum Archives Hendon. Sgt Stringer-Air gunner's flying log book ref B3139

Chapter Eleven
Counting the cost

When all the Plzeň force had landed and the weary crews had been to debriefing and breakfast, they stumbled into their beds exhausted. The day would reveal many empty beds to which their friends and fellow aircrew would not be returning. Linton-On-Ouse was the base with the most aircraft missing from the two squadrons 76 and 78 with six Halifaxes missing. One of these was (JB870) on the Mannheim raid. 408 Squadron Six Group, had the most aircraft missing from one squadron. Four Halifaxes and twenty-nine men would not be at the breakfast table and as many families would be receiving telegrams displaying the *dreaded* words, …

'I regret to inform you that your son (serial number) Sergeant ------- Number.--- squadron, Royal Air force is missing, the aircraft of which he was the air bomber having failed to return to its base on the night of the 16/17th April 1943 from an operational flight'……

This would be followed by a letter and then another communication; more often than not confirming the loss on operations.

249 aircraft claimed to have attacked the target however most of the aircraft dropped their bombs on or around Dobřany 7 miles south west of the target destroying a lunatic asylum and a German military barracks. 28 Aircraft reported attacking alternative targets. 4 attacked Saarbrücken, 3 Nürnberg, 3 München, 2 Mannheim, 2 Karlsruhe, 2 Stuttgart, Koblenz, Erlangen, Rothenburg, Worms, Trier, Neustadt and Würzburg. Five attacked unidentified towns or factories. 11 sorties were aborted due to defect, 1 due to illness, 1 due to mistaken pinpoint and 1 due to flak. There were 38 aircraft lost (almost 12%).

409 tons of high explosive bombs were dropped in the area of the primary target, and 131 tons of incendiaries. Alternative targets received 59 tons of high explosives and 10 tons of incendiaries. 105 4,000lb High Explosive 'cookies' were dropped on the 'primary.'

The south east part of the town of Dobřany was illuminated by the P.F.F. markers and had taken the brunt of the bombing. Its population of 4,000 were mostly of German origin.

A large 80-hectare psychiatric hospital near the town had been built there in the 19th century, which had wards, a water tower, boiler house and a large chimney. One kilometre east of the hospital was a training centre for the Wermacht in a former cavalry barracks. The casualties included 1000 German soldiers, 250 civilians and 300 hospital patients. In Nová Ves eleven people died. Hundreds of tons of bombs dropped within a 2-3 kilometre area around Dobřany a third of which were incendiaries. Many bombs however did not explode due to the low dropping altitude including several small bomb containers containing incendiary bombs.

Regarding damage to the works itself on the 17th April 1943, the Škoda Fire Brigade diary records the following;

No bomb hit the Škoda Works area or its immediate vicinity. Negligible damage was caused to only a small number of glazed roofs and windows of the production halls. Only one young German worker manning the anti-aircraft guns in the factory premises was injured by flak splinters. German apprentices who were working at the factory also operated anti-aircraft guns on the periphery of the works.

The bombs fell not only on Dobřany but in about a 15 kilometres long zone southwest from Plzeň along the river Radbuza and railway tracks in the direction of Plzeň, mostly in fields and woods. The nearest bombs to the western part of Škoda Works fell in the fields near the village Křimice (Grünhof) about 4 kilometres from Škoda Works.[155]

The human cost to the people on the ground around Dobřany was high as was the cost in lives of Bomber Command crews. One hundred and ninety-nine Bomber Command aircrew lost their lives on the Plzeň raid. The crews consisted of British, Australian, Canadian, American, New Zealand, Norwegian airmen and many other nationalities. As mentioned earlier the youngest of these was probably Leonard Jonasson of 76 Squadron, a 17-year-old mid-upper gunner who had lied about his age in order to enlist. He died on his third operation.

A small measure of consolation was the fact that there were fifty two airmen who survived to become prisoners of war and thirteen who had evaded captivity. One of the airmen who survived the raid and returned to base was to have a final desperate tragedy as he was murdered by the Gestapo on the Great Escape from Stalag Luft III on the 29th March 1944, having been shot down on a later raid. Another was killed on the 19th April 1945 when R.A.F Typhoons strafed what they thought was a column of German troops at Gresse. These in fact were p.o.w.s being force marched by the Germans to avoid the rapidly approaching Russian troops. The story of these marches is told in John Nichol and Tony Rennel's book 'The Last escape.' New Zealander Phil Langsford (78 squadron Halifax DT773) also got caught up in a strafing incident on the 11th of April 1945 when four R.A.F. Typhoons attacked his column on prisoners killing two and injuring seven in the group to his rear.

The bombers of the Plzeň force recorded 14 combats. A further 54 reported sightings of fighters but were not attacked. The German night-fighter force lost only a few fighters on operations, resulting in some wounded and three killed in action.

Night fighter loss summary.
10./NJG4 Bf110 of Oblt. Friedrich was shot down in return fire by gunners on Halifax HR758 of 158 sqn. The crew were wounded.
6./NJG4 Bf110 Wn. 4087 of Fw. Rase, was shot down by return fire from 10 sqn. Halifax JB910 crashing at St. Menehould near Châlons-sur-Marne (pilot OK, bordfunker killed)
6./NJG4 Bf110 Wn. 4756, force-landed near Joinville, 25 km. SE St. Dizier after air combat, Lt. Schäfer and his bordfunker were wounded.
1./NJG3 Bf110 loss on 16/17.4.43, a Me110 Wn. 3962 crashed 3 km. N. Bissel near Ahlhorn, probably due to air combat, Uffz. Heinrichs and his Bordfunker were killed.

The raid had been a failure. The Gee navigation system had been heavily jammed by the enemy on the Virginia frequency and in any case only yielded a range of about 200-miles for the MkI System and a little more for Gee MkII. The advantages of using new tactics in broad moonlight at low level had been negated by the many disadvantages.

Very similar geographical layouts concerning the rivers and landmarks at Plzeň and Dobřany led to the Pathfinders dropping their flares and target indicators in the wrong place. This was compounded by only one operational H2s navigation aid being used over the target area and a layer of cloud at around 10,000 feet, which had obscured the target

Some main force aircraft bombed early and smoke had drifted across the area making subsequent target recognition more difficult. Other aircraft whose navigators and bomb-aimers knew they were in the wrong place bombed on the markers anyway. The highly industrial appearance of the asylum south of Dobřany caused the P.F.F. to think they were over the Škoda factory and several crews were convinced enemy decoys fires or lights were in use to confuse the attacking force.

---

[155] Dr. Krátký, Škoda Museum

A green field site project for a dummy Škoda Works started in the year 1940 and was situated in the fields between the villages of Vochov and Vejprnice, about 6.5 km west of the western end of Škoda Works. It was 80 hectares in area. The plan and its realization had been carried out under the guidance of 'Luftgaukommando XVII, Verwaltung in Wien' with the participation of Škoda Works. During the year 1942 the decoy was finished and for the first time put into operation during autumn 1943. The Germans went to a lot of trouble to attract bombs to this decoy. At night time they switched on the lights to give the appearance of work going inside. Perhaps even though not completed at the time of April 1943, the structure may have caused further confusion.

In a bilateral contract between Luftgaukommando XVII and Škoda Works in Prague from 9. 2. 1943 was given, for other decoys – a military airfield and typical star shaped prison building in Plzen. Škoda would guarantee the personnel and surveillance. But these two decoys were never built and no traces have been found. Perhaps wartime problems stopped the realization. The prison building was covered in the year 1942 by a big round and dense camouflage net.[156]

The failure of the raid was soon apparent when the bombing photographs were developed. Two hundred and eleven photographs were examined. Of which only 6 were plotted within three miles of the aiming point. 52 were plotted outside 5 miles. Photographs taken by photo-reconnaissance aircraft soon after the raid, showed heavy damage at Dobřany and Nová Ves. Cloud cover over the works prevented complete observation but no damage was seen in the works. Some crews were convinced they were to bomb on the target indicators whilst others as mentioned in the official raid report, thought they were to bomb visually using the target indicators as a guide. F/Lt. Desmond of 467 squadron, stated that despite the ease of pinpointing, the hazards of such a long trip over well defended territory far outweighed the slight advantage.[157]

Churchill sent a telegram to Stalin on the 17th April on the subject of this and other raids,

'We have struck three good blows this week, namely Spezia, Stuttgart and, last night, both the Škoda works and Mannheim. In the first, 174 aircraft dropped 460 tons of bombs but hit the town of Spezia more than the shipping in the harbour owing to the haze and smoke. The second Stuttgart, was a flaming success. 462 bombers took part throwing 750 tons. Last night we sent 598 aircraft on the two targets, and about 850 tons were dropped. Reports about Škoda damage so far are good though the photographs have not yet come in. It was particularly important to go for Škoda as workmen and vital tasks have been transferred thither owing to damage at Essen. In these three raids we lost 81 bombers of which 64 were heavies, with about 500 highly trained air personnel. I repeat my assurance that attacks will continue throughout the summer on ever increasing scale.'[158]

On May 2nd he again wrote to Stalin by telegram,

'In the raid on Plzen we did not hit the Škoda works with any great concentration but this target will not be forgotten when the exceptional conditions, which alone render it practicable, recur.'[159]

---

[156] Dr. Krátký Škoda Museum
[157] Australian National Archives A9186/153/1191790 Unit history ORB 467 sqn. page 1160
[158] CHAR 20/110/38 Churchill Archives Centre Churchill College Cambridge
Reproduced with permission of Curtis Brown Ltd, London on behalf of The Estate of Winston Churchill-
Copyright Winston S. Churchill.
[159] CHAR 20/111/40-41 Source and permission for reproduction as per ref 158. Copyright Winston S. Churchill

In fact the Škoda works was attacked again on the night of May 13/14th 1943 when 156 Lancasters and 12 Halifaxes were sent with the loss of 9 aircraft. Only 60 aircraft got near the target and only five hit the industrial complex. Most of the bombs fell in open fields to the north of the works. The steel casting shop suffered damage, as well as the gun shop and the shop producing grenade fuses and the works power house. Some of the bombs fell on the factory housing estate at Karlov in the north east part of the city. In Radcice 16 people died. It is thought altogether 25 were dead and 54 injured.[160]

16/17 April 1945

222 Lancasters and 11 Mosquitos of No 5 Group carried out an accurate attack on the railway yards at Plzeň. One 463 squadron Lancaster crashed in France, the victim of a night fighter and one aircraft swung on take off from Metheringham, the crew escaping uninjured.

25th April 1945

The last heavy bomber attack by United States Eighth Air Force was made on 25th April 1945 with B-17s attacking the Škoda armaments factory at Plzeň. Even at the end of the war the complete set of jigs, gauges and equipment for the production of the Me109 was still intact. The Czechoslovaks later produced them for the Israeli Air Force.

Latterly the Škoda works has been occupied with more peaceful products such as the well known brand of cars and the main support for the 'London-eye' tourist attraction by the river Thames. The factory possesses some of the largest casting and machining facilities in the world.

---

[160] Dr. Vladislav Krátký

A Shaky do. The Plzen raid April 16/17th April 1943

CHURCHILL ÜBER DEN WIEDERAUFBAU EUROPAS

WINSTON CHURCHILL, Premierminister Grossbritanniens, gab der Welt am Sonntag, dem 21. März, abends 9 Uhr, im Rundfunk eine Erklärung über die praktischen Massnahmen, die Grossbritannien zum Wiederaufbau Europas ergreifen wird.

Diese praktischen Massnahmen sind :

Zunächst die Vernichtung der nazistischen und faschistischen Tyranneien.

Sodann, während Japan niedergerungen wird, der sofortige Beginn des europäischen Wiederaufbaus, im Zusammenwirken mit den Vereinigten Staaten von Amerika, Sowjetrussland und den übrigen Vereinten Nationen. Die britischen Pläne für diesen Wiederaufbau umfassen :

Ernährung der Gebiete Europas, die durch den Krieg gelitten haben.

Bestrafung der Kriegsverbrecher.

Besetzung der besiegten Länder. Aufschub der Demobilisierung aller dafür benötigten britischen Truppen.

Verhinderung künftiger Kriege durch Entwaffnung der schuldigen Staaten.

Schaffung eines Europäischen Rates zur Wiederherstellung der Herrschaft des Rechts in Europa und zur Erhaltung von Frieden und Freiheit.

Zusammenfassung der kleineren Nationen zu Staatenbünden mit Vertretung im Europäischen Rat.

Aufrechterhaltung nationaler oder internationaler Streitkräfte zur Durchsetzung von Recht und Ordnung.

Regulierung des internationalen Handels und Verhütung von Inflation und Wirtschaftskrisen in der Nachkriegszeit. Entsprechende Massnahmen sind bereits in Vorbereitung.

„Inzwischen wird in Grossbritannien selbst sofort nach dem Siege in Europa der Wiederaufbau mit einem Vierjahresplan für Grossbritannien beginnen, der einem neugewählten Parlament vorgelegt werden soll. Der Vierjahresplan wird, entsprechend der britischen Tradition, die Vorteile von Staatsplanung und Privatinitiative miteinander verbinden und dem Wohl aller Klassen gleichermassen dienen. So wird Grossbritannien, sozial, politisch und militärisch stark, voll gerüstet sein für seine Rolle bei der Sicherung des europäischen Schicksals."

G. 16

A Shaky do. The Plzen raid April 16/17th April 1943

Nickel G16

CHURCHILL ON THE RECONSTRUCTION OF EUROPE

Winston Churchill, prime Minister of Great Britain, broadcast to the world at 21 hours on Sunday 21st of March, a declaration on the practical measures which Britain will take in the reconstruction of Europe.

These practical measures are:

First of all to smash the Nazi and Fascist tyrannies.

Then, while smashing Japan, to begin at once the RECONSTRUCTION OF EUROPE.

Punishment of war criminals.

Occupation of the conquered territories. Postponement of demobilisation for all British troops needed for this purpose.

Prevention of further war by disarmament of the guilty states.

Creation of a council of Europe for the restoration of the rule of law in Europe for the protection of all its peoples and the revival of their freedom.

Setting up of confederations of smaller states represented in the Council of Europe, thus avoiding the cardinal mistakes of the last peace settlement.

Maintaining of armed forces national or international for the enforcement of law and order.

Regulation of international trade and prevention of post-war inflation and slumps, measures for which are now in preparation.

Meanwhile within Britain herself reconstruction will begin at once after victory in Europe, with a FOUR YEAR PROGRAMME FOR BRITAIN to be presented to a newly elected parliament. The Four Year Plan will combine, according to British tradition, the advantages of state planning with private enterprise, with equal benefit for all social classes. So that Britain, strong socially, politically and militarily, will be supremely fitted for her part in guaranteeing Europe's destiny.

A Shaky do. The Plzen raid April 16/17th April 1943

16 year old Lothar Stattmüller. A member of the Luftwaffe battery crew Grossraum Flak battery 1/902 between Ludwigshafen am Rhein and Mannheim, which shot down 103 Sqn Lancaster W4848

Some of Lothar's friends were killed and wounded when the Lancaster crashed on their position.

ROLL OF HONOUR
Plzen 16/17th April 1943

35 Sqn Halifax W7873
P/O Cruickshank G.
Sgt. Martyn J.R RCAF
F/S Bourne J.F.
Sgt. Young J.W.

49 Sqn Lancaster ED441
Sgt Penry D.T.
Sgt Bamford C.G.
F/S Dixon A.M.
Sgt Robertson R.C.
Sgt Fletcher J.F
Sgt James C.L.

49 Sqn Lancaster ED427
F/O Bone A.V.
Sgt Foster N.
Sgt Yelland C.W
Sgt White R.C.
Sgt Cope R.
Sgt Rooney R.J.
Sgt Watt B.E.

50 Sqn Lancaster ED784
F/O Elderfield H
Sgt Hinchcliffe H.
P/ Cotter P. C.

50 Sqn Lancaster ED800
Sgt J G Duncan
Sgt Spiers J.
Sgt Smellie D. M.
Sgt Bates J.A.
Sgt Payne C.
Sgt Berry A. W
Sgt Barnes H R

50 Sqn Lancaster ED691
F/O Day H.H.

51 Sqn Halifax DT670
Sgt Inch D.M.
Sgt Riley H
F/O Clements R.F
F/S Lancaster E.L. RAAF
Sgt Hayden T.P.

51 Sqn Halifax DT561
Sgt Cox E.W.
Sgt Burt R.G.
Sgt McCardle F.G. RCAF
Sgt Rogers W.A.
Sgt Briffett S.J.
Sgt Bray L.R.
Sgt McLaren R.A.

51 Sqn Halifax HR729
W/O Edwards J.G
Sgt Kitchen R.D.
F/O Brisbane W.C.
Sgt Lewis A.O.
Sgt Roberts G.E.
Sgt Ray H.
F/O Walters L

51 Sqn Halifax HR784
F/S Stewart R.H. RCAF
F/O Robinson T.C.
F/S Axtell D.
Sgt McBriar W.R.
Sgt Reid D.H.
Sgt Thompson F.M.

61 Sqn Lancaster W4317
P/O Macfarlane W.
Sgt Keay P.J. RAAF
F/O Williams C.F.
F/S Dawson W.W.
F/S Edwards J.F. D.F.M.
Sgt Rees J.V.
Sgt Holdsworth D.A.
Sgt Davidson E.R. (1654 H.C.U.)

76 Sqn Halifax JB800
Sgt Wright G.C
P/O Cooper A.N.
P/O Smith E.H.
P/O Webb J.F.
Sgt Robb F.A. RCAF

76 Sqn Halifax DT575
Sgt Wedderburn B.
Sgt Ross F.O RCAF
Sgt Clinging B.J.
Sgt Fidgeon F.C.
Sgt Jonasson L.N. RCAF
Sgt Strachan J.
Sgt Brown S.H.C.

76 Sqn Halifax DK165
Sgt Webb E.K.
Sgt Kay J.
Sgt Williams K.R.G
Sgt Ross A.R. RCAF
Sgt Braybrook S.
F/S Brown G

77 Sqn Halifax JB908
Sgt Pullen D.I.
Sgt Fernee G.R.
Sgt Edgar A. K.
Sgt Robinson R.W.

78 Sqn Halifax DT773
F/L Dowse A.P. D.F.C. (Ireland)

78 Sqn Halifax HR659
F/L Mortenson E.G.
Sgt Pitman D.A.

83 Sqn Lancaster R5484
P/O McNichol G.A. RCAF

83 Sqn Lancaster R5622
F/S Milton F.C.
F/S Beavan R. D.F.M
F/O Wells W.B.
Sgt Podolsky A
. F/O McLellan N.M
F/S Rodgers J. RCAF
Sgt Klienhorn M. RCAF

A shaky do-The Skoda works raid of 16/17th April 1943

ROLL OF HONOUR
Plzen 16/17th April 1943

100 Sqn F/L Milliken RNZAF
R.E. Lancaster ED564
Sgt Jones T.E.
Sgt George W.H. RCAF
Sgt Walton W.H.
Sgt Hunt R.E.J.
Sgt Good G.J.
Sgt Whitby M.

100 Sqn Lancaster ED563
Sgt Atkinson D.K RNZAF
Sgt Vanston N.
Sgt Brown I.S. RCAF
Sgt Rutter J.
Sgt Clutterbuck R.F.
Sgt Ruddick P. RCAF
F/S Monk P.V. RAAF

101 Sqn Lancaster ED379
F/S Menzies C.K. RAAF
Sgt Upton H.A.
Sgt Evans H.
P/O Taylor T.M. RAAF
Sgt Fitch J.H RCAF
Sgt Monks J.

102 Sqn HR663
P/O Williams G.G. G.M

103 Sqn Lancaster W4848
Sgt Mooney J.O.B. RNZAF
P/O Gipson A.H. RCAF
P/O Hudson F.J
Sgt Merefield V.J.
Sgt Harley R.W

156 Sqn Lancaster W4854
W/O Andersen H.R.DFC
P/O Bordycott K.W. DFC DFM
P/O Smith F. DFM
Sgt Brougham-Faddy P.L.
Sgt Gooding B.H.
Sgt Stephens J.T.
Sgt Woolnough W.O.

156 Sqn Lancaster W4930
Sgt Gonce H.B
Sgt Dean J.C.
Sgt Rowe H.D.
Sgt Muirhead Mck. M
P/O Anastassiades M (Cyprus)
. Sgt Boyd J.
Sgt Corley L.E RCAF

158 Sqn Halifax HR758
F/O Jay B.P. RAAF
P/O Barratt K.A.

408 Sqn Halifax JB925
F/L Hatle C.O. RCAF
P/O Holmes L. H.
Sgt Osmond S.F.
Sgt Richmond H. RCAF
Sgt Gibson J.W. RCAF
Sgt Tschantre A.A. RCAF/USA
Sgt Kapuscinski W.G. RCAF
P/O O'Connell T.N RCAF

408 Sqn Halifax DT752
F/O Sergent J.R.L. RCAF
Sgt Hill G.M.
Sgt Cocks F.R.
Sgt Gargrave D.F.
Sgt Kwasney W. RCAF/US
Sgt Heming C.D. RCAF
Sgt Machell H.G. RCAF

408 Sqn Halifax BB343
W/O Guay J.A. RCAF
Sgt Pilon F.R. RCAF
Sgt Haines L.G. RCAF
Sgt Winter R.H.
Sgt McDonald I. RCAF
Sgt Gielty A.P.
Sgt Fill H.W. RCAF

408 Sqn Halifax JB854
Sgt Heming G.C. RCAF
F/S Birchall R. RCAF
Sgt Zaleschuck D. RCAF
Sgt Mason R.W.
Sgt Jorgensen S.J. RCAF
Sgt Archie S. RCAF
Sgt Cantley A.C. RCAF

460 Sqn Lancaster ED711
Sgt White D.E. DFM RAAF
Sgt Stewart J.S. RAAF
W/O Charlton W.R.K. RAAF
F/S Ward F.H RAAF
F/S Parker A.K. RAAF
F/S Baker R.H RAAF
F/S Smith A.K
Sgt Knilands B. RAAF

460 Sqn Lancaster W4331
Sgt Miller I.G. RAAF
Sgt Richmond R.P.
Sgt Wilson G.J.
Sgt Curtis D.
Sgt Hall R
Sgt Capon M.G.A.
Sgt Beaumont R.

460 Sqn Lancaster W4942
Sgt Williams J.N. RAAF
Sgt King E.R. RAAF
Sgt Ebott E.C. RAAF
Sgt Smith L.C.
Sgt Bell J.C. RAAF
Sgt Ablethwaite E.J.
Sgt Clark A.W.

467 Sqn Lancaster ED780
Sgt Stuart R.C. RAAF
Sgt Martin
Sgt McDonald A.F.T.
F/O McNair B.R. DFC
Sgt Anderson R.C. RNZAF
Sgt Boase P.L. RAAF
Sgt Johnson R.J.

467 Sqn Lancaster ED651
Sgt Pallender R.H
. Sgt Goode H.F.
Sgt Dunn R.
Sgt Bannatyne W.W.

A shaky do-The Skoda works raid of 16/17th April 1943

Glossary

Coned	Aircraft held in a group of searchlight beams
Cookie	4000 lb high explosive blast bomb
Corkscrew	Violent evasive action to avoid attack
D.C.O	Completed operation. Duty carried out
D.F.C.	Distinguished Flying Cross
D.F.M.	Distinguished Flying Medal
D.N.C.O	Incomplete operation. Duty not carried out
D.R.	Dead reckoning-navigational technique
E/A	Enemy aircraft
F.T.R	Failed to return
Feathering	The process of disengaging a propeller.
G.C.I.	Ground controlled [Night fighter] interception
G.P.	General purpose (bomb)
Gardening	Mine laying operations
Gee	Navigational aid
George	Automatic pilot
H.C.U.	Heavy conversion unit.
H.E.	High explosive
I.C.B.	Incendiary bomb
I.F.F.	Identification friend or foe equipment
Inter-com	Crew communications system aboard aircraft.
K.I.A.	Killed in action
L.W.T.	Lost without trace
M.R.E.U.	RAF Missing Research & Enquiry Unit.
Mae West	Life saver jacket
Mandrel	Radio transmitters to jam and swamp ground radars Freya/ Würzburg.
O.T.U.	Operational training unit
Odd Bod	Non-regular crew member
Photoflash	Phosphor flash to light up target for bombing photo.
Q.F.E.	Barometric pressure reading at airfield level
S.B.C.	Small bomb container (incendiary carrier)
Shaky do	'A Shaky do' is term often used by R.A.F. aircrew to describe a raid beset with difficulties and heavy enemy opposition.
Second Dickey	Second pilot under training
Sprog	Inexperienced crew member
T.I.	Target indicator
T.I. L.B.	Target indicator long burning
Tinsel	Microphone attached to the engine and noise transmitted on the enemy fighter frequencies.
T.N.A.	The National Archives U.K.
Very cartridge	Warning flare sent up at airfields
Wind-milling	Condition caused when an engine lost power, the propeller rotated in the slipstream causing excessive drag and possible loss of control.

Bibliography

Avro Lancaster	Holmes, Harry
Bale out!	Martin, Alfie (Colourpoint)
Bomber Barons	Boyer, Chaz
Bomber Command war diaries	Middlebrook & Everitt
Escape or die	Brickhill, Paul
Escape to Freedom	Johnson, Tony
Flying for freedom	Redding, Tony
Footprints in the sands of time	Clutton-Brock, Oliver
In Brave Company	Chorley, Bill
Lancaster verliezen in Belgie	Govaerts, Wim
Nachtjagd	Boiten, Dr. Theo
Night after Night	Lambert, Max
Night Air War	Boiten, Dr.Theo
Past tense Charlie's story	Hobbs, Charlie
R.A.F Bomber Command Losses	Chorley, W.R.
Stuttgart Im Luftkrieg	Bardua, Heinz
The Blue Emu,	Catt, Charlie
The valley of the shadow of death	Phillips, J.Alwyn
For your tomorrow	Martyn, Errol

Suggested reading

An Airman remembers	Patterson, John
Bomber Boys	Wilson, Kevin
Enemy in the dark	Spoden, Peter
Hell on earth	Rolfe, Mell
It's suicide but it's fun	Goss, Chris
Lancaster at War	Garbett & Golding
Lancaster target	Currie, Jack
Looking into Hell	Rolfe, Mell
Strike and return	Firkins, Peter
Tail end Charlies	John Nichol & Tony Rennel
The last escape	John Nichol & Tony Rennel
The other battle	Hinchliffe, Peter
The pendulum and the scythe	Marshall, Ken
The Warlord and the Renegade (story of Hermann & Albert Goring)	Wyllie, James
To Hell and back	Rolfe, Mell
Ace of diamonds (Heinz Schnaufer)	Peter Hinchliffe
The Lent papers (Helmut Lent)	Peter Hinchliffe

APPENDIX A

MISCELLANEOUS BIOGRAPHICAL INFORMATION

AND OPERATIONAL DATA

PLZEN EVADERS AND POWS DATA

Name	Sqn A/C	P.O.W. Evaded	Camp
Sgt McKay J. A. RCAF	12 W4366	Pow1083	L1?L6 L4
Sgt Hutton T. H.		Evaded	
Sgt Rudkin L.		Evaded	
F/L Owen W.R.	35 W7873	Pow1272	L3
F/S Allen W.G.		Evaded	
F/S Bradley V.R.		Evaded	
Sgt Kerr H.W.G.	49 ED441	Pow	Sole survivor of seven crew
F/O Trotman D.A.	50 ED691	Evaded	Switzerland
Sgt Salmon R.C.		Pow 1167	L3?L6? 357
Sgt Holland H.E. RAAF		Pow 1072	L3
Sgt Hodgkinson G.A.E.		Pow 1151	L3?L6?/357
Sgt Rossbotham J.A.		Pow 1091	L1 L6?/357
Sgt Evans M.I.		pow 1241	L1 L6?/357
Sgt Symes S.R.A. RCAF			Camp not known repatriated May 1944
Sgt Riley H.	51 DT670	Evaded	Sailed on the SS "Esneh" from Seville to Gibraltar 11-13 August 1943 U.K. 17TH Aug.
Sgt Dards E.P.	51 DT670	Pow1146	L3? L6/L357
Sgt McCrea J.E.	51 DT690	Evaded	Via Spain
Sgt Allerdice J.		Evaded	Via Spain
F/O Spencer D.G.		Pow 2195	L3. camp given as L6 in AIR20/2336 UK archives
Sgt Ings C.B.		Pow 222519	4B captured sth. Perpignan 26/4/43
F/S Simpson J.E.C.		Pow 222554	4B/4C/4B captured 5/5/43
Sgt Jones D.L.		Evaded	Via Spain
Sgt Davis A.W.		Pow 1147	L3? L6/L357
F/O Marriot J.W.	51 HR729	Pow 42734	Dulag Luft 18/4/43-20/4/43 IXb Statroda 20/4/43-30/5/43 Stg. Luft III Sagan 30/5/43-28/1/45 Stg. IIIa Luckenwalde 4/2/45-20/5/45

A Shaky do. The Plzen raid April 16/17th April 1943

PLZEN EVADERS AND POWS DATA

Name	Sqn A/C	P.O.W. Evaded	Camp
W/O Keirnan W.R.	51 HR784	Pow 14	L6/357 Sole survivor of seven crew
Sgt Read A.G.C.	76 J B800	Pow 1029	L1 L6?/357 Killed by RAF Typhoons 19/4/45
Sgt Wombwell D.B.		Pow 1054	L3 /L6?/L357
Sgt Mitchell L.B.	76 DK165	Pow 42735	IX Arbeits/KDO 1170 Hosp. Statroda 22/4/43-6/43, Stg. Luft III Sagan, 6/43-7/43 Stg. Luft VI, Heidekrug 7/43-14/7/44 Stg. Luft IV, Gross Tischau 19/7/44-6/2/45 Stg. IIc, Greifswald 3/3/45-14/4/45 Stg. Luft I Barth 18/4/45-Repatriation
Sgt Wall F.S.	77 JB908	Pow 1163	Dulag Luft 20/4/43-17/5/43 Stg. Luft 6 Barth 20/5/43-27/10/43 Stamm Lager 357 Thorn 19/7/44-9/8/44 Stamm Lager 357 Fallingbostel 11/8/44-6/4/45
Sgt Tullet R.M.	77 JB908	Pow 1044	L3 /L6?/L357
Sgt Johnson L.	77 JB908	Pow	Stlag. Luft I Barth 23/4/43-28/10/43 Stlag. Luft VI Hydekrug 1/11/43-6/44 Stlag. 357 Thorn 7/44-8/44 Stlag. 357 Fallingbostel 8/44-6/4/44
Sgt Slater T.T.	78 DT773	Pow 1038	L1/L6?/357
F/S Desjardins R. RCAF		Pow 1148	L3?L6?/357
Sgt Thompson H.E.		Pow 43236	344 later repatriated amputated leg.
Sgt Langsford RNZAF		Pow 1154	Dulag Luft, L3, L6 Hydekrug, L3
Sgt Hoare A.W.		Pow 1002	L1/L6/357
F/O Orr A.N.		Pow 1102	L3

A Shaky do. The Plzen raid 16/17th April 1943

PLZEN EVADERS AND POWS DATA

Name	Sqn A/C	P.O.W. Evaded	Camp
Sgt Bell J.A.	78 HR659	Pow 1144	L3?L6?/357
P/O Dennis R.C.W.		Pow 1096	L3
F/O Fisher W.G.		Pow 1099	L3
Sgt Steven C.A.		Pow 1039	L3
Sgt Minshaw L.C.		Pow 1155	L3?L6?/357
Sgt Mott G.C.	83 R5484	Pow 1152	L1/L6?/357
P/O Beaupre H.H.F. RCAF		Pow 1253	L3
P/O Lewis T.W. RCAF		Pow 1270	L3
Sgt McFarlane G.S.		Pow 1079	L1/L6?/357
Sgt Willis H.R.		Pow 1113	L1/L6?/357
F/S Hobbs C.E. RCAF		Pow 1071	Dulag Luft, L1 Barth, L6 Hydekrug, 357 Thorn, Fallingbostel, escaping latterly.
Sgt Green L.	101 ED379	Pow 996	L1/L6/357 Sole survivor of seven crew
S/L Lashbrook W.I.	102 HR663	Evaded	Evaded via Spain
F/S Knight D.C.		Pow 250739	4B/L3 'The captain'
F/O Bolton K.G.		Evaded	
F/O Martin A.		Evaded	
Sgt Laws W.R		Evaded	
Sgt Neill L.		Pow 1192	L1?L6L4
Sgt Biggs S.	103 W4848	Pow 979	L1/L6?/357
Sgt Rowse H.J.D.		Pow 1033	L1?/L6?/357

A Shaky do. The Plzen raid April 16/17th April 1943

PLZEN EVADERS AND POWS DATA

Name	Sqn A/C	P.O.W. Evaded	Camp
Sgt Holmes F.E.	158 HR758	Pow 1004	L1/L6?/357
Sgt Scholes G.D.W.		Pow 1162	L3/L6/357
Sgt Ford A.		Pow 993	L1/L6/357
Sgt Newdick R.		Pow 1020	L1/L/6L4
Sgt Fawcett C.D. RCAF		Pow 991	L1/357
Sgt Wilson B.C. RAAF	467 ED651	Pow 10623	Reserve Lazarette Hohenlind Köln 30/5/43-30/6/43 Reserve Lazarette Munstereifel 1 month 30/5/43-30/6/43 Dulag Luft 3 weeks 30/6/43-23/7/43 Stg. Luft VI Hydekrug 29/6/43-25/8/44 Stg. 357 Thorne 27/8/44-27/10/44 Stg. 357 Fallingbostel 1/11/44-16/4/45
Reprisals were made by Depriving P.O.W.s of Mattresses tables & seats At Fallingbostel			
P/O Boswell F.G.		Pow Number?	Camp unknown
P/O Stitt R.		Pow 10621	6G

Camp & POW numbers provided by Oliver Clutton-Brock from 'Sands of Time' with exception of Wilson ED651, Hobbs R5484 from Charlie's Story (General Store Publishing House). Pow info for crews of JB908, DK165 found in WO344/221 TNA UK.

A Shaky do. The Plzen raid April 16/17th April 1943

Reflections at an air show
By Fred Mitchell Navigator, 103 sqn.

A damp, cold blustery day buffeted the brown dreary fields of Lincolnshire, the wartime home of much of Bomber Command. A thin yellow moon peeps cautiously through the watery clouds as the aircrew in Mae Wests, parachute harnesses and flying boots board the aircraft. The starting drill commences with the starboard inner; the whining electric starter pulls the engine through the compression as the propeller turns over in short jerks. There is a momentary ragged misfiring; a stab of flame from the exhaust stubs and a cloud of grey smoke are whipped away by the wind. The flight engineer scans gauges and flicks switches. The crackling backfire of four throttled back Merlins echoes across the airfield, the matt black aircraft rumbles forward to the runway in use, then with increasing characteristic sound, there is no going back it is committed; faster and faster until the controls feel spongy and the wings pull the weight off the wheels. Almost running out of runway, the roaring, straining Merlins haul the bomb and fuel laden bulk of the Lancaster off the ground and the slow laborious climb to altitude commences. The crew can see the nauseous heaving grey swell and chop of the relentless North Sea. Ice starts to spread its fingers along the leading edge of the wings.

Enemy coast ahead, the first shadows of fear and apprehension of the dangers that lie ahead flit into the minds of the aircrew.

****

The sky was clear blue, a glorious summer day at R.A.F. Scampton, the visiting spectators, families and enthusiasts were eagerly waiting the fly past. Over she comes in a bomb doors open banking turn, seeming to hang in the air, leaving four faint trails of exhaust smoke. That shape. That sound. The people fall silent.

Back around the circuit for a low level pass down the centre of the runway and the crisp crackling, whistling note of those four magnificent Rolls-Royce Merlins brings back to the veterans' eyes the prick of tears. Now she is a diminishing dot on the horizon and disappears, as if all had been a dream. Some small children were giggling, happily playing and chattering as children do. They know nothing of the Lancaster. They are here for the fairground rides and their packets of crisps and cans of Coke.

We know something they do not; fifty five thousand men of Bomber Command never came back.

They gave their lives for children's laughter and freedom.

A Shaky do. The Plzen raid April 16/17th April 1943

Fred Mitchell tour of ops 103 squadron

Op	Date	Target	Hours	Load	A/C	Method	Notes
1	26th/27th 3 43	Duisburg	4:05	1x4000+12 sbc	W4363 U	Wanganui	Med. flak
2	3rd/4th 4.43	Essen	5.0	1x4000+6x4lb sbc 6x30lb sbc	W4901 W	Parramatta	Heavy flak
3	4th/5th 4.43	Kiel	5:30	11 x 1000 2xLd 9 inst.	W4901 W	Wanganui	Medium flak
4	10th/11th 4.43	Frankfurt	7.0	1x4000+6x20lb 6x4lb	ED751 S	Wanganui	Medium flak
5	13th/14th 4.43	La Spezia Divert Westcott	10:10	5x1000+ 2x4lb 2x30lb sbc icbs	ED751 S	Parramatta	Weak opposition
6	16th/17th 4.43	Plzen	7:45	1x4000+3x1000	ED528 Z		Jettisoned Stuttgart Coned and hit by flak
7	18th/19th 4.43	La Spezia	10:10	5x1000+4x sbc icbs	ED751 S	Parramatta	Medium flak
8	20th/21st 4.43	Stettin	8:05	1x4000 6x4lb 6x30lb	W4364 T	Parramatta	Moonlight Map read
9	26th/27th 4.43	Duisburg	4:50	1x4000+icbs and Nickels	ED751 S	Wanganui	Heavy accurate flak
10	27th/28th 4.43	St Jean de Luz Biscay	8:20	5x1000 lb Mines	ED751 S		Heavy tracer
11	30th Apr.1st May 43	Essen	4:30	1x4000+12 sbc 4lb	ED751 S	Wanganui	Medium flak
12	12th/13th 5. 43	Duisburg	4:45	1x4000 icbs +Nickels	ED904 Y	Parramatta	Accurate flak
13	13th/14th 5. 43	Bochum	5:15	1x4000+icbs	ED904 Y	Parramatta	Heavy & accurate flak
14	23rd/24th 5. 43	Dortmund	4:40	1x4000+icbs and Nickels	ED904 Y	Parramatta	V. active S/Ls Med. flak
15	25th/26th 5. 43	Düsseldorf	4:50	1x4000+icbs	ED904 Y	Parramatta	Moderate flak
16	27th/28th 5. 43	Essen	4:50	1x4000+icbs and Nickels	ED904 Y	Wanganui	Hvy accurate flak 1st wave
17	29th/30th 5. 43	Wuppertal	5:10	1x4000+icbs and Nickels	ED904 Y	Parramatta	V. Heavy flak
18	11th/12th 6.43	Düsseldorf	4:50	1x4000+icbs Aiming point photo	ED904 Y	Parramatta	Coned/hit intense flak
19	12th/13th 6.43	Bochum	5:25	1x4000+icbs Aiming point photo	ED904 Y		Heavy flak eng. hit
20	14th/15th 6.43	Oberhausen	5:35	1x4000+4000lb icbs	ED904 Y	Wanganui	Air Bomber /hvy flak
21	16th/17th 6.43	Köln	4:15	1x4000+4x500	ED904 Y	DNCO	Heavy flak
22	21st/22nd 6.43	Krefeld	5:00	1x4000+icbs and Nickels	ED904 Y	DNCO	Mod flak/night-fighters

A shaky do-The Skoda works raid 16/17th April 1943

NOTEABLES

Squadron Leader Julian Sale
DSO bar DFC 35 Squadron P.F.F.

Of all the aircrew you will ever read about, you will find none braver of more well thought of than Julian Sale of 35 squadron P.F.F.

Sale was born in Penetanguishene, Ontario, 28 February 1914 and raised by foster parents (Mr. and Mrs. J.S. Holmested) as his parents Julian and Editha Sale of Toronto, were deceased. His last employment was as sales clerk and retail manager at Julian Sale Leather Goods Company, Toronto, a company founded by his grandfather. He enlisted in Toronto, 28th April 1941. Trained at No.1 ITS (graduated 25 August 1941), No.9 EFTS (graduated 10 October 1941), and No.1 SFTS (graduated 16 January 1942). Commissioned 1942.

On **ops Duisburg 12/13 May 43** 35 sqn crew Halifax II DT801 TL-A Sales's aircraft was outbound at 10,000 ft and shot up by night fighter flown by Oblt Gieger III./NJG1 02:00 near Buurse. Sale baled out and landed near Oldenzaal. He evaded capture travelling through Germany, Holland, Belgium and France finally reaching Spain from where he was returned to the UK via Gibraltar. The entire journey took him about 3 months! He had walked and cycled 800 miles except for three small journeys by train and bus. No help was received from any organisation, only local people.

The crew were on that occasion were;
F/L J Sale R.C.A.F. evd
Sgt C W Rowley pow
F/O G E Heard pow
P/O R C Sawyer +
Sgt S A Moores pow
Sgt D J Richards+
Sgt R O Elford R.C.A.F. pow

On ops to Frankfurt December 20/21 1943 35 sqn crew Halifax III HX328 TL-J Sale took off at 17:29 Gravely. On return a target indicator caught fire. The order to bale out given but Lamb's parachute was destroyed, so Sale landed the blazing bomber. Sale and lamb ran clear seconds before the aircraft exploded at 22:17.

S/L J Sale
W/O G H Cross DFM
F/L G H F Carter RCAF
S/L A J Dowling
W/O M Rees
F/L R L Lamb
W/O G Carpenter injured

19th Feb 1944 to Leipzig Halifax HX325 TL-J
Sale died in circumstances which were nothing short of tragic. Flying Halifax HX325 TL-J, on his 50th operation, one of his crew, Sgt Knight was killed in action when a Ju88 fighter attacked the Halifax. At the time of the attack they were flying at about 22,000 feet. The time was 02:43. The overload tanks were hit and exploded. During the attack the aircraft had been

A Shaky do. The Plzen raid April 16/17th April 1943

riddled with machine gun and cannon fire and Julian Sale was seriously wounded. He got the rest of the crew out before leaving the aircraft himself. He was picked up and taken to hospital. 'He was unable to cope or come to terms with his injuries as it was felt that he would end up a cripple so he jumped from a hospital window and ended his own life'.[161]
What an incredibly tragic ending for a brave and courageous man who had already endured so much in his short lifetime! Sale died on March 20, 1944, Age: 30.

S/L D J Sale	DSO & bar, D.F.C.
W/O G H Cross	D.F.C. D.F.M. pow
S/L G H F Carter	D.F.C. & bar RCAF pow
F/L B O Bodnar	D.F.C. R.C.A.F. pow
F/L H J Rodgers	D.F.C. pow
F/L R L Lamb	pow
F/S K Knight	+

Hamburg. 3/4 Feb 1943
Sales' crewmate P/O G H F Carter R.C.A.F. himself had a danger fraught tour. When on Ops to **Hamburg. 3/4 Feb 1943** flying 35 sqn Halifax II W7923 TL-D and was hit by flak which damaged undercarriage. On return they crash landed 01:27 wheels up.

Later when on Ops to Lorient.13/14 Feb 1943
P/O G H F Carter R.C.A.F. was flying on 35 sqn Halifax II W7885 TL-B The aircraft was hit by Flak over target the aircraft was later abandoned near Carhaix (Finistaire) France. F/O Freeman R.C.A.F. is buried there. Five of the crew evaded including Carter. One was P.O.W. (see also his ops mentioned previously when with Sale's crew.) Carter survived the war.

Flight Lieutenant Tom Wingham D.F.C.
(Halifax JB894 'X' Plzen raid)

Wingham joined the RAF in 1941 and trained as an Observer. He then joined 102 squadron in February 1943. He completed his first tour in June 1943. In April 1944 he joined 76 Squadron for his second tour of operations. On his third sortie, on the 22nd April, his aircraft was attacked and the order to bale out was given. Two of the crew were killed, three were taken prisoner of war and two evaded. Wingham made contact with the Resistance and then met up with the American forces returning home in September 1944.

In March 1945 he returned to operational flying with 105 Squadron equipped with the Mosquito and completed a further four operations before the end of the war in Europe. He was awarded the DFC by the Americans in April 1946.

---

[161] We Act With One Accord by Alan Cooper.

A Shaky do. The Plzen raid April 16/17th April 1943

4144

DOWSE, Arthur Patrick D.F.C.
78 Squadron

A.P. Dowse D.F.C. (Photo Gant)

Patrick Dowse, gave his life holding the blazing Halifax DT773 steady on 17th April 1943 until all his crew had baled out.

Paddy from Dublin Ireland, was on his second tour of ops, one tour usually being thirty operations. It is thought Paddy joined up in the first batch of aircrew in early 1939. Shortly before his death he had married a Canadian W.A.A.F. She was to be widowed twice more after her marriage to Paddy was so cruelly ended by war.

DOWSE, Arthur Patrick, P/O (88035, RAFVR*) - No.144 Squadron - Distinguished Flying Cross - awarded as per London Gazette dated 30 January 1942. Following text from RAF Quarterly, June 1942;

"This officer has always reduced height when finding it difficult to identify the target. He has displayed great courage and determination and has invariably completed successfully the tasks allotted to him."

His service number would indicate he enlisted in early September 1939 at Padgate. Paddy Dowse was probably in the first batch to enlist after 3/9/1939. He was posted to 2CFS Church Lawford W.E.F. 23/11/41 and did his first tour of operations on with 144 squadron in 1941 and 1942 earning a D.F.C., then posted to 78 Sqn. Linton On Ouse.

A Shaky do. The Plzen raid April 16/17th April 1943

Air Vice-Marshal A D Frank
10 squadron

Born in Cheshire, Frank attended Eton and joined the RAFO whilst an undergraduate at Magdalen College Oxford and learnt to fly with the University Air Squadron. He was mobilised in 1939 and posted to No 150 Squadron, with whom he flew Battles as part of the A.A.S.F. in France. On 19 May 1940 he was flying L5583, when he made a forced landing on Sommesous airfield, where he had to leave the aircraft and make his way back to his unit. Alan Frank survived and was still with 150 squadron when it returned to the U.K. after the Dunkirk evacuation, where it began converting to Wellingtons.

After a year with No 150 squadron, he moved to No 460 Squadron of the Royal Australian Air Force as a flight commander. When taken off operations in 1942, he travelled to the U.S.A. to act as a Liaison Officer, but was back in the U.K., later that year, where he assumed command of number 10 Squadron, equipped with Halifaxes. He took command of another Halifax unit, 51 Squadron, in April 1943, taking part in numerous raids over Germany, including Operation 'Gomorrah', the attack against Hamburg in July 1943 as well as operations against Italian targets.

He now had the opportunity to attend the RAF Staff College, following which he was assigned to the Air Staff of 'Tiger Force'. The force was due to take control of much of Bomber Command once Germany had been defeated, and join the fighting in the Pacific and Japanese home islands. However, the dropping of the atomic bombs brought the war to an end and with 'Tiger Force' no longer required it was disbanded. Frank transferred to the Air Ministry. He returned to flying, and was given command of the Aden Communications Flight, where he organised famine relief operations on the Hadhramaut plateau of southern Arabia.

In 1957, having completed the Vulcan conversion course at No 230 OCU he was tasked with forming the first operational Vulcan squadron, number 83 although the unit's first [162]aircraft did not arrive until July 1957. After commanding 83 squadron, he took command of the Victor base at Honington, before moving to HQ Bomber Command in 1960. In 1962 he returned to the Air Ministry as Director of Operational Requirements (C) and three years later returned to the U.S.A. as Air Attaché and Commander of the R.A.F. staff of the British Joint Services Mission. His final appointment was as Senior Air Staff Officer at H.Q. Air Support Command. From 1970 to 1974, he was Bursar of St Antony's College, Oxford.*

Brian Lawless Duigan DSO DFC
156 squadron

Brian Lawless Duigan, was born on November 15, 1914, the first son of Reginald Charles and Phyllis Mary Duigan and nephew of John Roberson Duigan. After leaving Geelong College in 1932, Brian worked as a drover on a cattle station in outback Queensland. In 1933 he travelled to South Africa where he worked as a Mining Engineer in Johannesburg and then in 1937, moved to Northern Rhodesia to work at the Hoan Antelope copper mine.

In 1938 sensing war was imminent he undertook a remarkable 4,000 mile motorcycle journey across equatorial Africa which saw him arrive in England in June 1939.

In August 1939 Brian joined the RAF, gained his 'wings' and as a commissioned officer was assigned to Bomber Command as a pilot in a Vickers Wellington squadron. At the end of his European 'Tour' he volunteered for a second tour, this time in the Middle East where he flew in North Africa, Greece, Syria and Iraq.

---

http://www.rafweb.org/Biographies/Frank_AD.htm*

A Shaky do. The Plzen raid April 16/17th April 1943

In July 1941 and during this second tour, he earned the D.F.C. for bravery shown under fire whilst bombing Benghazi harbour. A month later however his luck changed and his Wellington was shot down by Vichy French fighters over the Sahara and 100 miles from Port Said, he had to be rescued.

In April 1942 Brian earned a bar to his D.F.C. "on the completion of 20 consecutive low level attacks over enemy objectives" and upon returning to England in June 1942, was personally given the award by King George VI.

For six months he acted as a test pilot flying all sorts of aircraft 'traditional' and 'hush hush' but eventually was posted to a Lancaster Squadron in which now as a Wing Commander took part in the 1,000 bomber raids on Cologne and Essen.

In April 1943 he once again eluded the odds and whilst flying a disabled Lancaster on a bombing raid on the Italian naval base of La Spezia, he nonetheless successfully completed the mission and in doing so, won the D.S.O.

Brian married Phyllis Winifred Hales and had two children. He returned home to Australia ferrying one of the first English Electric Canberras. Brian stayed with the R.A.F. after the war and flew jets in Asia and the Middle-East. He even taught the Shah of Iran to fly. The family settled in Woodend Victoria, Australia where, uncharacteristically early for a 'Duigan', he died at 58 in 1972.[162]

****

Air Commodore Trotman
50 Squadron

Trotman was born in Wimbledon; educated West London schools; joined the RAF on leaving school in 1940; trained as a pilot; commissioned 1942 and eventually posted to 50 Sqn. Injured when he parachuted, pretended to be a French farm labourer; reached Switzerland and remained there until Oct 1944. He returned to the UK taking up various flying appointments; He was P.A. at HQ Air Command Far East; received the A.F.C. in January 1947; Air Ministry; air commodore Jan 1968; Cyprus; UK March 1971 and posted to Wilton (UK Land Forces near Salisbury). He remained at U.K.L.F. until his retirement in Nov 1976. He settled Laverstock; qualified at the Institute of Company Secretaries; joined a firm of chartered accountants in Salisbury. He was on Salisbury district council as member for Laverstock in 1983 and served in this capacity for 8 years. He was a school governor and member of Friends of Sarum. His wife predeceased him and they had no children. The Air Commodore was cremated Salisbury Crematorium on Tuesday 25th April 2006.[163]

****

Trotman as mentioned earlier had baled out on the Plzeň raid after his 50 squadron Lancaster ED691 'K' was flying at 19,000 feet over the Châlons-sur-Marne area. Though wounded in the leg by a cannon shell splinter Trotman landed a few miles north of Rosay. He destroyed his parachute and Mae West and walked due south until just before dawn, when he took refuge in a hut. At dawn he obtained food, rest, civilian clothes and information about the airfield at St Dizier and local curfews, then continued his journey in daylight. His original

[162] http://www.ctie.monash.edu.au
[163] Thursday, April 27, 2006 issue of the Salisbury Journal

A Shaky do. The Plzen raid April 16/17th April 1943

plan was to travel due south and meet up with a resistance organization or if no help was obtained to head for the Swiss border. Although his leg was giving him trouble he averaged 35-45 kms. per day along both major and minor roads, resting at nights in weeds or empty huts. He obtained a meal on average every two days but never managed contact with the resistance. On the 20th April he stopped at a Café in Colombey Les Deux Église and on the 22nd was given food at a private house between Langres and Champlitte and a raincoat at another village. Trotman passed through Besançon at midday on April 24th 1943 and mixed with shoppers to avoid detection. He attempted a border crossing on the evening of the 25th but failed due to the difficult hilly terrain and the river Doubs. On the 26th he continued up the frontier in the area of Maîche, St.Hippolyte, and Pont de roide receiving food and advice about the frontier. At a village near Maîche he stopped for food and drink at a café where he met an unknown contact who offered contact with Englishmen with French papers. They made plans for a rendezvous at the fountain in Montécheroux at 8 O'clock. At a Café Trotman was shown a map of the frontier and given a description of the defences, pillboxes motorcycle and dog patrol routes. He kept the rendezvous but no one turned up and he left at 20:07 hours passing through Chamesel and hid in woods until dark. He made the crossing through moderately undulating country during the night and without seeing any defined frontier or guards. The Swiss Douanier arrested Trotman on 27th April 1943 at Réclère, inside the Swiss Porrentruy sector. He had covered a total distance of approximately 400 kilometres.

****

Flt/Lt. Petrie-Andrews D.F.C. D.F.M.

Joe Petrie-Andrews was born in 1924. He enlisted at Uxbridge and his training was as follows; Initial Training Wing, Scarborough, Pilot Training in South Carolina, USA. He then was posted to 102 squadron at Pocklington (Jan 1943), to 158 Squadron at Rufforth (February 1943) where he did his first seven ops. 13/2/43 Lorient, 14/2/43 Cologne, 9/3/43 Munich, 11/3/43 Stuttgart, 12/3/43 Essen, 22/3/43 St. Nazaire, 26/3/43 Duisburg. He was then posted to 35 (Pathfinder) Squadron at Graveley (March 1943 11/7/44). Here he did another 61 ops.

Joe's D.F.M. was earned on a low level op to Stettin and they were coned for some several minutes. Explosions in the cockpit injured the navigator (P/O Armitage) and Wop/Ag. (Sgt. 'Jock' Berwick) The bomb sight, airspeed indicator, D.R. compass and intercom were all unserviceable. Petrie-Andrews was awarded an immediate D.F.M. [165]The crew carried on to the target and after bombing Stettin, managed to land at base on a standard runway 2,000 yards at night with no airspeed indicator or brakes.

Joe Petrie-Andrews was awarded the Distinguished Flying Cross as per London Gazette dated 18 February 1944 with 35 Sqn. Citation reads;

'This officer is a capable and courageous pilot whose example of devotion to duty has been highly commendable. His determination was well illustrated during a sortie one night in November 1943. Before reaching his target, one of the aircraft's engines failed.

---

[165] Although awards were most often given to the captain of the aircraft, the author has never talked to a captain yet who didn't feel his crew also richly deserved the same recognition. Petrie-Andrews is no exception.

A Shaky do. The Plzen raid April 16/17th April 1943

Nevertheless, he went on to reach and bomb the objective. Whilst over the area, a second engine failed. Thereupon, Pilot Officer Petrie-Andrews decided to set course for Sardinia. On his flight to the island a third engine became useless and Pilot Officer Petrie-Andrews was compelled to bring his aircraft down on to the sea. He and his crew got safely aboard the dinghy and paddled their way to the Sardinia coast which they reached 70 hours later. This officer has completed many sorties and his record is impressive.'

He was posted to 24 Sqn at Bassingbourne the King's long range flight with Lancastrians and also did 200 round trips on the Berlin Airlift.

He was awarded an immediate D.F.M. April 20 1943, and later the D.F.C.

Latterly he flew Spitfires Vampires, and Meteors with 615 (County of Surrey) Squadron, Royal Auxiliary Air Force.

****

Sgt Alan Egan and Crew 103 Sqn.

Essen 3rd April (ED389), Kiel 4th April (ED389), Frankfurt 10th April (ED767), La Spezia 13th April (ED767), Plzeň 16th April (ED767), Duisburg 26th April (ED773), Essen 30th April (ED879), Dortmund 4th May (ED879), Duisburg 12th May (ED879), Bochum 13th May (ED879), Dortmund 23rd May (ED879), Düsseldorf 25th May (ED879), Essen 27th May, Wuppertal 29th May (ED879), Düsseldorf 11th June (ED769), Bochum 12th June (ED731), Oberhausen 14th June (ED528), Köln 16th June (ED922), Mulheim 22nd June (ED528), Wuppertal 24th June (ED528), Gelsenkirchen 25th June.(ED528)

On Egan's 21st op they were hit by flak when details for the first wave to Gelsenkirchen. He decided to do a circuit as no P.F.F. flares had dropped. At approximately 01:00 and 19,000 feet, there was a heavy bump and the two port engines caught fire, the controls were useless and the escape hatch jammed. The aircraft exploded before anyone could bale out and the nose of the aircraft broke away. Miller and Johnson survived the explosion. The pilot Egan was unconscious and came to falling through the air and landing near Ludinghausen. He was taken prisoner of war as were Johnson and Miller. Miller evaded capture for 19 days and stated that he had been shot at twice by a fighter on his way down. It was thought possible but unconfirmed that the two gunners got out but were killed by the fighter; an extremely rare occurrence. A German flak soldier claimed the next day to have shot the aircraft down with his first salvo. Sgts. Brown, Britton, Horrell and Flt.Sgt. Elliot were killed.

A Shaky do. The Plzen raid April 16/17th April 1943

Eugene Rosner 106 Squadron

Eugene 'Gene' Leon Rosner was born on 17th April 1920 into a Jewish family in Wilkes Barr, Pennsylvania. He was the eldest son of Isidore Harry and Esther Rosner (nee Marcovici), both originally from Romania, but emigrated to America before the first world war. Gene was raised in a mining town and after school went onto Ohio University in Athens, from 1938-40. After the war had broken out in Europe Gene volunteered to become a Cadet in the United States Army Air Corps in mid 1940.

He trained at the Institute of Aeronautics in Tuscaloosa, Alabama, between August 1940 and January 1941, and passed his basic flying training. At this time however, the Air Corps was very selective, as America had not yet entered the war and did not have the need for vast numbers of pilots, and he was washed out before being commissioned. There is an alternative story within the Rosner family that Gene 'buzzed' a General's house, in order to impress his daughter, near the end of his pilot training and because of this incident was not given his commission, but it is not confirmed! He therefore left the Air Corps in April 1941 but was still really desperate to fly, so joined the RCAF in July 1942. He was accepted and a month later found himself aboard ship bound for the UK, to continue his flying training at No. 15 (P) AFU at Leconfield, Lincolnshire. After only a week or so there he was deemed suitable for operational training and went to No. 14 OTU RAF Cottesmore where he formed his initial crew of 5 training on Wellingtons.

Two theories exist as to the events of the loss after being shot down by fighter in July 1943. One was that they collided with the attacking fighter. Another that they collided with another Lancaster lost that night.

Rosner's operational sorties

Op	Target	Date	Aircraft	Duration	Notes
2nd Dickie	Berlin	27/28th March	ED708 'O'	07-40	F/O Brodrick
1	Lorient	2/3rd April	R5492 'S'	05-45	P/O Rosner
2	Essen	3/4th April	W4256 'D'	05-15	P/O Rosner
3	Frankfurt	10/11th April	ED649 'X'	06-10	P/O Rosner
4	La Spezia	13/14th April	ED819 'U'	10-15	P/O Rosner
5	Stuttgart	14/15th April	ED649 'X'	07-00	P/O Rosner
(DNCO)	Plzen	16/17th April	ED649 'X'	03-35	P/O Rosner
6	Essen	30th Apr/1st May	ED819 'U'	05-05	P/O Rosner
7	Dortmund	4/5th May	ED819 'U'	05-55	P/O Rosner
8	Duisburg	12/13th May	R5611 'W'	04-20	P/O Rosner
9	Plzen	13/14th May	R5612 'P'	07-50	P/O Rosner
10	Dortmund	23/24th May	ED649 'X'	05-55	P/O Rosner
11	Düsseldorf	25/26th May	ED649 'X'	05-00	P/O Rosner
12	Essen	27/28th May	ED649 'X'	05-15	P/O Rosner
13	Wuppertal	29/30th May	ED649 'X'	05-20	P/O Rosner
14	Krefeld	21/22nd June	ED303 'J'	04-55	P/O Rosner
15	Mulheim	22/23rd June	ED409 'E'	04-20	P/O Rosner
16	Wuppertal	24/25th June	ED801 'N'	05-15	P/O Rosner
17	Gelsenkirchen	25/26th June	R5614 'Z'	04-35	P/O Rosner
18	Köln	28/29th June	ED360 'K'	04-45	P/O Rosner
19	Köln	8/9th July	ED720 'R'	03-50	1st Lt. Rosner

(info Clive Smith)

Flt. Sgt. William W. Dawson 61 sqn. Lancaster W4317

William Waller Dawson the son of John Michael Dawson a coal merchant and Betsy Waller, was educated at Sedbergh public school. He then joined Provincial Insurance in Kendal. After this he joined the R.A.F. in 1940 and trained in Rhodesia and South Africa under the Empire training scheme. William's Father John was a Methodist local preacher and William was following in those footsteps. Two of William's school friends, Harry Batty, and Charlie Lowis were also killed on ops. Batty's 115 sqn Wellington was lost on ops to Stuttgart in May 1942. Lowis' 78 sqn. Halifax was lost without trace 04/05/1943 on ops to Dortmund.

A shaky do-The Skoda works raid 16/17th April 1943

Flt. Sgt. William W. Dawson 61 sqn.

Op	Target	Date	Aircraft	Notes
1	Genova	13/11/42	Lanc. W4192	
2	Torino	18/11/42	Lanc. W4192	
3	Mannheim	06/12/42	Lanc. R5859	
4	Essen	11/01/43	Lanc. ED359	
5	Essen	12/01/43	Lanc. W4357	
6	Essen	13/01/43	Lanc. ED359	
7	Berlin	16/01/43	Lanc. ED359	
8	Berlin	17/01/43	Lanc. ED359	
	Düsseldorf	23/01/43	Lanc. R5618	Returned. Escape hatch blew off damaging turret.
9	Düsseldorf	27/01/43	Lanc. W4198	
10	Hamburg	30/01/43	Lanc. ED359	
11	Köln	02/02/43	Lanc. W4830	
12	Turin	04/02/43	Lanc. W4326	
13	Wilhelmshafen	18/02/43	Lanc. W4830 E	
14	Bremen	21/02/43	Lanc. W4830 E	
15	Köln	26/02/43	Lanc. W4357	
16	St Nazaire	28/02/43	Lanc. W4763	
17	Hamburg	03/03/43	Lanc. W4317 'R'	
18	Essen	05/03/43	Lanc. R5618	
19	Nürnberg	08/03/43	Lanc. W4317 'R'	
20	München	09/03/43	Lanc. W4317 'R'	
21	Stuttgart	11/03/43	Lanc. W4900	
22	Danzig	13/03/43	Lanc. W4236	
23	St.Nazaire	22/03/43	Lanc. W4317 'R'	
24	Duisburg	26/03/43	Lanc. W4317 'R'	
	Berlin	27/03/43	Lanc. W4798	Returned
25	Berlin	29/03/43	Lanc. ED718	
26	La Spezia	13/04/43	Lanc. W4317 'R'	
27	Stuttgart	14/04/43	Lanc. W4317 'R'	
28	Plzen	16/04/43	Lanc. W4317 'R'	Failed to Return

Operations completed by W.W. Dawson 61 sqn.

Peter Keay Flight Engineer W4317 61 sqn
By Chris Keay

Peter's father was John Arthur Keay (known as Jack Keay) who was of British origin having been born in Walsall in Staffordshire, England in 1893. He emigrated to Australia in or about 1910 where he was firstly employed in the country and then moved to Sydney, having various clerical jobs before he enlisted from that City into the Australian Army on the outbreak of World War I. He served in Egypt and Gallipoli before being discharged for health reasons in 1917. He went to work in Government service.

Jack married Nancy Hilda Tarrant Smith in 1920 and there was only one child of their marriage, namely Peter John Keay who was born on the 6th of February 1921 in Sydney.

In 1924 the family went to live near Rocky Glen in central New South Wales, approximately 450 kilometres West of Sydney, where Jack became a farmer. To do this he took advantage of what was known as the 'soldier settler scheme' whereby the State Government acquired large tracts of farmland, subdivided them into farm size portions, which were then sold to ex-service men on terms.

The farm was named 'Bracklyn', I believe a name given to it by a previous owner, who had 'taken up' the farm but then did not proceed with the purchase. The land was substantially unimproved and required clearing of scrub to enable cultivation and grazing of stock, construction of fences and a dwelling house. I believe that for some time the family lived in a tent until Jack built his first house out of timber cut on the land.

Peter was therefore brought up on a farm. In the early 1930's and Jack and Nancy separated. Peter remained on the farm with his father who married again in 1936. Of that marriage Peter had a step sister: Frances Elizabeth Keay (now Frances Thomas) currently resident in Hawaii, USA, and a step brother Christopher Amos Keay.

Peter's schooling consisted attending a local one teacher school for primary school classes then subsequently high school at Bathurst , where it is thought he completed the third year of high school. He then returned to Bracklyn and lived and worked with his father Jack on the farm.

Rocky Glen had been a staging post for horse-drawn transport in the 19th Century and at one time boasted several buildings including a wine shanty, but by this time there was only one family living there, who ran the local post office from their home. The "village" is situated on a highway, and "Bracklyn" was some 8 or nine kilometres distant from the village, and away from the main road. The closest town is Coonabarabran, is approximately 30 Kilometres from Rocky Glen.

Peter and his father were very close as they had lived and worked together for a number of years until Peter enlisted in the air force on the outbreak of World War II. Peter and Chris's father Jack were almost like brothers, years later he would frequently inadvertently refer to him as 'Pete' in conversation. They shared a lot of experiences, including on one occasion the destruction of the farmhouse by fire. Peter was apparently very proficient with the rudimentary farm machinery of the day, which required a fair degree of rough mechanical skills to keep operating.

Jack also enlisted in the army on the outbreak of war with Japan, but this time was not posted outside Australia. Jack said that Peter from an early age had a passionate interest in flying. Jack was coerced into providing payment for the occasional joy flight in light aircraft: I understand that in these early days of flying pilots would make a tour of country towns taking people on short flights as a way of earning money.

Peter was a very tall man, six feet six inches in height when he enlisted but of slight build, his weight was then 11 stone seven pounds. He served as the flight engineer on Lancaster W4317 QR-R, being responsible for the engine management and fuel systems. He would have been trained to fly straight and level if the pilot was incapacitated. He was killed in action along with all his crewmates on the Plzen raid 16/17th April 1943.

Wing Commander R.A.V. Gascoyne-Cecil
61sqn (Plzen raid Lancaster ED718)

Had a distinguished career, doing two tours on Bomber Command and earning a D.F.C. and bar. Later he worked with Professor R.V. Jones and the Directorate of Scientific Intelligence at the Air Ministry working on plans to develop electronic counter-measures and to neutralise German coastal radars. After the war he completed a doctorate at Baliol and was the first dean and vice-principal at Linacre College Oxford. He died in 2004.

****

Tom Jackson and Crew
419 sqn. (Halifax II JB912 on Plzeň raid)

On the next operation after Plzeň the Stettin raid, Tom Jackson encountered a night fighter and saw tracers shoot past his left shoulder side between his position and the port inner engine. He remembered;

'The German fighter plane was right on me. If he had been any further away, the bullets would have crossed sooner and killed me.'

It was Jackson's 26th op. He was flying low in order to evade the German radar. With one engine left, he knew he would never reach his target so he jettisoned his bombs into the Baltic Sea and headed for the shore. When the aircraft was safely over land Tom gave the order to bale out. He knew as soon as he let go of the controls the plane would start to spin. He eased up on the throttle before he made his break for the door.   Immediately he was thrown across the fuselage which was engulfed in flames. Tom was held there for what seemed a long time burning his face badly. He only just got out in time.

Sadly Tom's second pilot and eighth crew member, Flight Sergeant Watkins D.F.M., was killed. Jackson was taken to Stalag Luft III and took part in the 'Great Escape.' Tom was number 139 to go and was waiting in hut 104 sitting on a pile of logs. He was ready to go down the tunnel when he heard the sound of machine gun fire and knew the game was up. He then promptly rushed back to his own hut to take off his civilian clothing and eat all the food he had saved up for the journey before the Germans could commandeer it!

Werner Hoffmann who shot down Tom and his crew, claimed his first victory on the 24th May 1940, when he shot down an R.A.F. fighter over Calais and went on to become one of the top night aces claiming 51 victories. Serving with ZG2, NJG3, NJG1 and NJG5 He survived the war.

****

Lancaster ED800

Roger Anthoine, a witness, went out the next day to the place were the aircraft had crashed. It was located in the 'Bois de Rosette' at Yves-Gomezée:

"I arrived with my bicycle at a huge crater in the forest. The area was guarded, but I was able to have a look and they even allowed me to take photographs. The bomber must have gone straight into the ground. I looked around, not one tree was hit, but there were four craters from the engines and one big hole in the middle filled with water and oil, where the fuselage went in. Not one piece could be found which identified the aircraft, and what about the crew?"

In a previous century, minerals were exploited for which underground galleries were made. When the aircraft crashed it went straight into one of the tunnels and was literally swallowed by the ground. On the 20th of April, a German recovery unit (Bergungscommando) from Deurne airfield arrived on the site but was only able to find some metal parts. In July, a second attempt was made without success. After the war when a recovery unit of the RAF came, they were to find only a carburettor with a serial number and where thus able to identify ED800. The families were notified of the crash-location but that it was not possible to recover the bodies. In 1951 they were officially noted as 'missing in action' and their names appeared on the Runneymede Memorial. In 1993 it was decided by the 'Comité en souvenir de Lancaster Englouti' from Yves-Gomzée that a fitting ceremony had to be made in honour of the crew. The families were contacted and together they stood at 'Bois de Rosette' on 17th of April 1993, where a monument was being unveiled for the Duncan-crew. One of the men present was Tom Speirs, the nephew of James Speirs. He is a well-known Scottish piper and he played the song, which was composed by his father for the wedding of his Uncle James in 1942. Shortly after the ceremony a formation of F-16's from Florennes airbase came over. Children of the village were standing at the crater, it rained, and again oil was seen to be floating on top of the water. As the F-16's were thundering away, the people at the ceremony each threw a flower in the water as a last tribute to this crew.[166]

****

Frank Ward

Lancaster ED711

Frank was born at Darlinghurst NSW on 13th July 1917. His father was Henry Herbert Ward, a Grocer and his mother was Ellen (Née Stewart). The Ward family lived in the Darlinghurst area and later moved to Ashfield NSW.

Frank had a brother, Jim and a sister, Vera, both older than he.

His primary schooling was at St. Mary's Cathedral School in Sydney. Later he attended Christian Brothers High School, Lewisham from February 1929 to July 1933. He sat for the Intermediate Certificate in November 1932 and gained passes in Physics, Chemistry, English, Maths II, French & Latin. He failed in History and Maths I. It appears that he left secondary school part of the way through fourth year and did not carry on to sit for the Leaving Certificate.

Frank was a keen sportsman playing Rugby, Tennis and Golf. He was also involved in swimming and athletics.

On 5th August 1937 he started work at Sydney Pincombe Pty Ltd, 48 Hunter Street, Sydney where he eventually held the position of Assistant Accountant and Credit Manager.

Frank commenced part time study in Accounting at the Metropolitan Business College and passed the Intermediate Accountants and Auditing examination in November 1939 with passes in Intermediate Accounting I & II and Intermediate Auditing. His aim was to qualify as an Accountant with the Association of Accountants of Australia.

At this early stage of Frank's life, the War with Germany intervened. His first experience of military life was three months compulsory training with the Army Signals Corps, 36 Bn. He also commenced voluntary attendance at N.C.O. classes, two nights per week.

Perhaps army life was not to Frank's liking and in July 1940 he applied for selection as air crew with the Royal Australian Air Force (RAAF). He was placed on the air crew waiting list.

In the meantime, Frank met Mary Thompson in August 1940 whilst holidaying with friends at Rosnel Guest House at Bundanoon NSW. He contacted Mary again and they started going out together. They became engaged on 6th May 1941.

Then, at the age of 23 years and 9 months, Frank was called up at No.2 Recruitment Centre, Lindfield NSW on 26th April 1941and was posted to No.2 ITS for initial flight crew training. On 26th June that year he was posted to No.5 Elementary Flight Training School at Narromine NSW where he undertook basic flying training on De Haviland DH82 Tiger Moth aircraft. He held the rank of Leading Aircraftman (LAC).

On 12th September 1941 he returned to No.2 ITS Lindfield.

---

[166] Wim Govaerts Belgie in Oorlog 36 Lancaster verliezen in Belgie 1941-1945

A Shaky do. The Plzen raid April 16/17th April 1943

Frank and Mary were married at St Josephs Catholic Church, Belmore on Saturday 20th September 1941.

On 11th October he was posted to No.2 ED at Bradfield Park, Sydney and embarked at Sydney with his unit for further training in Canada on 13th November 1941. He disembarked in Canada on 1st December 1941 and was posted to No.1 Air Observer School at Malton, Ontario.

In March 1942 he attended a Bombing and Gunnery School at Jarvis, Ontario and in late April he attended an Advanced Navigation School at Penfield Ridge. He was promoted to Sergeant on 25th April 1942. In late May he was posted to No.1 "Y" Depot at Halifax pending a posting to a unit in the UK.

On 14th June 1942 he embarked for the UK, arriving on 24th June. He was attached to the Royal Air Force (RAF) and posted to No.2 Operational Training Unit (O.T.U) at Tatenhill in Staffordshire. There he trained on Avro Anson and Vickers Wellington aircraft doing cross-country navigation, air gunnery, bomb aiming and second pilot duties.

Training at Tatenhill continued until early October, after which he was posted to 460 Squadron at Breighton based at in East Yorkshire. 460 sqn. was an Australian RAAF unit formed in November 1941. Initially it was equipped with Vickers Wellington aircraft and at the time of Frank's posting had been converted to the larger Avro Lancaster four-engine heavy bomber.

In December 1942 he commenced training on Manchester bombers at 1656 Conversion Unit, Lindholme. In January 1943, training commenced on Avro Lancaster heavy bombers at Lindholme, doing circuits and landings.

On 16th January 1943 after a final air test, Frank flew his first mission, which was a raid on Berlin in Lancaster No. 'D' 4776. He was the bomb-aimer. At this point he had a total of 224 flying hours logged, including 63 hours night flying. This first mission involved 7 hours 20 minutes night flying. Due to a late take-off (5.25pm) they did not reach Berlin and bombed a secondary target at Rostock from a height of 17,000 feet. No enemy aircraft were encountered but they flew through medium flak without suffering any damage.

His second mission on 17th January was also to Berlin, which they reached on time and successfully bombed. German defences were better prepared and the bombers faced determined and powerful opposition from both ground and air defences on this raid. Frank's aircraft was damaged by heavy flak but returned safely after 8.5 hours in the air. This was his first taste of real warfare and must have been a terrifying experience.

Further training in circuits and landings and all weather flying was done from Lindholme in late January. After 48 hours leave in Sheffield, he rejoined 460 Squadron at Breighton on 27th January 1943. Breighton is a small village about 20 kilometres south of the City of York. The airfield is right next to the village and is now used for general aviation. Frank wrote of Breighton in his diary

'When we arrived at Breighton found it the usual old place, unaltered from when we were here before. The place is covered with mud and to speak mildly, it is a bloody awful place'

Bomber Command was at this time under great pressure to escalate bombing attacks on Nazi Germany and other occupied countries. The targets were generally heavy industrial centres, munitions factories, arms and vehicle manufacturing plants, military bases, etc.

Frank's situation in being sent on night bombing missions with the barest of operational training was typical of the time. Unfortunately, the allied losses of aircraft and crews was heavy and the chances of any airman completing the required 30 missions before being

A Shaky do. The Plzen raid April 16/17th April 1943

allowed any respite were slight, to say the least.

After just 18 months since joining the R.A.A.F. and only eight weeks since leaving Sydney, Frank and his mates found themselves in one of the darkest periods of the war facing the very real prospect of not returning from each mission. After 8 or so hours in the air at night over enemy territory, the crews returned mentally and physically exhausted, sometimes in a badly damaged aircraft barely able to stay in the air. Daylight hours would have been spent in fitful sleep followed by the essential briefing sessions before the next mission.

On one occasion Frank and his fellow crew were given weekend leave, so they headed for Doncaster and stayed in a hotel. They were so exhausted that they spent most of the weekend sleeping, so a weekend of fun and frivolity was out of the question.

Upon joining 460 Squadron at Breighton, Frank and his crew mates did local and cross country flying with their new pilot, Flight Sgt White. The crew were: Flight Sgt D E White Pilot, Flight Sgt F H Ward bomb-aimer & air gunner, Flight Sgt. A. K. Parker Wireless Operator, W/O W R K Charlton Navigator, Sgt B Knilands Flight Engineer, Sgt N Simpson air Gunner and Flight Sgt A. K. Smith (RAF) air Gunner

All were Australians except Smith who was attached to the Squadron from the RAF. White was from Colac Victoria, Charlton was from Sydney, Alan Parker was from Mosman NSW, Knilands was from Hornsby NSW and Simpson from Queensland.

On 4th February 1943 Frank flew his third mission bombing Turin in Italy, a nine hour operation. Missions against Lorient (2), Bremen and Milan followed during February without mishap. They aborted the Milan flight one and a half hours out from base due to an oxygen system failure. Of the Bremen mission Frank wrote in his diary

'not a bad trip - 10/10ths cloud most of the way & over target. Bags of flak over target and all the way out. Didn't know whether we were coming or going half the time'

In March they flew missions against Hamburg, Essen (twice), Nürnberg, Munich, Stuttgart and St Nazaire. All went without suffering any damage except for the last mission against a German submarine base at St Nazaire on 22nd of March.

Just before reaching the target they were shot-up by a JU88 German night fighter. The rear and mid-upper gun turrets returned fire. In the ensuing engagement the rear turret, fuselage, tail-plane and starboard wing were damaged by cannon fire. The rudder and elevator trim were shot away and the aircraft went out of control, diving steeply. White managed to regain control, pulling out of the dive at 4000 feet. Although the damage was serious, they continued on and bombed the target.

On completion of the bombing run, Frank discovered that one bomb had not released from the bomb bay. Facing a certain crash landing back in England their attempts to jettison the bomb were unsuccessful until Frank managed to dislodge it after half an hour of effort. He then assisted White who was having great difficulty controlling the damaged aircraft. They crash-landed on British soil in South Cerney. The plane was destroyed by fire. No mention is made in Frank's log book and diary about any injuries or loss of crew from this crash. They all must have been able to get clear of the aircraft before it caught fire.[166]

At the end of March 1943 Frank had flown 87.4 hours on operations, all at night.

Following the loss of their Lancaster 'D' W4879 on the St Nazaire raid, Frank and Flight Sgt White tested a new aircraft on 2nd April and found it to be unserviceable. The following night they resumed operations in Lancaster serial number ED711 with a raid on Essen. On the

---

[166] D.F.M. citation for this action PWC

A Shaky do. The Plzen raid April 16/17th April 1943

return leg, they landed at Church Fenton base where they stayed until 6th April, possibly due to aircraft problems. The day they returned to Breighton they practiced cross country, low level, and formation flying involving 60 aircraft for three hours.

Missions to Duisburg and La Spezia followed on the 13th and 14th of April. Then on the 16th April Frank and his crew mates set out with fourteen other Lancasters from 460 Squadron to bomb the Škoda arms works at Plzeň in Czechoslovakia.

The Plzeň raid was different from the previous missions they had done. It was staged during a full moon period in the hope that the target could be identified visually, and to offset the danger from fighters, full-scale diversionary raids were made on cities in Western Germany.

Navigational difficulties were encountered in locating Plzeň. We know that one Australian crew bombed Nürnberg instead whilst two others searched over a wide area without finding the Pathfinder flares that were supposed to have been dropped beforehand on the Škoda works and then set course for base, attacking Erlangen and Koblenz en route. Night fighters harried the Lancasters, which found the bright moonlight a hazard that outweighed the expected advantage of easier navigation. Consequently, heavy losses were experienced.

460 Squadron lost three aircraft that night, including Lancaster ED711.

Postscript

Frank Ward was a typical Australian young man of his time who enlisted to help defend the British Empire against the Nazi tyranny unleashed by Adolf Hitler. Married to Mary only weeks before he left Australia, he found himself embroiled in an air war far worse than anyone could have foreseen.

The final months of his life at the 460 Squadron base at Breighton were miserable with the cold winter weather, the stress from undertaking night-time sorties over enemy territory and a longing for Australia and his loved ones. Frank and his crew mates would have developed a strong bond, as most bomber crews did, and the short leave breaks would have been largely spent together over drinks, card games and story telling. They flew together during one of the most dangerous periods of the war when bomber crew losses were very high, particularly amongst the Australian Squadrons.

The war dragged on for another two and a half years after the ED711 crew met their fate. Many more airmen died over Europe before Nazi Germany was forced in to submission. The missions they flew played a major part in crippling the German war machine.

I hope that this account of Frank's short life will serve to perpetuate his memory across future generations of his descendants, so that his sacrifice will not be forgotten.

BruceHall
Bowral NSW

December 1999

A Shaky do. The Plzen raid April 16/17th April 1943

Ops in a Halifax
(To the tune Waltzing Matilda)

Now the first silly blighter opened up the throttles wide,
Sped down the runway fast and free,
And he sang as he swang and pranged upon a boundary,
Who'll come on ops in a Hali with me?

Chorus;
Ops in a Hali, ops in a Hali,
Who'll come on ops in a Hali with me?
And he sang as he swang and pranged upon a boundary,
Who'll come on ops in a Hali with me?

Now the second silly blighter, he got off the deck alright,
Got over Flamboro' and pranged in the sea,
And he sang as he swam all up and down the coast again,
Who'll come on ops in a Hali with me?

Chorus, (Third line as above verse).

Now the third silly blighter, he got over Germany,
Up came the fighters One Two Three,
And the crew all sang as they went into a power-dive,
Who'll come on ops in a Hali with me?

Chorus, (Third line as above verse).

Now the fourth silly blighter, he got over Hannover,
Up came the flak like a Christmas tree,
And the crew all sang as they buckled on their parachutes,
Who'll come on ops in a Hali with me?

Chorus, (Third line as above verse).

Now the fifth silly blighter, he got over Magdeburg,
Ten tenths cloud so he dropped 'em in the sea,
And the navigator sang as the captain tried to shoot himself,
Who'll come on ops in a Hali with me?

Chorus, (Third line as above verse).
Now the last silly blighter, he got there and back alright,
They gave him a green but he couldn't find the Tee,
And the crew all sang as they landed on a hangar roof,
Who'll come on ops in a Hali with me?

Chorus, (Third line as above verse).

(Petrie-Andrews)

A Shaky do. The Plzen raid April 16/17th April 1943

Target Stettin
April 20th 1943

(Personal Experiences of a Bomber Command Raid)
Walter William (Bill) Garbett – Flight Engineer – Lancaster
('Steve' Stephen's crew of 106 sqn. Lancaster R5551 on Škoda raid)

At 11:00 hrs on 20th April 1943 our Squadron was detailed for yet another raid on Germany, the target being unknown to us. All crews, including my own, were detailed to test their own aircraft, which they were going to take on the raid that evening. The air test only took 45 minutes then we proceeded to lunch.

Briefing, was at 16:00 hrs and every one was most anxious to find out the target and the extent of its defences

At 16:15 hrs all this curiosity was solved and we found our target to be 'Stettin', a vital supply port to Germany in her supply to the Russian Front.

The briefing Officer told us of the nature of the Port's defences and the dock areas were the points of concentration for the bombing. We were to go low level up to the islands north of Denmark; there we were to climb to 14,000 feet to bomb our target. The object of the low level route, was to avoid lights and their radio location, as, on that night the moon was to be full.
At 16:45 hours, all crews began to go out to the aircraft. These were inspected every vital point, paying very great attention to the armament and the security of the bomb load.

I forgot to mention, on this particular raid, there were to be, 500 aircraft, comprising of Lancasters and Halifaxes.

Our bomb load was 1 four thousand pound bomb and 288, 30lb incendiaries.

Dead on 17:30 hours the aircraft of the Squadron began to start their engines for take off. We were 4th off the ground, and commenced our trip out. We flew at 1500 feet to the coast of England and aircraft were all around us, their navigation lights, giving us some idea of their position.

We crossed the English coast at 18:00 hours and from there on, all lights were put out and every one was on their toes. From this stage on, we were briefed to fly below 500 feet, and the moon began to shine on us, just as if it were daylight. Occasionally we could see another aircraft, which indicated we were still on track, and not alone.

Just before 20:30 hours we saw the coast of Denmark coming up, this we knew would mean action, as when the first of our aircraft crossed that coast, their defences would immediately come into action, we saw anti-aircraft fire commence, and assumed the first of the boys were across.

A Shaky do. The Plzen raid April 16/17th April 1943

The moon was shining very brilliantly now, and as we crossed the coast out altitude being no more than 50 feet, we could see the Promenade and bedroom windows open. On our starboard side light anti aircraft guns were blazing away, but being so low, and our speed being in the region of 200 miles per hour, our aircraft was quite a difficult target.

We continued across Denmark low level, and shortly we came across an anti aircraft Battery on our port bow, these fellows were firing at us, so our Pilot gave orders to the gunners to open fire. In a few seconds, our front gunner had silenced the gun post.

From there on we met very little opposition.

About an hour after our little battle with the gun post, we saw a car coming towards us with an extremely bright headlight, so, assuming it was an enemy staff car, the gunners gave it one burst and the light went out.

Our next bit of fun was a train, enemy gunners were firing from the top of it, and so we got as near as we could and our gunners strafed it from stem to stern.

From there on, our journey was uneventful, and as we crossed the north coast of Denmark, we began our climb over the Baltic to our bombing height. A few flak ships fired at us, but with very little accuracy.

During our flight across the Baltic, we could see the Stirlings, bombing Rostock and the fires were going very nicely, occasionally we could distinguish our aircraft going down in flames, which was not a pretty sight.

At 21:00 hours, we were approaching the target, and flak and searchlights, seemed to be plentiful. A 21:30 hour was zero hour and soon we were on the outskirts of the target.

On our first bombing run, we were covered in searchlights, and could not bomb and as the bombing is done straight and level searchlight avoiding action would have only resulted in wrong and inaccurate bombing.

After 40 seconds of violent evasive action, we got out of those searchlight beams and came around again for the final bombing run. This time we had a very nice run up, but on the words "bombs gone" from our bomb aimer, we were covered by searchlights for the second time.

This time we got a shell under our bomb bay, and it tore a very nice hole in our fuselage. There was no time to waste now if we were to get out of the target alive, so the skipper put the nose down and we came out of that target at 280 miles per hour, until we were once more 50 – 100 feet above the Baltic outside the target area. By this time, bombs were exploding with great flashes, and the fires were very bright and extending. So the bomber force had once more completed its task.

Now came the hazardous journey back to base. By this time, the whole of northern Germany was alive, and possibly aware of our homeward route, so we could expect opposition now until we got well into the North Sea once again.

A Shaky do. The Plzen raid April 16/17th April 1943

The Baltic now seemed to hold a number of flak ships, all of which were out to shoot us down.

Ten minutes out of the target, we had a minor battle with one of these flak ships, but the fire from our aircraft soon demoralised them, and all was quiet once more, but not long after this we were flying along quite nicely just above the water and a searchlight came on from nowhere, this light we found only too soon, was on a German destroyer, which meant business.

Our pilot immediately took evasive action and told all gunners to open fire, which they did without any hesitation. After a second or two one of the Destroyers shells tore away our starboard rudder, which made the aircraft difficult to handle, but our Pilot was one of the best, and kept up his evasive action, but before we finally evaded our enemy, we were hit once more in the fuselage below my feet. This time the shell had blown all our hydraulic pipes apart, which meant a belly-landing if we got back.

For some time later, we had no opposition and sailed along on top of the water, until our navigator came up to the cockpit, and looked down for a map reading, this he soon got, and said "Good Heavens SYLT!" This being a German naval base, the name brought very quick action to both the Pilot and me, and we had all the engines wide open in no time at all.

Beneath us were the battle ships, but we were over them so soon, they never heard anything but the roar of our engines and we were past them on our final leg home.

Now we could relax a little, and our navigator informed our time of reaching base was 02:10 hours, this meant a dark landing with a badly damaged aircraft. None of the crew seemed very worried, but we were all very pleased to be on our way home and finally clear of enemy territory.

01:50 hours we could see our aerodrome lights ahead, which to us were a very pleasant sight, and we could see the other aircraft returning from the raid.

We called up the aerodrome and asked for permission to land, this was soon got, and within 5 minutes we were on English soil once again. None of us hurt in any way, we proceeded to interrogation and a nice big meal. Then away to a well deserved sleep.

Thus ended another blow against the enemy in the war, which was forced upon us all.

(Walter William) Bill Garbett April 1943)
(Reproduced from the transcript by Bruce Nigel Garbett)

Additional comment by Pilot 'Steve' Stephens;

'From Stettin we knew we had no hydraulics but could only wait and see what the effect was. We found that the undercarriage could not be lowered normally but the emergency bottle worked OK. The flaps could not be selected and the landing was fast and ended in a ground loop near the end of the runway with no serious damage.'

A Shaky do. The Plzen raid April 16/17th April 1943

Nat Bury D.F.M. citation

LG 7/12/43 F/S Bury as Flight Engineer, has participated in successful attacks upon Essen, Kiel, Berlin and many distant targets such as La Spezia, Plzeň and Peenemünde. In September 1943, during an attack on Hannover, one engine of his aircraft caught fire while over the target and immediately afterwards the bomber was attacked by an enemy fighter. These airmen at once extinguished the fire which enabled the captain and gunners to concentrate on the combat. F/S Bury's devotion to duty during long flights has inspired confidence in the other members of his crew and contributed to the successful completion of many sorties.

Incidents on Nat Bury's Tour

Date	Target	Incident	Result
2.4.42	Bay of Biscay	Starboard Inner engine u/s shut down, feathered. Port Outer on ½ power.	DNCO
10.4.43	Frankfurt	Compasses U/S	DNCO
16.4.43	Plzeň	Shot up by flak. Badly holed	DCO
02.5.43	Duisburg	Well coned. Targeted by flak lost a great deal of height	DCO
13.5.43	Plzeň	Jettisoned two 500lb bombs	DCO
11.6.43	Düsseldorf	Attacked by fighter 02:02 hrs.	DCO
14.6.43	Oberhausen	Coned. Shot up by flak 01:08 hrs.	DCO
5.7.43	Köln	hit by 30lb I.C.B over target 01:22 hrs through starboard aileron. Badly damaged	
9.7.43	Gelsenkirchen	Starboard Inner at half power 00:13 hrs jettisoned two 500lb bombs & two more at 00:23	DCO
10.8.43	Nürnberg	Gee unserviceable	DCO
17.8.43	Peenemünde	Extreme fighter activity bombed from 6,000 ft.	DCO
23.8.43	Berlin	Caught up in ack ack barrage on return journey.	DCO
22.9.43	Hannover	Engaged by Bf110- returned fire	DCO
23.9.43	Mannheim	Engaged by Bf110, port outer eng. on fire-shut down and feathered. rear turret and Gee. U/S near Troyes at 23:12 hrs.	DCO

Prangs

20.9.43 Langar Night bombing exercise. Overshot runway on landing. Funnel lights not operating. Disagreement with control. Very bad damage. (and language)

5.3.44 Syerston Night flying exercise. Snow covered runways. Pranged on landing. Drifted into snow piled either side of runway. Very bad damage.

25.3.44 Syerston Circuits and bumps, Burst tyre on take off. Pranged on landing. Very bad damage. Last two incidents with student crews when instructing.

A Shaky do. The Plzen raid April 16/17th April 1943

Nat Bury D.F.M. Flight Engineer 207 Squadron tour of operations from Langar

Date	Target	Duration	Aircraft	Result
28th Mar 1943	St.Nazaire	5:20	ED550 'K'	DCO
2nd April 1943	Bay of Biscay, gardening	4:20	ED498 'D'	DNCO
3rd April 1943	Essen	6:05	W4129 'L'	DCO
4th April 1943	Kiel	5:15	ED554 'Q'	DCO
10th April 1943	Frankfurt	4:15	ED498 'D'	DNCO
14th April 1943	La Spezia	9:45	ED498 'D'	DCO
15th April 1943	Stuttgart	6:25	ED498 'D'	DCO
16th April 1943	Plzen (Skoda works)	8:25	ED412 'Q'	DCO
	Diverted Tangmere			
	Returned from Tangmere	1:00		
18th April 1943	La Spezia	9:55	ED498 'D'	DCO
4th May 1943	Dortmund	7:00	ED586 'F'	DCO
	Diverted to Predanack			
5th May 1943	Returned from Predanack	2:10		
12th May 1943	Duisburg	4:35	ED586 'F'	DCO
13th May 1943	Plzen	7:55	ED586 'F'	DCO
23rd May 1943	Dortmund	5:10	ED498 'D'	DCO
25th May 1943	Düsseldorf	5:00	ED498 'D'	DCO
11th June 1943	Düsseldorf	5:05	W5006 'G'	DCO
12th June 1943	Bochum	5:45	ED586 'F'	DCO
14th June 1943	Oberhausen	5:05	ED486 'F'	DCO
21st June 1943	Krefeld	4:30	ED486 'F'	DCO
25th June 1943	Gelsenkirchen	5:05	ED550 'K'	DCO
5th July 1943	Köln	5:30	ED586 'F'	DCO
8th July 1943	Köln	5:20	ED498 'D'	DCO
9th July 1943	Gelsenkirchen	6:20	ED586 'F'	DCO
7th August 1943	Genova	8:35	W5006 'G'	DCO
9th August 1943	Mannheim	4:45	EE126 'A'	DCO
10th August 1943	Nürnberg	7:10	ED586 'F'	DCO
15th August 1943	Milano	7:40	ED586 'F'	DCO
17th August 1943	Peenemunde	6:55	ED550 'K'	DCO
23rd August 1943	Berlin	7:15	ED586 'F'	DCO
27th August 1943	Nürnberg	7:10	ED586 'F'	DCO
22nd September 43	Hannover	5:50	R5895 'B	DCO
23rd September 43	Mannheim	6:50	DV243 'D'	DCO

A shaky do-The Skoda works raid 16/17th April 1943

Bill Harrall ops 44 and 582 PFF sqn.

Number 2 A.G.S 11th Sept.42-24th Oct 42 31 course Dalcross
1654 Con Unit Wigsley 21st Nov. 42-9th Dec.42
20th Dec. 42 to 44 Sqn. 582 Sqn. P.F.F. 5th April 44-18th Aug.1944.
 # landed Tangmere

Op	Target	Date	Aircraft	Duty	Notes
1	Essen	13th Jan 43	Lanc. ED314	A/G	4:45 duration. Pilot F/Lt Osborn
2	Berlin	16th Jan 43	Lanc. ED314	A/G	8:00 duration Pilot F/Lt Osborn
3	Düsseldorf	23rd Jan 43	Lanc. ED314	A/G	5:35 duration Pilot Pennington
4	Köln	2nd Feb 43	Lanc.W4137 'L'	A/G	6:20 duration Pilot Pennington
DNCO	Hamburg	3rd Feb 43	Lanc. W4831	A/G	Rtnd-bad weather 4:00 duration Pilot Pennington
5	Lorient	13th Feb 43	Lanc. W4199	A/G	6:15 duration Pilot Pennington
6	Lorient	16th Feb 43	Lanc. W4305	A/G	5:50 duration Pilot Pennington
7	Wilhelmshafen	18th Feb 43	Lanc. W4838	A/G	6:05 duration landed Leeming Pilot Pennington
8	Bremen	21st Feb 43	Lanc. W4831	A/G	5:35 duration Pilot Pennington
9	Nürnberg	25th Feb 43	Lanc. R5898	A/G	8:50 duration Pilot Pennington
10	Köln	26th Feb 43	Lanc. W4831	A/G	5:50 duration Pilot Pennington
11	St Nazaire	28th Feb 43	Lanc. W4831	A/G	5:40 duration Pilot Pennington
12	Berlin	1st Mar 43	Lanc. W4831	A/G	7:30 duration Pilot Pennington
13	Essen	5th Mar	Lanc. W4831	A/G	4:30 duration Pilot Pennington
14	Nürnberg	8th Mar 43	Lanc. W4831	A/G	7:30 duration Pilot Pennington
15	Danzig	10th Mar 43	Lanc. W4831	A/G	8:30 Gardening Swinemünde Pilot Pennington
16	Essen	12th Mar 43	Lanc. W4831	A/G	5:00 duration Pilot Pennington
17	Kiel	4th Apr 43	Lanc. W4935	A/G	5:40 duration Pilot Pennington
18	Duisburg	8th Apr 43	Lanc. W4831	A/G	6:00 duration Pilot Pennington
19	Duisburg	9th Apr 43	Lanc. W4831	A/G	4:30 duration Pilot Pennington
20	La Spezia	13th Apr 43	Lanc. W4935	A/G	Returned/engine fire 4:40 hrs.# Pilot Pennington
21	Plzen	16th Apr 43	Lanc. ED611 'J'	A/G	8:30 duration Pilot Pennington
22	Stettin	20th Apr 43	Lanc. W4831	A/G	8:00 duration Pilot Pennington
23	Bay of Biscay	22nd Apr 43	Lanc. W4831	A/G	9:00 duration. Gardening. Pilot Pennington

A shaky do-The Skoda works raid 16^{/17th} April 1943

BILL HARRALL 1ST TOUR CONT.

	Target	Date	Aircraft	Duty	Notes
24	Bordeaux	27th Apr 43	Lanc. W4831	A/G	8:30 duration Gardening Pilot Pennington
25	Essen	30th Apr 43	Lanc. W4831	A/G	4:50 duration Pilot Pennington
26	Düsseldorf	11th Jun 43	Lanc. ED716	A/G	4:15 duration Pilot Pennington
27	Bochum	12th Jun 43	Lanc. ED716	A/G	5:30 duration Pilot Pennington
28	Freidrichshafen	20th Jun 43	Lanc. EE185	A/G	10:00 hrs. Base-target-Algiers Pilot Pennington
29	La Spezia	23rd Jun 43	Lanc. EE185	A/G	9:30 Algiers-target-Base Pilot Pennington
	11th July 43	17 O.T.U.	Silverstone	Intructor	
	1st August 43	17 O.T.U.	Turweston	Screened A/G	
	28th Jan 1944	1481 Gunnery Flt.	Binrook	R.Gnr.	58 'B' Course
	15th Feb 1944	1656 C.U	Lindholme	A/G	
	9th Mar 1944	No.1 L.F.S.	Lindholme	A/G	
	30th Mar 1944	N.T.U.	Warboys	A/G	

Bill Harrall 2nd tour 582 P.F.F. sqn.
Pilot Flt/Lt Walker (Coleman*)

Op	Target	Date	Aircraft	Duty	Notes
30	Lille (supporter)	9th Apr 44	Lanc. ND816	A/G	2:50 duration 13,000 lb HE Pilot F/Lt. Walker
31	Aachen (ditto)	11th Apr 44	Lanc. ND438	A/G	3:35 duration 13,000 lb HE Pilot F/Lt. Walker
32	Noisy-le-Sec	18th Apr 44	Lanc. ND502	A/G	3:55 duration 13,000 lb HE Pilot F/Lt. Walker
33	Düsseldorf	22nd Apr 44	Lanc. ND502	A/G	4:05 duration 6 x 2000 HE Pilot F/Lt. Walker
34	Montdidier	3rd May 44	Lanc. ND187	A/G	3:15 duration 13 x 1000 lb Pilot F/Lt. Walker
35	Mantes-Gassicourt	6th May 44	Lanc. ND816	A/G	3:20 duration 12x1000 lb Pilot F/Lt. Walker
36	Louvain (Support)	11th May 44	Lanc. ND899	A/G	3:00 duration Pilot F/Lt. Walker
37	Boulogne	18th May 44	Lanc. ND812	A/G	2:45 duration 18 x 500 lb Pilot F/Lt. Walker
38	Duisburg	21st May 44	Lanc. ND812	A/G	4:20 dur. 1x4000 8x500 lb Pilot F/Lt. Walker
39	Dortmund	22nd May 44	Lanc. ND812	A/G	4:00 dur. 1x4000 8x500 lb Pilot F/Lt. Walker
40	Rennes (Illumin')	27th May 44	Lanc. ND812	A/G	3:55 duration 8 x 1000 lb Pilot F/Lt. Walker
41	Tergnier (Illumin)	30th May 44	Lanc. NE169	A/G	3:35 duration 8 x 1000 lb Pilot F/Lt. Walker
42	Longues 'D-Day'	6th Jun 44	Lanc. NE169	A/G	3:15 dur. 11x1000 lb 4x500 lb Pilot S/Ldr.
43	Lens	16th Jun 44	Lanc. ND348	A/G	2:20 dur. Pilot S/Ldr. *Coleman 11 x 1000 lb 4 x 500 lb
44	Coubronne	23rd Jun 44	Lanc. PB136	A/G	2:00 dur P-pln base Plt F/Lt. Walker 11x1000 lb 3x500 lb

A Shaky do. The Plzen raid April 16/17th April 1943

BILL HARRAL 2ND TOUR CONT.

No.	Target	Date	Aircraft		Details
45	Middel Straete	25th Jun 44	Lanc. PB136	A/G	2:00 18 x 500lb HE p-plane base Pilot F/Lt. Walker
46	Blainville (Illum')	28th Jun 44	Lanc. PB136	A/G	6:05 duration. 6x4x7 flares 7x1000lb HE. Stbd. outer on fire. Pilot F/Lt. Walker
47	Oisement Neuville	2nd Jul 44	Lanc. PB136	A/G	2:25 duration. P-plane base Pilot F/Lt. Walker
48	Wizernes	5th Jul 44	Lanc. NE130	A/G	2:00 duration P-plane base Pilot F/Lt. Walker
49	L'Hay	9th Jul 44	Lanc. PB136	A/G	2:05 duration P-plane base Pilot F/Lt. Walker
50	Nucourt	10th Jul 44	Lanc. PB136	A/G	2:50 duration P-plane base Pilot F/Lt. Walker
51	Gappennes	11th Jul 44	Lanc. PB136	A/G	2:45 duration P-plane base Pilot F/Lt. Walker
52	Rollez	12th Jul 44	Lanc. PB136	A/G	2:20 duration P-plane base Pilot F/Lt. Walker
53	St.Philbert Ferme	14th Jul 44	Lanc. PB136	A/G	2:45 duration P-plane base Pilot F/Lt. Walker
54	Nucourt	15th Jul 44	Lanc. PB136	A/G	3:05 duration P-plane base Pilot F/Lt. Walker
55	Cagny (Caen)	18th Jul 44	Lanc. PB136	A/G	3:05 duration Monty's breakthrough. Pilot F/Lt. Walker
56	Mont Candon	19th Jul 44	Lanc. PB149	A/G	2:35 duration P-plane base Pilot F/Lt. Walker
57	Forêt Du Croc	23rd Jul 44	Lanc. PB136	A/G	3:00 duration P-plane base Pilot F/Lt. Walker
58	Kiel	23rd Jul 44	Lanc. PB136	A/G	5:20 duration secondary blind marker Pilot F/Lt. Walker
59	Stuttgart	25th Jul 44	Lanc. ND880	A/G	7:40 duration Blind marker Pilot F/Lt. Walker
60	Stuttgart	28th Jul 44	Lanc. ND182	A/G	6:40 duration. Blind marker. S/Ldr. Walker
61	Dijon	10th Aug 44	Lanc. PB182	A/G	5:40 duration Blind marker-Illuminator S/Ldr. Walker
62	Russelheim	12th Aug 44	Lanc. PB182	A/G	4:30 duration Prim-blind marker S/Ldr. Walker
63	Volkel Airfield	15th Aug 44	Lanc. PB182	A/G	2:55 duration V.B.U. S/Ldr. Walker
64	Stettin	16th Aug 44	Lanc. PB182	A/G	7:35 duration Prim.blind marker. Illumin'tr. S/Ldr. Walker
65	Bremen	18th Aug 44	Lanc. PB182	A/G	5:05 duration Prim blind marker. Illum. S/Ldr. Walker

Ops 60-65 Pilot was same, now Squadron Leader Walker. Bill Harrall flew on Defiants, Manchesters, Lancasters, Wellingtons and Halifaxes.

A Shaky do. The Plzen raid April 16/17th April 1943

F/L Ken Dean 51 Squadron

Ken Dean flew with 51 Squadron as a Bomb Aimer and later became the Group Bombing Leader with 4 Group to which 51 Squadron was attached. He rose to Flight Lieutenant towards the end of the War and received his D.F.C. at Buckingham Palace. He took part in most of the major raids including all of the 1,000 bomber raids over Cologne, Munich etc., and the all important Peenemünde raid (the attack on the V1 sites). He later became a Navigator on the Halifax.

At the end of the War he was posted temporarily to 617 Squadron when they carried out a "Goodwill Tour" of Canada and the US; at that stage in the War 617 had been badly mauled and needed to make up numbers for the US trip. They flew the Avro Lincoln on this trip.

Ken Dean's son Michael spent some time at the Chingford CID (North London) and arrived for duty early one morning to find to find a young man had been arrested for breaking into a deceased person's bungalow. He gives his account of an interesting meeting during his investigations;

'*I then contacted the witness and made an appointment to obtain a statement from him that morning.*

I attended his address and he invited me into the kitchen and provided me with a cup of coffee. As I was starting to take the written statement I glanced up and noticed a picture rail with a number of clearly hand painted dinner plates of family pets, Leopard's, Tigers etc and I complemented him on his collection, he then indicated his wife was a talented painter and had done them herself.

I then looked further around the picture rail I noticed a plate with the old Bomber

A Shaky do. The Plzen raid April 16/17th April 1943

Command crest on it; knowing his age and also his military bearing I asked him if he had served in bombers during the War and he replied "Yes". I then asked him where he had been stationed and he said something like "Oh it was a little airfield you have probably never heard of, it's called Snaith in East Yorkshire." I said something like "Ah 51 Squadron then Sir!"

There was a stunned silence from him for a good couple of minutes; he may well have been thinking that the Metropolitan Police was using some form of black art to obtain this information. Then the penny dropped and he said "You introduced yourself as Detective Constable Dixie Dean. Was your Father with 51 Squadron as Flt. Lt. Dixie Dean?" and I nodded. He was quite stunned that he had just met the son of a Group bombing Leader who had actually had at least one flight with my Father on board. The Group Bombing Leader used to fly in every aircraft in the Group to ascertain the efficiency of the bomb aimer and each trip was therefore quite hazardous.'

Info Michael Dean

Albert Goering

Much had been written about the infamous Nazi leader Hermann Goering but little has been said or heard of his bother Albert. Albert's connection with the Skoda works is that he was export director in 1939 and began his roving brief at the end of 1940. From that point on he was almost always on the move, with a base in Bucharest. He did return to Plzen as his wife was still based in Prague, however his direct involvement in the Skoda factory itself was negligible from that time on, It is not known if he was at the works on the night of the 16/17th April 1943.

Albert was a vehement anti-Nazi and due to his influences at least 50 people but possibly several hundred more were saved from death. He also turned a blind eye to the work of the Czech resistance and sabotage in the works itself. He indirectly reduced production of military equipment by deliberately encouraging non-military output. His story is not unlike that of Oscar Schindler and he is known to have sent trucks to the concentration camps requesting workers which he then released. There are plenty of rumours that during his time in Hungary in 1944, that he was there energetically helping as many as he could get out. After the war Albert Goering was interrogated at the Nuremberg Trials and many survivors testified on his behalf. The story of Albert and his brother is ably covered by James Wyllie in his book 'The warlord and the renegade' (Sutton Publishing).

APPENDIX B

Operations records listing aircraft and crew on Plzen raid 16/17th April 1943

AIRCRAFT	SERIAL	CODE	SQN.	CREW	TRADE	UP	DOWN	BOMBED	NOTES
Lancaster	ED558	WS-N	9	Sgt Brown R.	Capt	21:19	06:00	01:44	No green TI until after bombing
				W/O Wood W.E.	2nd Pilot			8,000 ft	Illuminators did not illuminate factory
				Sgt Storey R.	F/E				on first or second run, only river and
				F/O Carey B.	Nav				Wood.
				Sgt King C.P.	B/A				Flak hole in port wing. Trailing aerial
				Sgt Jenkins H.	W/Op				shot away
				Sgt Cox R. J. M.	M/U				
				Sgt Bland J.A.	R/G				Landed Tangmere
Lancaster	ED831	WS-H	9	F/O Fox C.W.	Capt	21:20	05:40	02:07	Green TI seen then Illuminators.
				Sgt Pratt J.	F/E			6,000 ft	These showed only woods.
				Sgt Hodson W.H.	Nav				
				Sgt Piper J.	B/A				
				Sgt Robinson T.N.	W/Op				
				Sgt Russel P.	M/U				
				Sgt Sargent C.F.	R/G				
Lancaster	W4133	WS-S	9	P/O Boczar S.	Capt RCAF	21:27	06:00	01:48	One green TI seen far side of
				Sgt Vinall J.	F/E			10,000 ft	Illuminators. Failed to light up factory
				P/O Carrere J.P.H.	Nav RCAF				owing to haze and smoke.
				Sgt Watts C.S.	B/A				
				Sgt Webb R.S.	W/Op				
				F/S Burgar R.K.	M/U				
				F/S Browell G.W.	R/G				
Lancaster	ED836	WS-T	9	Sgt Turp K.	Capt	21:25	05:55	01:58	Green TI seen. Nickels dropped over
				Sgt Bailey D.	F/E			6,000 ft	target. Contact with fighter.
				P/O Clark H.A.	Nav				
				Sgt Freeze W.	B/A				
				Sgt Pimm J.E.W.	W/Op				
				Sgt Silvester S.E.	M/U				
				Sgt Shelmerdine T.P.	R/G				Landed Tangmere

A Shaky do-The Skoda Works Raid of 16/17th April 1943

AIRCRAFT	SERIAL	CODE	SQN	CREW	TRADE	UP	DOWN	BOMBED	NOTES
Lancaster	ED499	WS-X	9	F/L Robertson G.F.	Capt	21:24	06:02	01:45	No green TI seen. Flares seen but
PANIC II				Sgt Nunez G.A.	2nd Pilot			8,000 ft	failed to penetrate thick smoke
				Sgt Brown W. E.	F/E				Nunez from Trinidad, lost ops Essen 1
				P/O Smith R.H.	Nav				may/Photo ED499
				P/O Knell E.J.	B/A				
				F/S Greene K.	W/Op				
				Sgt. Pelly J.	A/G				
				Sgt Allan G.	A/G				Landed Tangmere
Lancaster	ED654	WS-W	9	Sgt. McCubbin J.	Capt	21:24	05:43	01:56	Made three runs. Too much smoke to
Cutty Sark				Sgt Owen N.D.	F/E				7,000 ft ID'd factory
				Sgt SherryB.	Nav				
				Sgt Dagnall K.J 'Joe'	B/A				
				Sgt Smith A.M.	W/Op				
				Sgt Lynam P.	M/U				
				Sgt Stewart C.	R/G				
Lancaster	ED480	WS-U	9	Sgt Saxton G.	Capt	21:35	06:04	Not known	All crew KIA 13th May on Plzen op
				Sgt Ferris D.C.	F/E				
				Sgt Macdonald W.C. RCAF	Nav				
				Sgt Morris R.M.	B/A				
				Sgt Reddish J.	W/Op				
				Sgt Owen J.C.	M/U				
				Sgt Buntin J.	R/G				Landed West Malling
Lancaster	ED799	WS-G	9	F/O Hale C.A.	Capt	21:18	05:45	01:45	Green markers only seen after
				Sgt Dodds J.G.	F/E			7,000 ft	bombing. Saw bursts of many other
				Sgt Powell R	Nav				aircraft
				Sgt Hales G.E.	B/A				
				Sgt Piper R.V.	W/Op				
				Sgt Clark C.	M/U				
				Sgt Jones H.L.	R/G				

171

A Shaky do-The Skoda Works Raid of 16/17th April 1943

AIRCRAFT	SERIAL	CODE	SQN	CREW	TRADE	UP	DOWN	BOMBED	NOTES
Halifax	DT785	ZA-Q	10	F/L Munro	Capt	20:57	06:32	01:39	Visual ID
				Sgt Arriette C.M.	Nav			8,500 ft	
				F/S Deveraux	W/OP				4x1000 1x500 Gp
				F/S Butler C.T.	A/B				
				F/S Robinson	M/U				
				Sgt Langworthy A.L.	F/E				
				Sgt McDougle G.O. D.F.M.	R/G				
				Sgt Winn	2nd pilot				
Halifax	JB910	ZA-R	10	F/S Virgo W. RAAF	Capt	21:02	06:56	01:45	
				Sgt Furlong N.J.	Nav			7,000 ft	4x1000 1x500 Gp
				Sgt Hulley J.R.	A/B				
				Sgt Driver A.	W/OP				
				Sgt Tester D.	M/U				
				Sgt Gabbut	F/E				
				F/S Hill W.L.H.	R/G				Shot down a Bf110 near Rethel
				Sgt Solomon	2nd Pilot				
Halifax	HR691	ZA-W	10	F/O Dawes A.R.	Capt	21:15	06:00	01:36	
				P/O Parry A.W. RCAF	Nav			10,000 ft	
				Sgt Bradshaw R.	A/B				4x1000 1x500 Gp
				Sgt Johnson J.L.	W/OP				
				F/S Brennan D. RCAF/US	M/U				Also did two tours with USAAF
				Sgt Edwards A.G.	F/E				
				Sgt McDaniel H.H.L. RCAF	R/G				D.F.C. 1st Sept. 1943 Bn. Dublin 1919

A Shaky do-The Skoda Works Raid of 16/17th April 1943

AIRCRAFT	SERIAL	CODE	SQN	CREW		TRADE	UP	DOWN	BOMBED	NOTES
Halifax	HR697	ZA-F	10	S/L Frank A.D.		Capt	20:52	05:45	02:05	Bombs wouldn't release over target.
				W/O E.W. Todd		Nav				Dropped live 52 Miles N.E. Nurnberg.
				F/L Minchinton G.G.		A/B				S/L Frank Flew Battles in 1940 & was
				F/S Harris V.A.		W/OP				83 sqn Vulcan c/o May 1957
				Sgt. Fletcher A.		M/U				eventually A.V.M. DSO DFC CBE CB
				Sgt McCann T.L.		F/E				4x1000 1x500 Gp
				P/O Fynn N.D.		R/G				
Halifax	DT791	ZA-K	10	F/L Wood J.A. 'Timber'		Capt				Crash landed Lewes. P.O. u/s flak ov'r
				P/O Whynes K.F.		Nav				target. At channel coast Port/l hit
				P/O Stepney G.C.		A/B				believed flak. Crossed channel on two
				Sgt Walshaw G.		W/OP				eng. A/c written off
				Sgt. O'Kill P.G.		M/U				8 crew injured
				Sgt. Beare F.W.		F/E				4x1000 1x500 Gp
				Sgt Prebble F.N.	RCAF	R/G				
				Sgt Rooney R.W.S.	RAAF	2nd Pilot				Rooney 1658 CU D.F.C. LG 06/10/1944
										Did tour with 640 sqn.
Halifax	HR698	ZA-E	10	P/O Hollis		Capt	20:53	05:39	01:47	Attack made visually, some icbs seen
				Sgt Poulton A.C.	RCAF	Nav			10,000 ft	moderate opposition
				F/S Craft		A/B				4x1000 1x500 Gp
				Sgt Bullock K.J.		W/OP				
				Sgt Larkins		M/U				
				Sgt Blair A.L.		F/E				
				F/S Gardner		R/G				
Halifax II	DT784	ZA-M	10	Sgt Cozens R.W.		Capt	20:51	06:15	01:40?	Green markers
				Sgt Davies C.E.		Nav			10,000 ft	
				Sgt Harris D.		A/B				4x1000 1x500 Gp
				Sgt Fenwick J.E.		W/OP				
				Sgt Taylor		M/U				
				Sgt Moss A.L.		F/E				
				Sgt Atkinson J.		R/G				

A Shaky do-The Skoda Works Raid of 16/17th April 1943

AIRCRAFT	SERIAL	CODE	SQN	CREW	TRADE	UP	DOWN	BOMBED	NOTES
Halifax II Z	DT789	ZA-A	10	F/O Vinish G.A.	Capt	20:46	06:15	01:48	Light flak +6 searchlights over target
				F/O Kitchen E.E.	Nav			9,000 ft	4x1000 1x500 Gp
				F/S Janes A.J.	A/B				
				Sgt Black A.E.	W/OP				Landed Enstone
				Sgt Heap R.E.	M/U				
				Sgt Crouch A.J.	F/E				
				Sgt Rafferty E.H.	R/G				
				Sgt Hatchard	2nd Pilot				
Halifax II Z	HR695	ZA-D	10	Sgt Wade G.K.	Capt	20:46	06:15	01:45	Visual ID & markers. Haze and 8/10ths
				P/O O'Toole W. G.	Nav			4,000 ft	Cloud hinderd ID.
				Sgt Pullen N.	A/B				Smasmodic flak, few lights
				Sgt Gale R.A.	W/OP				4x1000 1x500 Gp
				Sgt Beaton A.N.	M/U				
				Sgt Gladwell	F/E				
				Sgt Hainsworth R.	R/G				
				Sgt Knox J.	2nd Pilot				
Halifax II	DT786	ZA-P	10	Sgt Beveridge G.T.	Capt	20:56	05:55	01:45	Visual ID & markers
				Sgt Gordon-Powell				11,000 ft	
				Sgt Billet H.C.					4x1000 1x500 Gp
				Sgt Taylor R.J.					
				Sgt Hughes W.					
				Sgt Carey L.E.					
				Sgt Compton F.C.					
Halifax II	JB930	ZA-H	10	Sgt Glover F.	Capt	20:55	06:05	01:55	Visual ID & markers
				Sgt Taylor D.E.	Nav			11,000 ft	3 small flak hits starboard & port
				Sgt Bell R.	A/B				wing. 9 search lights in target area
				Sgt Phillips E.J.	W/OP				4x1000 1x500 Gp
				Sgt Hobbs F.	M/U				
				Sgt Burr R.S.	F/E				
				Sgt Everett R.E.	R/G				

A Shaky do-The Skoda Works Raid of 16/17th April 1943

AIRCRAFT	SERIAL	CODE	SQN	CREW		TRADE	UP	DOWN	BOMBED	NOTES
Lancaster III	ED408	PH-A	12	Sgt G Elsworthy		Pilot				All this crew and aircraft lost April
				Sgt Pye E.A.		F/E				28/29th Gardening in the Baltic
				F/O Vierra B.V.L.	RCAF	Nav				
				P/O Haddow J.L.		A/B				
				F/S Freeman W.E.		W/op				
				Sgt Downes C.W.S.		M/U				
				Sgt Grant R.C.		R/G				
Lancaster I	W4366	PH-R	12	Sgt Mizon W F	RAAF	Pilot				Three of crew baled out not hearing
				Sgt Peckham H. E.		F/E				rescinded order over intercom.
				Sgt Stenborg H. O.	RAAF	Nav				
				Sgt Smale T.G.		A/B				
				Sgt Hutton T. H.		W/op				Evaded
				Sgt McKay J. A.	RCAF	A/G				POW
				Sgt Rudkin L.		A/G				Evaded
Lancaster III	ED818	PH-Y	12	S/L J C Richards		Pilot				
				F/O G F Jones		Nav				
				Sgt H V Durrant		F/E				
				Sgt F T Peake		Wop/Ag				
				Sgt L A Rummery		A/B				
				Sgt W J Colwill		M/U				
				P/O R P Cryer		R/G				
Lancaster 1	ED357	PH-S	12	Sgt Tribe D.	RCAF	Pilot				Flew very low level
				F/O Furrell H.		Nav				
				Sgt Collier G.		F/E				
				Sgt Moore G.		A/B				
				Sgt Thompson T.		Wop/Ag				
				Sgt Hilldebrand H.		M/U				
				Sgt Hill J.		R/G				

A Shaky do-The Skoda Works Raid of 16/17th April 1943

AIRCRAFT	SERIAL	CODE	SQN	CREW	TRADE	UP	DOWN	BOMBED	NOTES
Lancaster I	ED522	PH-U	12	Sgt Lawrence C. DFM	Pilot				
				F/O Kettles W.M.	Nav				
				Sgt Jackson A	Wop/ag				
				F/S Cruse B C RCAF	A/B				
				Sgt Harper P H J	M/U				
				Sgt Hill W G	F/E				
				Sgt Drake C	R/G				
Lancaster I	ED548	PH-X	12	F/L Potts J. W.	Pilot				
				F/Sgt Sheldon					
				F/Sgt Hall K. DFM					
				Sgt Thomas					
				P/O Stewart					
				Sgt Martin R.					
				Sgt Harris J.S.					
Lancaster I	W4380	PH-E	12	F/S Head L.W.G. D.F.M.	Pilot	21:30			Missed target and bombed a railway Junction. Shot up three trains. All this crew lost April 28/29th Gardening in the Baltic.
				Sgt Short J	Nav				
				Sgt Gibbs F.G.R.	Wop/ag				
				Sgt Willatt J.	A/B				
				Sgt Murphy P.T.	M/U				
				Sgt Wensley H.H	F/E				
				Sgt Payne D.W.	R/G				
Lancaster I			12	Unknown crew					
				*					
				*					
				*					
				*					
				*					
				*					

A Shaky do-The Skoda Works Raid of 16/17th April 1943

AIRCRAFT	SERIAL	CODE	SQN.	CREW		TRADE	UP	DOWN	BOMBED	NOTES
Lancaster I			12	Unknown crew						
				*						
				*						
				*						
				*						
				*						
Halifax	JB787	TL-Z	35	S/L Lane R.J.	RCAF	Capt	21:11	05:36	01:32	Ground marker
				W/O Bodnar B.	RCAF	A/B			14,000 ft	6x4 white flares dropped by H2s by
				S/L Tricket R.I.		Nav			010° mag	DR from Straubing Yellow TIs
				P/O Thorpe L.S.	RCAF	W/op/Ag				dropped there at 01:12
				Sgt. Tulloch D.		R/G				Coned over Frankfurt
				F/S Seannal J.		M/U				
				F/S Haxby H.		F/E				
Halifax	DT804	TL-G	35	S/L Johnson P.		Capt	21:13	05:48	01:50	Ground marker
				P/O Wood R.		A/B			11,000 ft	1 long burning TI & 6x4 white flares
				F/L Powell P.G.		Nav			330° mag	Dropped. Pinpoint obtained on river
				F/S Royall B.T.	RCAF	W/op/Ag				Green TIs already there.
				P/O Rogers H.J.		R/G				Attacked by fighter Crailsheim 00:30
				Sgt. Cowan A.W.	RCAF	M/U				14,000 ft. Sustained burst tyre &
				Sgt Jarvis F.J.		F/E				bullet holes.
Halifax	BB320	TL-S	35	F/L Lane T.H.	RCAF	Capt	21:14	23:31	Returned	22:40 from 50.05N-01.30 E
				W/O Darling G.W.		A/B				Ground marker
				F/O Jackson P.M.		Nav				3 guns unserviceable
				F/S Balson A.P.	RAAF	W/op/Ag				1 TI Yellow 2xTI Grn, 2x TI red & 6x4
				F/S MacDonald R.H.		R/G				Flares brought back
				F/O Alexander D.R.		M/U				
				F/S Rogers F.J.		F/E				

A Shaky do-The Skoda Works Raid of 16/17th April 1943

AIRCRAFT	SERIAL	CODE	SQN	CREW	TRADE	UP	DOWN	BOMBED	NOTES
Halifax	W7873	TL-M	35	F/L Owen W.R.	Capt	21:16	POW		Shot down by Lt Helmut Bergmann StbIII./NJG4 23.03 hrs Sevigny
				Sgt Martyn J.R. RCAF	A/B		KIA		Equipped H2s, 4x250lb TI, 24 flares
				P/O Cruickshank G.	Nav		KIA		
				F/S Bradley V.R.	W/op/Ag		Evaded		
				F/S Bourne J.F.	R/G		KIA		
				Sgt Young J.W.	M/U		KIA		
				F/S Allen W.G.	F/E		Evaded		
Halifax	W7825	TL-V	35	F/L Howe S.G.	Capt	21:17	05:27	01:49	Ground marker
				F/O Watts G.P.	A/B			14,000 ft	Flares fell amongst others.
				P/O Burgess W.H.	Nav			330° mag	Green TI not dropped as target not ID'd. H2s Unserviceable.
				F/S Jamieson H.A. RNZAF	W/op/Ag				
				F/S Barry F.W. RCAF	R/G				6 this crew lost on DT805 ops
				W/O Dunhill W.E.	M/U				Munster
				Sgt Mundy H.	F/E				12th June '43, 5 pow 1 (Howe), kia
Halifax	DT803	TL-O	35	F/L Cranswick A.P.	Capt	21:18	05:34	01:35	Illuminator
				Sgt Williams A.T.	A/B			14,000 ft	6x4 white flares dropped
				W/O McRobbie W.	Nav			028° mag	Aiming point not I.D.'d
				F/S McKenzie D.	W/op/Ag				1 TI green & 1 LB TI green dropped in
				F/S Howard D.	R/G				light of flares. 2 TI Red & 1yellow
				Sgt. Arnott M.	M/U				brought back, not required.
				Sgt. Johnson F.	F/E				
Halifax	DT801	TL-A	35	F/L Sale J. RCAF	Capt	21:19	05:53	01:40	Illuminator
				P/O Sawyer R.C.	A/B			14,000 ft	6X4 White flares
				P/O Heard G.E.	Nav			01:50	
				Sgt Moores S.A.	W/op/Ag			6,500ft	1TI Green+ 1 Lb TI Red Dropped vis.
				Sgt Richards D.N.	R/G			010° mag	
				Sgt Elford R.O.	M/U				
				Sgt Rowley C.W.	F/E				

A Shaky do-The Skoda Works Raid of 16/17th April 1943

AIRCRAFT	SERIAL	CODE	SQN	CREW	TRADE	UP	DOWN	BOMBED	NOTES
Halifax	W7779	TL-U	35	Sgt Petrie-Andrews J.R.	Capt	21:20	06:01	01:54	Main Force
				Sgt. Backhouse H.J.	A/B			10,000 ft	Port wing +bomb doors hit, hvy flak
				P/O Armitage J.W.	Nav			030°	
				Sgt Berwick R.B.	W/op/Ag				
				Sgt Barnet N.W.	R/G				
				Sgt Dale G.	M/U				
				Sgt Morgan J.H.	F/E				
Halifax	DT489	TL-Y	35	F/L Pexton H.C.	Capt	21:20	06:07	02:05	Main Force
				Sgt. Fenton F.	A/B			14,000 ft	3x1000lb dropped on Green TI.
				Sgt Hughes C.D.	Nav			045° Mag	Several sticks of ICBs seen betw'n TIs
				Sgt Weldon C.J.	W/op/Ag				WT & Gee U/s due to enemy action at
				Sgt Walters W.O.R.	R/G				Mannheim 03:08 hrs. Ammo track &
				P/O Warren J.W.	M/U				petrol tank damaged
				P/O Stocker E.E.	F/E				Landed Ford
Halifax	DT805	TL-T	35	F/L MacDonald H.B.	Capt	21:26	23:59	Returned	22:47 From 6 mile South of Abbeville
				F/L Rome K.D.	A/B				6 guns and H2s unserviceable
				F/L Baker J.	Nav				
				F/S Whitter E.	W/op/Ag				
				F/S Carpenter G.	R/G				
				F/S Ely J.R.	M/U				
				F/S Jones J.E.	F/E				
Lancaster	W4936	KM-W	44	P/O Taylor H.H. DFM	Capt	21:09	05:49	01:59	No target attacked bombs dropped
				Sgt Baczinski M.	F/E			12,000 ft	over Germany
				F/S More E.G.	Nav			270°	
				Sgt Hutchinson J.A.	B/A				
				Sgt Cass R.	W/op				
				Sgt Betteley L	M/U				
				F/S Bursey W.E.	R/G				
				P/O Wallace	2nd Pilot				

AIRCRAFT	SERIAL	CODE	SQN	CREW	TRADE	UP	DOWN	BOMBED	NOTES
Lancaster	W4961	KM-S	44	F/O Pilgrim L.W.	Capt	21:19	06:21	01:49	Markers late at Position C, the
				Sgt Skilton J.A.	F/E			9,000 ft	last turning point at Straubing on the
				P/O Benner K.J.	Nav			030°	River Danube (Danau).
				Sgt Williams J.O.	B/A				
				Sgt Fanning G.	W/op				
				Sgt Short G.T.	M/U				
				Sgt Kethro R.M.	R/G				
Lancaster	W4838	KM-B	44	S/L Jennings P.N.	Capt	21:15	06:00	01:50	Nickels dropped
				Sgt Stamford J.W.E.	F/E			8000 ft	Bombs aimed to overshoot Green TIs.
				P/O Parker F.	Nav			038°	
				Sgt Tibbs R.	B/A				
				Sgt Ball P.	W/op				
				P/O Etheridge R.C.	M/U				
				Sgt Dearman D.	R/G				
				Sgt Cockbain	2nd Pilot				
Lancaster	R5740	KM-O	44	F/Sgt Shnier C. RCAF	Capt	21:10	06:00	01:45	ABS bomb sight full auto
				Sgt Gibbons A.N.	F/E			10,000 ft	Nose of aircraft damaged heavy flak
				Sgt Laidler N.	Nav			360° mag	Over Nürnberg at 7,000 ft for 7
				Sgt Wigley H.T.	B/A				minutes
				Sgt Evans P.C.	W/op				
				Sgt Knoesen B.G.	M/U				
				Sgt Croft D.E.	R/G				Pilot M/U & R/G Killed 29/30 July
				Sgt Gollogey	2nd Pilot				Ops Hamburg 97 sqn
Lancaster	W4949	KM-H	44	Sgt Shearman P.J.	Capt	21:18	06:40	01:57	Holes in Port rudder
				Sgt Pugh E.L.	F/E			9,000	Illuminator flares and green TIs seen
				Sgt Ballamy N.L.	Nav			360° mag	Nickels distributed in target area
				Sgt Smith A.R.	B/A				
				Sgt Card B.W.	W/op				
				Sgt Zedy G.C.A.	M/U				
				Sgt Akeister C.W.	R/G				

A Shaky do-The Skoda Works Raid of 16/17th April 1943

AIRCRAFT	SERIAL	CODE	SQN	CREW		TRADE	UP	DOWN	BOMBED	NOTES
Lancaster	ED611	KM-J	44	Sgt Pennington J.C.		Capt	21:17	05:46	01:47	Nickels dropped 10 miles before
				Sgt Dowding K. B.		2nd Pilot			8,000 ft	target
				Sgt Morrison D.		F/E			048° mag	Duration 8 hrs 30
				Sgt Hewitt J.R.		Nav				
				Sgt Hawkes L.		B/A				
				Sgt Betts D.	RCAF	W/op	Odd bod.			Did 2nd tour with 582 PFF sqn.
				Sgt Harrall W.A.		M/U				
				Sgt Homewood G.		R/G				
Lancaster	ED716	KM-L	44	F/L Robinson R.D.		Capt	21:21	05:53	00:45	Bombs dropped Munich. Coned and
				Sgt Metalfe N.		2nd Pilot			9,000 ft	ran into full defences there
				Sgt Hayward E.E.C.		F/E			104°mag	Cont. to target to keep with stream.
				F/O St. C. Millar A.A.		Nav				Rear turret u/s earlier in journey
				Sgt Parsons L.A.T		B/A				
				Sgt Woodgate A.J.		W/op				
				Sgt Broome F.P.L.		M/U				
				Sgt Weller G.M.E.		R/G				
Lancaster	W4268	KM-Q	44	F/O Moodie D.M.		Capt	21:26	06:18	01:57	Small hole port wing
				Sgt Melbourne L.F.		F/E			8,000 ft	bullet holes in fuselage
				Sgt Bundle J.T.		Nav			020° mag	Flares illuminated rivers
				Sgt Clausen H.W.N.		B/A				
				Sgt Stamp T.F.		W/op				
				Sgt Drummond L.A.		M/U				
				Sgt Hughes F.A.		R/G				
Lancaster	ED307	KM-R	44	F/L Haywood G.B.		Capt	21:20	06:30	02:00	Coned over Nürnberg took evasive
				Sgt Foot R.G.		F/E			7,000 ft	action
				F/L Asson B.		Nav			035° mag	
				Sgt Boardman R.		B/A				
				Sgt Rivers R.W.		W/op				
				Sgt Brand R.C.H.		M/U				
				Sgt Armstrong J.H.		R/G				

A Shaky do-The Skoda Works Raid of 16/17th April 1943

AIRCRAFT	SERIAL	CODE	SQN	CREW		TRADE	UP	DOWN	BOMBED	NOTES
Lancaster	ED723	KM-U	44	Sgt Drysdale J.L.	RCAF	Capt	21:16	06:24	01:50	Smoke over target
				Sgt Lester J.F.		F/E			8,000 ft	All crew and a/c lost on ops to
				P/O Marsden W.A.		Nav			091° mag	Dortmund 23/24th May
				Sgt Hyett H.W.E.		B/A				
				Sgt Jones S.		W/op				
				Sgt Bushill A.S.		M/U				
				Sgt Doherty F.A.	RCAF	R/G				
Lancaster III	ED783	KM-F	44	Sgt Ellis L.J.		Capt	21:47	05:56	01:45	Illuminator flares lit up area. Grn TIs
				Sgt Le Page R.L.		F/E			7,000 ft	Seen after leaving. 'Factory' chimney
				Sgt Rollings W.A.	RCAF	Nav			90-40° mag	Seen in bomb sight. Flares caused
				Sgt Browne J.B		B/A				glare.
				Sgt Ellis H.C.		W/op				
				Sgt Williams R.		M/U				
				Sgt McClellan S.S.		R/G				
Lancaster	R5733	KM-P	44	Sgt Sharp D.M.		Capt	21:13	06:46	01:54	Green TIs western edge. Red TIs in
				Sgt Johnstone T.		F/E			8,500 ft	bomb sight. Fires at Mannheim seen
				Sgt Dash R.J.		Nav			045°Mag	70 miles away.
				Sgt Palmer D.J.N.		B/A				
				Sgt Morris N.H.		W/op				
				Sgt Griffiths E.R.H.		M/U				
				Sgt Langstaff K.W.		R/G				
Lancaster	ED441	EA-E	49	Sgt Penry D.T.		Capt	21:11	KIA		Crashed Camon, Somme Abt. 05:00
				Sgt Bamford C.G.		F/E		KIA		
				F/S Dixon A.M.		Nav.B		KIA		
				Sgt Robertson R.C.		WT/AG		KIA		1260x4lb incendiaries
				Sgt Fletcher J.F.		A/G		KIA		
				Sgt James C.L.		A/B		KIA		
				Sgt Kerr H.W.G.		A/G		P.O.W.		

A Shaky do-The Skoda Works Raid of 16/17th April 1943

AIRCRAFT	SERIAL	CODE	SQN	CREW	TRADE	UP	DOWN	BOMBED	NOTES
Lancaster	ED427	EA-O	49	F/O Bone A.V.	Capt	21:14	KIA		Crashed due to Flak 02:00 flying west
				Sgt Foster N.	F/E		KIA		at Laumersheim
				Sgt Yelland C.W.	Nav/B		KIA		1x4000lb 2x1000lb .025
				Sgt White R.C.	WT/RG		KIA		
				Sgt Cope R.	A/G		KIA		
				Sgt Rooney R.J.	A/B		KIA		
				Sgt Watt B.E.　RCAF	A/G		KIA		
Lancaster	ED597	EA-	49	F/L Allsebrook R.A.P.	Capt	21:12	06:27	01:47	Running in on 040° when green TI
				Sgt Moore P.	F/E			6,000 ft	went down ahead. Many cookies
				W/O Botting N.A.	Nav			040°	seen to burst.
				F/O Grant J.M.	Wop				Moore listed as Front gunner
				F/L Bain J.	M/U				in his log book
				Sgt Lulham R.B.S.	A/B				
				Sgt Hitchen S.	R/G				
				S/L Storey G.G.	2nd Pilot				Landed Scampton
Lancaster	ED805	EA-S	49	S/L Gilpin G.W.	Capt	21:13	05:45	01:48	Saw attack open and made three runs
				Sgt Taylor J.T.	F/E			8,000 ft	at target
				Sgt Pennels P.	Nav				
				Sgt Wynn J.	Wop				
				Sgt Lund E.E.T.	M/U				
				Sgt Wilkinson H.	A/B				
				F/S Cook T.S.	R/G				
Lancaster	ED426	EA-	49	Sgt Price J.N.　USA	Capt	21:17	06:00	01:46	One green Ti seen 1 mile sth of A.P.
				Sgt Pearman T.F.	F/E			7,000 ft	ID by PFF & positive pinpoint.
				Sgt Potts D.E.	Nav				Tall chimney seen in bomb sight
				Sgt Greavison H.E.	Wop				
				Sgt King A.L.	M/U				
				Sgt Glover G.G.	A/B				
				Sgt Hefferon	R/G				

A Shaky do-The Skoda Works Raid of 16/17th April 1943

AIRCRAFT	SERIAL	CODE	SQN	CREW	TRADE	UP	DOWN	BOMBED	NOTES
Lancaster	ED702	EA-	49	W/Co Johnson	Capt	21:15	05:52	01:44	ID'd by woods south west of target.
				Sgt Gottwaltz	F/E				Made two runs. First run Id'd factory.
				P/O Kelly P.	Nav				second run smoke prevented this
				Sgt Hudson J.W.	Wop				
				Sgt Hall	M/U				
				Sgt Taylor R	A/B				
				F/O Chandler	R/G				
Lancaster III	ED448	EA-	49	Sgt Tolchard L.N.	Capt	21:16	05:56	01:59	Visibility 5 miles. Skoda works clearly
				Sgt Best A.E.	F/E			8,000 ft	ID'd. Fired at by a Lancaster 3/4th
			28th op	F/O Hastings L.R.	Nav				April ops Essen and by own guns at
				F/S Arnold V.M.	Wop				Folkestone on ops Stuttgart
				Sgt Doe D.	M/U				14/15th April
				F/S Coburn G.W.	A/B				8 hrs 40 mins.
				Sgt Porter G.H. RCAF	R/G				
Lancaster III	ED784	VN-N	50	F/O Elderfield H	Capt	21:43	KIA		Elderfield missing. Ditched 6 miles off
				Sgt Chambers R.	F/E				French coast approx. 04:00 17th April
				Sgt Laing J. M.	Nav				Damaged by Fighters +flak
				Sgt Hinchcliffe H.	A/B		KIA	Drowned	Crew picked up by M.T.B. 18th April
				Sgt Harman R.S.	Wop/Ag				1260x4lb Incendiaries
				Sgt Hammond J.	M/U				Equipped Gee, IFF
				Sgt Webster H.	R/G				Aircraft came down near Berck-sur-mer
				P/O Cotter P. C.	2nd Nav		KIA	Drowned	
Lancaster III	ED800	VN-O	50	Sgt J G Duncan	Capt				Shot down by
				Sgt Spiers J.	F/E				Wilhelm Herget Stab I./NJG4
				Sgt Smellie D. M.	Nav				Yves-Gomezée 2.500 m. 04.23
				Sgt Bates J.A.	A/B				
				Sgt Payne C.	Wop/Ag				
				Sgt Berry A. W.	M/U				
				Sgt Barnes H R	R/G				

A Shaky do-The Skoda Works Raid of 16/17th April 1943

AIRCRAFT	SERIAL	CODE	SQN	CREW	TRADE	UP	DOWN	BOMBED	NOTES
Lancaster III	ED712	VN-T	50	F/S Weber A.J.	Capt	21:39	00:07		Return'd to base due to Pilot sickness
				Sgt Carter M.C.	F/E				
				F/S Felsen M.R. RCAF	Nav				
				F/S Norman F.	A/B				
				Sgt Goldstraw R	Wop/Ag				
				P/O Ferguson C.W. RNZAF	M/U				
				Sgt Kerley R.C.	R/G				
Lancaster III	ED468	VN-A	50	P/O Chopping D.H.	Capt			Nürnberg	Circled target 3 times. Two rows of
				Sgt Wooding F.A	F/E				Regular red lights see. Pilot convinced
				F/O Parsons E.	Nav				dummy target. Coned and chased by
				F/O Webster M.D.	A/B				JU88 fighter on this sortie.
				Sgt Thomas A.J.	Wop/Ag				
				Sgt Twitchett T.F.	M/U				
				Sgt Ruppert J. C.	R/G				
Lancaster III	ED475	VN-D	50	F/O Hollis A N	Capt	21:32	06:01	01:43	'Factory' clearly seen in light of flares
				Sgt Adshead D.S.	F/E			7,000 ft	Czech Nickels dropped over target
				F/O Palmer R. RCAF	Nav				and German Nickels over Germany
				Sgt Cheshire T.G.	A/B				
				Sgt Kemp R. A.	Wop/Ag				8 hrs 30 duration
				Sgt Yates R.G.	M/U				
				Sgt Walker W.	R/G				
Lancaster	ED691	VN-K	50	F/O Day H.H.	Capt	21:31	FTR	KIA	Shot down by fighters 00:30 near
				Sgt Salmon R.C.	F/E			P.O.W	Epense, Challons Sur Marne.
				Sgt Holland H.E. RAAF	Nav			P.O.W	Holland Initially in Rennes prison
				Sgt Rossbotham J.A.	Wop/Ag			P.O.W	Equipped Gee
				Sgt Hodgkinson G.A.E.	A/B			P.O.W.	
				Sgt Evans M.I.	M/U			P.O.W.	
				Sgt Symes S.R.A.	R/G			P.O.W.	Bomb load 1260x4lb ICB
				F/O Trotman D.A.	2nd Pilot			Evaded to	Switzerland

A Shaky do-The Skoda Works Raid of 16/17th April 1943

AIRCRAFT	SERIAL	CODE	SQN	CREW	TRADE	UP	DOWN	BOMBED	NOTES
Lancaster	ED693	VN-B	50	Sgt Duncan D.A.	Capt	21:33	06:49	01:48	Good concentration of fires
				Sgt Cable C.				8,000 ft	9 hrs 35 Minutes in the air
				Sgt Evans W.J.					
				Sgt Hayter R.L.					
				Sgt Fulton J.					
				Sgt Dooley I.C.V.					
				Sgt White K.D.					
Lancaster	ED810	VN-Z	50	Sgt McCrossen J.M.	Capt	21:36	06:04	01:43	Outline of factory buildings bombed
				Sgt Wilkinson J.T.				8,000 ft	Believed Skoda Works. Dummy fires
				Sgt Buchan D.McD					seen S.W. of target
				Sgt Morgan J.K.					
				Sgt Stewart G.L.					
				Sgt Stone H.R.					
				Sgt Aitken J.A.					
Lancaster	ED828	VN-S	50	S/L Birch P.C.		21:41	06:07	02:01	Searched the target for 25 mins.
				Sgt Mooney W.				7,000 ft	decided flares did not cover target.
				P/O Medani J.	DFM				bombed factory in proximity of target
				F/S Allan S.					Many 4000lb seen to burst in open
				F/L Wood E.C.J.					country
				F/O Gray C.W.					Fighters over Mannheim
				Sgt Hartman J.M.					
				F/O Lewis					
Lancaster	ED755?	VN-	50	F/L Gilmour B.M.	Capt	21:30	05:57	01:58	Attacked several railway engines and
				Sgt W.J. Madder				8,000 ft	airfield at Leon-Athies
				F/O Benefield C.F.					
				F/O Mathieson R.M.					
				F/O Randle T.E.					
				Sgt Box G.					
				Sgt Tanner A.					
				Sgt Garvey					

A Shaky do-The Skoda Works Raid of 16/17th April 1943

AIRCRAFT	SERIAL	CODE	SQN	CREW	TRADE	UP	DOWN	BOMBED	NOTES
Halifax II	DT690	MH-A Bar	51	Sgt McCrea J.E.	Pilot	20:32	McCrea	4x1000 GP 1x500 MC	Shot down Missy les Pierrepont approx 03:25 Probably by Hptm. Haesler I./NJG4
				F/O Spencer D.G.	Nav		Evaded		
				Sgt Ings C.B.	A/B		P.O.W.		
				F/S Simpson J.E.C.	W/Op		P.O.W.		killed after war in flying accident.
				Sgt Allerdice J.	F/E		Evaded		
				Sgt Davis A.W.	M/U		P.O.W.		
				Sgt Jones D.L.	R/G		Evaded		
Halifax II	DT670	MH-M	51	Sgt Inch D.M.	Pilot	20:23	KIA		Oblt Hans Autenrieth 6./NJG4 Pocancy 3600 metres 03:50
				Sgt Riley H.	Nav		Evaded		
				F/O Clements R.F.	A/B		KIA		
				F/S Lancaster E.L. RAAF	W/OP		Injured	Died hospit'l	Injured crash Wimpy HE102 15 OTU Hampstead Norris 11 Sep 1942
				Sgt Hayden T.P.	F/E		KIA		Bomb load 4x1000 GP 1x500 MC
				Sgt Dards E.P.	M/U		P.O.W		1x500? Equipped Gee
				Sgt Mumme R.M.	R/G		KIA		
Halifax II	DT561	MH-K	51	Sgt Cox E.W.	Pilot	20:46	KIA		Shot down at Hadamar. Lt Otto Blohm 10./NJG4
				Sgt Burt R.G.	Nav		KIA		
				Sgt McCardle F.G. RCAF	A/B		KIA		
				Sgt Rogers W.A.	W/OP		KIA		4x1000 GP 1 x 500 MC
				Sgt Briffett S.J.	F/E		KIA		Equipped Gee R3003S
				Sgt Bray L.R.	M/U		KIA		
				Sgt McLaren R.A.	R/G		KIA		

AIRCRAFT	SERIAL	CODE	SQN	CREW	TRADE	UP	DOWN	BOMBED	NOTES
Halifax II	HR729	MH-R	51	W/O Edwards J.G.	Pilot	20:43	KIA		Shot down by fighter Bechtolsheim
				Sgt Kitchen R.D.	2nd Pilot		KIA		Lt Hebert Jung 12./NJG4 02:32
				F/O Brisbane W.C.	A/B		KIA		
				Sgt Lewis A.O.	Nav		KIA		4x1000lb GP 1x500 lb MC
				F/O Marriot J.W.	W/OP		POW		
				Sgt Roberts	F/E		KIA		
				Sgt Ray H.	M/U		KIA		
				F/O Walters L.	R/G		KIA		
Halifax II	HR784	MH-	51	F/S Stewart R.H. RCAF	Pilot	20:42	KIA		Shot down by fighter Eppeville
				W/O Keirnan W.R. D.F.M.	Nav		POW		Hptm Hans-Karl Kamp 04:36
				F/O Robinson T.C.	A/B		KIA		4x1000 1x500 MC
				F/S Axtell D. D.F.M.	W/OP		KIA		Equipped Gee, R3003A, IFF
				Sgt McBriar W.R.	F/E		KIA		
				Sgt Reid D.H.	M/U		KIA		
				Sgt Thompson F.M.	R/G		KIA		
Halifax II	W1212	MH-	51	F/S Collins J.H.	Pilot	20:36	05:40	01:43	Many HE seen exploding & buildings
				Sgt Green L.	Nav			8,000 ft	disintegrating.
				Sgt Parker J.H.	A/B				On return trip, fighter seen, no
				Sgt Spreckley P.G.	W/OP				combat
				Sgt Toole E.	F/E				
				Sgt Fry R.S.	M/U				5 Crew+ a/c lost ops Stettin20th April
				Sgt Uppington B.S.	R/G				
Halifax II	DT628	MH-B	51	Sgt Brett B.T.	Pilot	20:34	05:30	01:47	Target ID'd visually by pinpoints on
				Sgt Lyster R.F.	Nav			7,000 ft	buildings
				P/O Glover R.	A/B				4x1000 gp 1x500 gp
				Sgt Shortland P.	W/OP				Landed Tangmere on two engines.
				Sgt Waring C.G.	F/E				
				Sgt Vandy C.	M/U				
				Sgt Alp P.L.	R/G				

A Shaky do-The Skoda Works Raid of 16/17th April 1943

AIRCRAFT	SERIAL	CODE	SQN	CREW	TRADE	UP	DOWN	BOMBED	NOTES
Halifax II	HR788	MH-	51	Sgt Haly E.F.M.	Pilot	20:35	06:15	01:51	Target ID'd visually. No cloud slight
				Sgt Wright A.	Nav			5,000 ft	haze
				F/S Bramfitt C.L.	A/B				4x1000 gp 1x500 gp
				F/S Woods P.	W/OP				
				Sgt Marks K.G.	F/E				
				Sgt Baldwin L.S.	M/U				
				Sgt Johnstone C.G.	R/G				
Halifax II	DT580	MH-	51	S/L Moore D.H.A.	Pilot	20:41	05:52	01:49	Smoke over target caused by PFF
				F/O Bond G.	Nav			5,400 ft	flares
				Sgt Dean A.K.	A/B				4x1000 gp 1x500 gp
				P/O Annand F.C.	W/OP				
				Sgt Forbes A.W.	F/E				
				P/O Price S.G.	M/U				
				Sgt Evans A.C.	R/G				Landed Abingdon
Halifax II	HR787	MH-J	51	F/S Brigden C.M. RAAF	Pilot	20:31	05:45	01:39	Several buildings observed being hit
				Sgt Griffith W.D.	Nav			4,500 ft	Medium flak
				Sgt Peters G.C.	A/B				Crew+ a/c lost ops Duisburg 27th Apr.
				Sgt Holding W.	W/OP				
				Sgt Sees R.G.H.	F/E				
				F/S Green B.F.K. RAAF	M/U				4x1000 gp 1x500 gp
				Sgt Chittock W.V. RAAF	R/G				Landed Harwell
Halifax II	DT513	MH-	51	Sgt Tay J.P	Pilot	20:45	05:20	4,500 ft	PFF flares bombed, 'factory' seen
				P/O Popley T.D.					4x1000 gp 1x500 gp
				Sgt Redshaw A.C.					6 this crew lost ops Köln 29th June
				F/S Houlston J.L.					
				Sgt Smith A.					
				Sgt Lynch J.P.					
				F/S Vidal W. RCAF					Landed Harwell

A Shaky do-The Skoda Works Raid of 16/17th April 1943

AIRCRAFT	SERIAL	CODE	SQN	CREW	TRADE	UP	DOWN	BOMBED	NOTES
Halifax II	HR782	MH-	51	Sgt Richards N.C.	Pilot	20:37	06:23	01:42	One of first aircraft on target
				Sgt Barnicoat J.H.	Nav			8,000 ft	Bombed with aid of PFF flares
				St McKeown G.	A/B				4x1000 gp 1x500 gp
				Sgt Holland L.	W/OP				
				Sgt Stow R.	F/E				
				Sgt Tidmarsh A.F.	M/U				
				Sgt Grisdale K.	R/G				
Halifax II	DT685	MH-	51	P/O Woodward G.W.	Pilot	20:29	06:29	01:45	Pinpoints obtained on buildings
				Sgt Wilson E.	2nd Pilot			6,000 ft	P.A.F.U.
				P/O Glover G.G.	Nav				
				F/O Gibb M.	A/B				4x1000 gp 1x500 gp
				Sgt James W.W.	W/OP				
				Sgt Tipton F.	F/E				
				Sgt Clark L.	M/U				
				Sgt Fyfield B.I.	R/G				
Halifax II	HR728	MH-	51	Sgt Williams J.J.	Pilot	20:48	06:45	01:41	Bombed with aid of pinpoints & PFF
				Sgt Casey J.	Nav			9,000 ft	Flares.
				Sgt Tucker R.C.	A/B				Bombed with aid of PFF flares
				Sgt Hurley G.J.	W/OP				
				Sgt Barrie J.I.	F/E				
				F/S Brown E.C.	M/U				
				Sgt Bishop T.C.	R/G				

A Shaky do-The Skoda Works Raid of 16/17th April 1943

AIRCRAFT	SERIAL	CODE	SQN	CREW	TRADE	UP	DOWN	BOMBED	NOTES
Halifax II	DT671	MH-S	51	W/O Clayton B.W.	Pilot	20:39	06:41	01:43	Target easily ID'd visually &by PFF flares
				Sgt Buttle W.	Nav			6,500 ft	flares
				Sgt Watson J.E.	A/B				Bombed with aid of PFF flares
				Sgt Bibby J.	W/OP				
				Sgt Hill A.	F/E				
				Sgt Hume W.	M/U				
				F/S Stacey S.G. RCAF	R/G				
Halifax II	HR790	MH-C	51	P/O Byres G.W.H.	Pilot	20:45	07:02	01:49	Caught in lights on 1st &2nd runs
				F/O Stark R.H.	Nav			5,000 ft	Target ID'd by chimneys
				Sgt Emes D.J.	A/B				Aircraft slightly damaged in
				Sgt Howell R.T.	W/OP				undercarriage door
				Sgt Thompson G.H.	F/E				4x1000 gp 1x500 gp. 10 hours 40 min
			3rd Op.	Sgt Stringer C.	M/U				6 of crew lost 14 May ops Bochum on
				Sgt Jacobs A.C.	R/G				HR790
	HR730	MH-W	51	Sgt Baldwin	Pilot			13,000 ft	Arrived over target found no trace of
				Sgt Ramskill	Nav				the raid therefore bombed
				Sgt Collop	A/B				Mannheim
				F/S Dudgeon W	W/OP				Large amount of black smoke & fires
				Sgt Thompson	F/E				
				Sgt Hill	M/U				
				Sgt Snaith T M	R/G				
Lancaster I	ED827	DX-Z	57	S/L Avis G.G.	Pilot	21:12	06:33	01:59	Saw burst 500 yards W.W. aiming
				F/O Crocker M.	2nd Pilot			7,000 ft	Point.
			16th Op.	F/S Lovejoy E.W.	Nav				1x4000 HC 2x1000 gp
				Sgt Edwards R.W.	F/E				
				Sgt Gibson J.	B/A				
				Sgt Philips H.W.	W/OP				
				Sgt King E.M.	M/U				
				F/S Wellard H.J.	R/G				

A Shaky do-The Skoda Works Raid of 16/17th April 1943

AIRCRAFT	SERIAL	CODE	SQN	CREW	TRADE	UP	DOWN	BOMBED	NOTES
Lancaster III	ED706	DX-	57	F/L Roberts W.E.	Pilot	21:12	06:53	02:05	Stb /Inner failed 20 miles S.E. Munich
				Sgt Parker G.A.N	2nd Pilot				A/c lost 1st May Ops. Essen
				Sgt McDonald C.A.	Nav				1x4000 HC 2x1000 gp
				Sgt Rea B.	F/E				
				F/O Torrisi V.F.J.	B/A				
				Sgt Davies D.J.	W/OP				
				Sgt Barnes R.H.	M/U				
				F/S Pratt G.A.	R/G				
Lancaster III	ED698	DX-	57	W/O Mapp I.P.	Pilot	21:06	06:23		Saw factory in moonlight aided by
				Sgt Barker M.E.	2nd Pilot				Flares. Clearly saw chimneys
				F/L Ciano C.V.	Nav				Claimed to have hit power station
				Sgt Baylis T.	F/E				1x4000 HC 2x1000 gp
				Sgt Erratt T.J.	B/A				
				Sgt Abraham R.G.	W/OP				
				Sgt Ovenden K.	M/U				
				P/O Sherratt R.J.	R/G				
Lancaster I	ED762	DX-	57	F/L Wareing S.	Pilot	21:02	05:53	01:52	Saw markers built up area obscured
				Sgt Daniels N.F.	Nav			7,000 ft	by smoke
				Sgt Ramsay G.L.	F/E				1x4000 HC 2x1000 gp
				Sgt Burt D.W.	B/A				
				Sgt Ewing M.M.	B/A				a /c crashed may 3rd in training
				Sgt Bryson H.	W/OP				
				Sgt Bryan E.F.	M/U				
				Sgt Harris A.J.	R/G				

A Shaky do-The Skoda Works Raid of 16/17th April 1943

AIRCRAFT	SERIAL	CODE	SQN	CREW	TRADE	UP	DOWN	BOMBED	NOTES
Lancaster I	ED778	DX-	57	F/L Jenks I.S.	Pilot	21:01	05:54	01:57	Saw TIs SW of target
				Sgt McDowell T.A. RCAF	Nav			6000 ft	1x4000 HC 2x1000 gp
				Sgt Bryant J.	F/E				6 this crew lost ED770 Stettin 21 Apr
				Sgt Britton A.J.	B/A				Hit by flak outward and return
				P/O Mathews G.	B/A				
				Sgt Smithdale J.	W/OP				
				Sgt Slade E.D.	M/U				
				Sgt Turvey L.	R/G				
Lancaster I	W4948	DX-	57	Sgt Grimwood R.P.	Pilot	21:04	06:00	01:44	Made dummy run
				Sgt Glotham W.J.	Nav			7,000 ft	1x4000 HC 2x1000 gp
				F/O Shaw C.	F/E				
				Sgt Thornicroft H.	2nd F/E				
				Sgt Frenchum C.J.	B/A				
				P/O Gibbons R.E.	W/OP				
				Sgt Hodges W.R.	M/U				
				Sgt Roberts W.M.	R/G				
Lancaster III	ED668	DX-	57	Sgt Hawkins P.H.	Pilot	21:03	06:21	01:55	Smoke hid ground detail
				Sgt Farmer V.D.	2nd Pilot			6,800 ft	1x4000 HC 2x1000 gp
				Sgt McKenzie L.E.	Nav				a/c lost Bochum 13th June
				Sgt Bamlett W.S.	F/E				
				Sgt Roach C.W.F	B/A				
				F/S Stevens K.G.	W/OP				
				Sgt Tuck F.A.	M/U				
				Sgt Kimber J.A.	R/G				

A Shaky do-The Skoda Works Raid of 16/17th April 1943

AIRCRAFT	SERIAL	CODE	SQN	CREW		TRADE	UP	DOWN	BOMBED	NOTES
Lancaster I	ED308	DX-	57	P/O Collins R.F.	RCAF	Pilot	21:18	05:59	Early Return	From near Regensburg
				Sgt O'Loughlin D.		Nav				Landed Beaulieu feared fuel shortage
				Sgt Emerson R.V.		F/E				
				P/O Tate F.R.		B/A				
				Sgt Fazackerly H.		W/OP				
				Sgt Norris K.		M/U				
				Sgt Whitcombe K.		R/G				
Lancaster I	R5751	DX	57	Sgt Gifford H.S.		Pilot	21:10	06:20	01:56	Timed run from markers
				Sgt Agnew J.T.		Nav			8,000 ft	112x30lb incendiaries
				Sgt Luke C.W.		F/E				
				Sgt Harrison A.G.		B/A				
				Sgt Tanner L.R.		W/OP				
				Sgt Cambell R.G.		M/U				
				Sgt Morris H.E.		R/G				
Lancaster I	W4944	DX-	57	F/O Wilson V.A.		Pilot	21:08	05:58	02:35	Not convinced primary had been
				Sgt Thomas R.B.		Nav			12,000 ft	found. Bombed Mannheim, well on
				Sgt Loughlin S.		F/E				fire
				Sgt Knight S.R.		B/A				1260xlb incendiaries
				P/O Armstrong T		B/A				
				Sgt Leverseed R.B.		W/OP				
				Sgt Gerding C.H.		M/U				
				Sgt Steele A.		R/G				
Lancaster I	ED777	DX-	57	F/S Leach G.B.	RCAF	Pilot	21:05	05:56	01:49	ID'd river in light of flares
				P/O McNiel H.C.	RCAF	Nav			7,000 ft	112x30lb incendiaries fell across
				Sgt Rees N.		F/E				'factory'
				Sgt Gregory T.		B/A				crew lost ED778 ops 13 May x2 pow
				Sgt Grace M.J.		B/A				
				Sgt Sheehan H.A.	RCAF	W/OP				
				Sgt Levins M.	RCAF	M/U				
				F/S Home A.L.	RCAF	R/G				

A Shaky do-The Skoda Works Raid of 16/17th April 1943

AIRCRAFT	SERIAL	CODE	SQN	CREW	TRADE	UP	DOWN	BOMBED	NOTES
Lancaster III	ED667	DX-	57	F/S Lovell R.P.	Pilot	21:11	06:11	01:54	Bombed markers. ID'd factory on run
				W/O English E.T.	Nav			5,030 ft	up 112x30lb incendiaries
				Sgt Cooper A.H.	F/E				Landed Waddington
				Sgt Bryans R.W.C.	B/A				
				F/S Taylor J.T.	W/OP				
				Sgt Willis R.A.	M/U				
				F/S Williams D.P.	R/G				
Lancaster III	ED413	DX-	57	Sgt Allwright E.G.	Pilot	21:07	06:46	01:51	Smoke over target
				P/O Kennedy B.J.N.	Nav			8,000 ft	112x30lb incendiaries
				Sgt Morrison A.	F/E				
				Sgt Lemarchant H.E.	B/A				
				Sgt Lammas A.J.	W/OP				
				Sgt Stevenson J.G.	M/U				
				Sgt Bracken E.	R/G				
Lancaster	W4899	QR-	61	Sgt Dashper F.	Capt	21:20	06:26	6,000 ft	Made 2nd run
				Sgt Faraday W.	F/E				
				Sgt Watkins H.	Nav				
				Sgt Carr K.S.	A/B				
				Sgt Daniels D.C.	WT/Ag				
				Sgt Fleming N.	AG1				
				Sgt Staves A.W.	AG2				
Lancaster	R5618	QR-	61	P/O Frost	Capt	21:19	00:01	Rtnd early	U/S elevator trim tab-
				Sgt Harris T.A.	F/E				Jettisoning bombs 53:12.5N 00:34E
				F/O Williams R.H.	Nav				Gee fix 53:49.5N 02:06E
				Sgt Hulland F.S.	A/B				
				Sgt Chorley V.J.	WT/Ag				
				F/S Graham J.	AG1				
				Sgt Culham G.W.	AG2				

A Shaky do-The Skoda Works Raid of 16/17th April 1943

AIRCRAFT	SERIAL	CODE	SQN	CREW		TRADE	UP	DOWN	BOMBED	NOTES
Lancaster	W4900	QR-	61	Sgt Parsons W.C.	RCAF	Capt	21:23	06:01	7,900 ft	
				Sgt Mullins A.G.		F/E				
				Sgt Lowe		U/T Nav				
				Sgt Dyson R.S.		Nav				
				Sgt Poole F.J.		A/B				
				Sgt Clark A.		WT/AG				
				Sgt Isaacs G.A.		AG1				
				Sgt Towse C.D.		AG2				
Lancaster	ED722	QR-	61	Sgt Madgett H.R.		Capt	21:15	05:25	8,000 ft	
				Sgt Robinson H.		F/E				
				Sgt Palk S.G.		Nav				
				Sgt Barker K.S.		A/B				
				Sgt Bradley R.	RCAF	WT/AG				
				Sgt Wakefield J.J.		AG1				
				Sgt Soutar A.W.A.		AG2				
Lancaster	ED718	QR-	61	S/L Gascoyne-Cecil R.A.V.		Capt	21:11	05:58	01:52	Did dummy run-saw. P. F. F. Lanc blow up on run up (R5622, 83 sqn.)
				P/O Jackson B.J.		F/E				
				W/O Ayles R.N.		Nav				
				P/O Brewer A.B.		A/B				
				F/L Neath W.C.		WT/AG				
				Sgt Hamment N.W.		AG1				
				F/S Say L.		AG2				
				Sgt Archer		U/T A/B				
Lancaster	W4898	QR-	61	F/L Benjamin E.G.		Capt	21:17	05:35	8,000 ft	Observed at least 5 a/c going down
				Sgt Stephenson K.J.		F/E				
				F/O Hewitt H.L.		Nav				
				Sgt Steed F.W.		A/B				
				Sgt Dinsdale R.D.		WT/AG				
				Sgt Frawley J.		AG1				
				Sgt Rankin H.		AG2				

A Shaky do-The Skoda Works Raid of 16/17th April 1943

AIRCRAFT	SERIAL	CODE	SQN	CREW	TRADE	UP	DOWN	BOMBED	NOTES
Lancaster	W4317	QR-R	61	P/O Macfarlane W.	Capt	21:13	FTR	All crew KIA	Shot down by Oblt. Rudolf Altendorf
				Sgt Keay P.J.	F/E				2./NJG4 at 04:02 Givry, Belgium
				F/O Williams C.F.	Nav				
				Sgt Dawson W.W.	A/B				Bomb load 1x4000 HC 2x1000
				F/S Edwards J.F. D.F.M.	WT/AG				Equipped ARI 5082, R3003A, Tinsel
				Sgt Rees J.V.	AG1				
				Sgt Holdsworth D.A.	AG2				
				Sgt Davidson E.R.	U/T Nav				Sgt Davidson 1654 O.T.U.
Lancaster	W4269	QR-	61	P/O Rawes D.A.	Capt	21:18	05:46	8,500 ft	Photo 6 Miles SW of target
				Sgt Lawrence L.	F/E				
				P/O Skilletter E.A.	Nav				
				Sgt Wilkes W.D.G.	A/B				
				Sgt White H.S.	WT/AG				
				Sgt Atkins W.J.	AG1				
				Sgt Mattick S.R.	AG2				
				F/O Clark	U/T Nav				
Lancaster	W4236	QR-K	61	Sgt Shipway A.G.	Capt	21:17	06:20	9,000 ft.	Port inner U/S on return journey
				Sgt Cummings E.	F/E				
				Sgt Moorcroft B.	Nav				1x4000lb, 2x1000lb
				F/S Brown F.	A/B				
				Sgt Silk R.W.	WT/AG				
				Sgt Denoon B.	AG1				
				Sgt Lewis P.L.T.	AG2				
Lancaster	W4279	QR-	61	F/L Cooper G.R.	Capt	21:22	05:40	8,500 ft.	Attacked visually
				Sgt Hamilton G.	F/E				
				F/O Le Sueur B.W.	Nav				
				F/O Miles A.W.	A/B				
				Sgt Nichols A.A.	WT/AG				
				Sgt Hodgkins J.G.	AG1				
				Sgt Homewood F.G.	AG2				

A Shaky do-The Skoda Works Raid of 16/17th April 1943

AIRCRAFT	SERIAL	CODE	SQN.	CREW		TRADE	UP	DOWN	BOMBED	NOTES
Lancaster	W4766	QR-J	61	F/O Thomas D.C.		Capt	21:16	06:33	9,000 ft	a/c lost Peenemunde 17/18th August
				Sgt Burrell G.L.		F/E				different crew
				Sgt Lewis R.F.		Nav				
				Sgt Watford R.H.		A/B				
				Sgt Pollitt J.C.		WT/AG				
				Sgt Davis L.G.		AG1				
				Sgt Little J.		AG2				
Lancaster	W4795	QR-	61	F/S Goodwin T.H.	USA	Capt	21:18	06:28	7,000 ft	9 Hours 10 Minutes. 'B' Flight
				Sgt Lewis R.		F/E				
				F/O McDowell W.H.		Nav				
				Sgt Lucas R.H.		A/B				
				Sgt Hamblett L.S.J.		WT/AG				
				Sgt Stone		AG1				
				Sgt Jones T.R.		AG2				
				Sgt Macphail		U/T A/B				
Lancaster	ED782	QR-	61	Sgt Allcroft F.C.		Capt	21:14	06:37	8,000 ft	
'Rings over				Sgt Coles H.		F/E				
the Ruhr'				Sgt Readman H.		Nav				
				Sgt Pemberton G.S.		A/B				
				Sgt Reynolds R.H.G.		WT/AG				
				Sgt McDonald A.		AG1				
				Sgt Hargreaves S.		AG2				

A Shaky do-The Skoda Works Raid of 16/17th April 1943

AIRCRAFT	SERIAL	CODE	SQN	CREW		TRADE	UP	DOWN	BOMBED	NOTES
Halifax II	BB365	MP-T	76	Sgt Hoover H.C.		Capt	20:36	06:23	01:51	
				Sgt McCann B.S.					9,000 ft	
				Sgt Bergey E.K.	RCAF					
				Sgt Howden G.M.	RCAF					
				F/S Mossop J.						
				Sgt Hill G.						
				Sgt Lloyd G.W.						
				F/S Tripp P.C.H.						
Halifax II	JB800	MP-U	76	Sgt Wright G.C.		Pilot	20:01	KIA		Shot down by Lt. Heinz Bock
				P/O Cooper A.N.		A/B		KIA		7./NJG101 at Holzweiler Hof 01:44
				P/O Smith E.H.		Nav		KIA		Mundelsheim
				P/O Webb J.F.		Wop		KIA		Aircraft exploded in the air after
				Sgt Wombwell D.B.		M/U		POW		steep dive.
				Sgt Read A.G.C.		F/E		POW		4x1000 lb RDX 1x500lb MC
				Sgt Robb F.A.	RCAF	R/G		KIA		19 April 45 Read mortally wounded
										by allied fighters at Gresse
Halifax II	DT575	MP-Y	76	Sgt Wedderburn B.		Pilot	20:49	KIA		Shot down by Uffz.Thiele 9./NJG4
				Sgt Ross F.O.	RCAF	A/B		KIA		Exploded in the air 03:38 Vesles et
				Sgt Clinging B.J.		Nav		KIA		Caumont.
				Sgt Fidgeon F.C.		Wop		KIA		4x1000lb GP 1x500 MC
				Sgt Jonasson L.N.	RCAF	M/U		KIA		Jonasson 17, amongst youngest
				Sgt Strachan J.		F/E		KIA		lost on ops with Bomber Command.
				Sgt Brown S.H.C.		R/G		KIA		
Halifax V	DK169	MP-E	76	Sgt Hickman S.W.		Pilot	20:37	22:48	Early rtn.	Rear turret U/S 20 miles 275°from
				Sgt Pring A.S.		A/B				Skegness. Bombs jettisoned
				F/O Keene C.W.		Nav				
				Sgt Smith D.A.		Wop				
				Sgt Jackson L.F.		M/U				
				Sgt Piller F.J.		F/E				
				Sgt Scott G.		R/G				

A Shaky do-The Skoda Works Raid of 16/17th April 1943

AIRCRAFT	SERIAL	CODE	SQN	CREW	TRADE	UP	DOWN	BOMBED	NOTES
Halifax V	DK165	MP-C	76	Sgt Webb E.K.	Pilot	20:42	KIA		5km N.E. Neustadt. Shot down 00:30
				Sgt Kay J.	A/B		KIA		by Oblt. Jakob Bender 7./NJG101
				Sgt Williams K.R.G	Nav		KIA		4x1000 lb RDX 1x500lb MC
				Sgt Ross A.R. RCAF	Wop		KIA		
				Sgt Mitchell L.B.	M/U		POW		
				Sgt Braybrook S.	F/E		KIA		
				F/S Brown G.	R/G		KIA		
Halifax II	JB872	MP-C	76	Capt. Halle B. RNAF	Pilot	20:44	06:45	01:49	ID visually by SW corner of 'factory' &
				S/L Bennett N.J.	A/B			8,000 ft	PFF Green markers. Centre of factory
				Lt Vikholt H. RNAF	Nav				in bomb sight.
				F/S Evans E.	Wop				
				Sgt Boanas G.R.	M/U				
				Sgt Watters J.	F/E				
				Sgt Jacobs E.R.	R/G				
Halifax II	JB874	MP-L	76	F/S Bawden E.A.	Pilot	20:40	06:21	01:46	Explosions observed when 80 miles
				Sgt Musgrove T.	A/B			8,000 ft	away.
				Sgt Thick L.W.S.	Nav				Bawden, Musgrove, Greenhalgh,
				Sgt Smith J.W.	Wop				Hitchcock all KIA 24th May Ops
				Sgt Greenhalgh C.	M/U				Dortmund. Rest were pow.
				Sgt Knowles T.	F/E				
				Sgt Hitchcock T.L.V.	R/G				
Halifax V	DK166	MP-D	76	Sgt Perks R.S.		20:38	06:30	01:48	Bombs burst Nth of rail line through
				F/O Adams				10,000 ft	'works'
				Sgt Shiplee E.J.					
				Sgt Strang C.R.					
				Sgt Lee P.E.					
				Sgt Stempniak T.					
				Sgt Hallidayn H.D.					
				Sgt Reader R.F.					

A Shaky do-The Skoda Works Raid of 16/17th April 1943

AIRCRAFT	SERIAL	CODE	SQN	CREW	TRADE	UP	DOWN	BOMBED	NOTES
Halifax II	DT541	MP-S	76	F/S Clarke P.E.	Pilot	20:46	06:42	01:43	Many HE bursts seen
				P/O Fielder R.J.	A/B			8,000 ft	Target visually identified by 'factory'
				Sgt Lewis J.	Nav				roofs.
				F/S Hipkiss H.	Wop				
				Sgt Wilson R.	M/U				
				Sgt Roberts W.J.	F/E				
				Sgt Smith P.E.C.	R/G				
Halifax II	HR748	MP-R	76	Sgt Sanderson J.E.	Pilot	20:52	06:26	01:41	Target ID'd by river east of 'works' &
				Sgt Robbins A.E.	A/B			8,500 ft	White flares
				Sgt Curtis J.A.E.	Nav				Photo showed ground detail and a
				F/S Robinson H.G.M.	Wop				wood on fire.
				Sgt Morgan R.G.	M/U				
				Sgt Shillcock A.	F/E				
				P/O Morris J.E.H.	R/G				
Halifax II	JB846	KN-L	77	F/S Maslin S.A.	Pilot	20:37	05:35	9,500 ft	Nickels dropped.
				Sgt Crane E.R.	F/E				Large square building to SW of grn TIs
				P/O Dungey F.A.	Nav				Bombs seen to enter building
				P/O Simpson L.	A/B				BFX'd Landed Harwell
				F/S Greenwood F.J.	Wop/Ag				48x30 450x4 90x4 X type
				Sgt Boulton S.H.	A/G				
				Sgt Lewis W.	A/G				
Halifax II	DT736	KN-M	77	Sgt Ellis G.B.	Pilot	20:35	06:24	9,000 ft	Dropped bombs at end of Green and
				Sgt Brierley F.	F/E				White flares
				F/O Ashman M.R.	Nav				BFX'd Landed Harwell
				Sgt Gilbey F.R.	A/B				48x30 450x4 90x4 X type
				Sgt Walsh G.A.	Wop/Ag				
				Sgt Richardson S.A.	A/G				
				Sgt Mayo G.W.	A/G				

A Shaky do-The Skoda Works Raid of 16/17th April 1943

AIRCRAFT	SERIAL	CODE	SQN	CREW	TRADE	UP	DOWN	BOMBED	NOTES
Halifax II	JB804	KN-Q	77	F/L Lea T.S.	Pilot	20:36	05:34	10,000 ft	crew (except w/t) and a/c lost Stettin
				Sgt Cruxton G.H	F/E				20/21 Apr
				F/S White R.J.	Nav				Dropped Bombs on Railway line.
				P/O Chitty D.J.D.	A/B				Attacked by fighter at Noyon 23:30
				F/O King D.F.	W/T				49.37N 00.00E
				Sgt Carter E.	M/U				48x30 450x4 90x4 X type
				Sgt Lambert R.W.	R/G				Landed Ford
Halifax II	JB853	KN-T	77	Sgt Gawler H.V.	Pilot	20:38	06:50	8,800 ft	Green TIs showed row of sheds
				Sgt Cotterall A.	F/E				2 columns of smoke rising to 1000 ft
				Sgt Leicester J.J.	Nav				
				Sgt Langston S.C.	A/B				48x30 450x4 90x4 X type
				Sgt Burgess A.	Wop/ag				Landed Elvington
				Sgt Kitchen P.W.	A/G				
				Sgt Todd T.	A/G				
Halifax II	JB865	KN-J	77	S/L Bainbridge F.	Pilot	20:39	05:50	7,000 ft	Search lights 49.15N 08.40E Nth of
				Sgt Shaw F.G.	F/E				Bruchsal East of the Rhein? ? ?
				Sgt Randall J.R.	Nav				Landed Abingdon
				Sgt Walton E.	A/B				
				Sgt Rees W.D.	Wop/ag				48x30 450x4 90x4 X type
				Sgt White P.B.	A/G				
				Sgt Bacon J.A.	A/G				
Halifax II	DT793	KN-F	77	Sgt Canton E.J.	Pilot	20:48	06:47	4,000 ft	Large number of white flares burning
				Sgt McElroy W.	F/E				on ground. Holed by light flak over
				P/O Jousse P.	Nav				target
				Sgt Myers J.	A/B				BFX'd Landed Harwell
				Sgt Godwin R.	Wop/ag				
				Sgt Huxley L.	A/G				48x30 450x4 90x4 X type
				F/S Polston F.B.	A/G				

A Shaky do-The Skoda Works Raid of 16/17th April 1943

AIRCRAFT	SERIAL	CODE	SQN	CREW	TRADE	UP	DOWN	BOMBED	NOTES
Halifax II	JB911	KN-X	77	Sgt Smith R.F.	Pilot			10,000 ft	White flares used as aid on run up
				Sgt Jones R.C.C.	F/E				Bombs released on Green Tl.
				Sgt Page A.J.	Nav				48x30 450x4 90x4 X type
				Sgt Cork H.	A/B				
				Sgt Jones G.E.	Wop/ag				
				Sgt Jones F.S.	A/G				
				Sgt Pollock F.H.	A/G				Landed Elvington
Halifax II	JB908	KN-W	77	Sgt Wall F.S.	Pilot	20:46	POW		A/C abandoned low altitude
				Sgt Pullen D.I.	F/E		KIA		Chute did not open
				Sgt Fernee G.R.	Nav		KIA		Chute did not open
				Sgt Tullett R.M.	A/B		POW		P.O.W
				Sgt Edgar A. K.	Wop/ag		KIA		Chute did not open
				Sgt Johnson L.	A/G		POW		Bomb load as JB911
				Sgt Robinson R.W.	A/G		KIA		Found dead in the aircraft
							over-flew	Ehningen	on fire. Crashed Mauren valley.
Halifax II	JB852	KN-C	77	F/S Goodwin G.R.	Pilot	20:43	06:29	8,000 ft	Vast amount of smoke. Huge block of
				Sgt Jones J. H.	F/E				buildings well ablaze making I.D.
				P/O Wood A.	Nav				difficult.
				P/O McClelland J.	A/B				BFX'd Harwell
				F/S Daborn C.J.	Wop/ag				48x30 450x4 90x4 X type
				Sgt Sutton T.H.	A/G				
				Sgt Cocks J.	A/G				
Halifax II	DT796	KN-D	77	W/O Pye J.D. RAAF	Pilot	20:41	06:29	9,500 ft	Two large explosions seen.
				Sgt McCulloch W.	F/E				Pye K.I.A. 26/27 April 43 Duisberg op
				P/O Stewart R.C.	Nav				Stewart P.O.W 26/27 April43. M.I.D.
									Murdered by Gestapo 29th Mar 1944
				P/O Atter D.W.	A/B				P.O.W 26/27 April 43
				Sgt Marlow G.	Wop/ag				Bombload as JB852
				Sgt Gibbs P.	A/G				P.O.W 26/27 April 43
				Sgt Wells J.R.	A/G				K.I.A. 26/27 April 43 Duisberg op

A Shaky do-The Skoda Works Raid of 16/17th April 1943

AIRCRAFT	SERIAL	CODE	SQN	CREW	TRADE	UP	DOWN	BOMBED	NOTES
Halifax II	JB892	KN-E	77	F/O Puddephatt D. P.	Pilot	20:40	05:50	7,500 ft	White flares aided I.D. long sheds seen
				Sgt Brookes M.J.H.	F/E				
				Sgt Morgan J.I.P.	Nav				All crew and a/c lost ops Bochum
				Sgt Bolton L.W.	A/B				13/14th May 43 to Night fighter
				Sgt Walton G.S.	Wop/ag				
				Sgt McKillop A.W.	A/G				
				Sgt Halestrap R.A.	A/G				48 x 30 450x4 90x4 X type
Halifax II	JB803	KN-G	77	Sgt Watson G.	Pilot	20:45	06:35	8,000 ft	Dropped Nickel, sheds seen
				Sgt Crawford I.D.	F/E				Landed Elvington
				F/O Parsons A.E.	Nav				
				Sgt Hannam L.	A/B				48 x 30 450x4 90x4 X type
				Sgt Louth W.R.	Wop/ag				
				Sgt Fedi E.	A/G				
				Sgt Scarff T.	A/G				
Halifax II	JB856	KN-H	77	Sgt Symmons A.	Pilot	20:42	06:45	10,000 ft	Green TIs in bomb site, thick smoke over target. One big explosion.
				Sgt Johnstone K.E.	F/E				
				F/S Fulsmer J.I.	Nav				Nickels dropped
				F/S Whitney J.L.	A/B				Landed Elvington
				Sgt Simonson R.E.	Wop/ag				
				Sgt Fleming W.A.	A/G				
				F/S McQueen F.C.	A/G				48x30 450x4 90x4 X type
Halifax II	JB850	KN-B	77	S/L Surtees W.	Pilot	20:44	06:37	01:44	H.E.s seen to throw up debris.
				Sgt Brown E.J.	F/E			8,500 ft	Bombs dropped onto buildings with tall chimneys
				F/L Newsham G.	Nav				
				Sgt Wooley H.G.W.	A/B				Landed Harwell with engine trouble
				P/O Penny H.A.	Wop/ag				
				Sgt Shepherd R.	A/G				
				P/O Wallace A.V.	A/G				48x30 450x4 90x4 X type

A Shaky do-The Skoda Works Raid of 16/17th April 1943

AIRCRAFT	SERIAL	CODE	SQN	CREW	TRADE	UP	DOWN	BOMBED	NOTES
Halifax II	DT807	R	77	P/O Williams J.H.	Pilot	20:47	06:07	4,000 ft	Onto Green Tls.
				Sgt Newstead F.L.	F/E				Suffered minor damage light flak en route.
				Sgt Anstee L.J.	Nav				
				Sgt Isherwood F.A.	A/B				BFX'd Landed Harwell
				Sgt Williams G.	Wop/ag				
				Sgt Bradbury P.R.	A/G				
				Sgt Marden-Mowbray K.D.	A/G				48x30 450x4 90x4 X type

F/Sgt Anstee, Navigator, 2nd from left Sgt Bill McCulloch, flight engineer,5th from left Sgt A Isherwood, A/B
SGT G Williams, Wop/Ag. Crew of 77 squadron DT807 a few weeks after Plzen.

A Shaky do-The Skoda Works Raid of 16/17th April 1943

AIRCRAFT	SERIAL	CODE	SQN	CREW	TRADE	UP	DOWN	BOMBED	NOTES
Halifax II	HR684	EY	78	S/L Neal R.J.	Capt	20:55	06:48	01:48	Target I.D.'d by River, Cathedral &
				P/O Conlon W.	Nav			7,000 ft	built up area. Bombs fell on 'factory'
				Sgt Hailey F.W.	B/A				sheds
				F/O Pledger T.O.	W/OP				
				P/O Cooper F.C.	F/E				
				Sgt Winter K.	A/G				
				Sgt Tait	A/G				
Halifax II	DT768	EY-W	78	F/S Marshall O.P.	Capt	21:03	05:45	9,300 ft	No Green markers seen.
				P/O Gibson D.J.	Nav				Landed Stanton Harcourt
				P/O Reid N.S.M.	B/A				
				Sgt Sansum J.	W/OP				
				Sgt Ablett D.	F/E				
				Sgt Bell H.	A/G				
				Sgt Lee B.A.	A/G				
Halifax II	W7932	EY-	78	Sgt Hemmings F.	Capt	20:53	06:52	9,500 ft	Target attacked, located by P.F.F. on.
				Sgt Stone J.	Nav				SW corner of 'factory'. Bend in river
				Sgt Foale W.C.R.	B/A				seen
				Sgt Shaw A.	W/OP				
				Sgt Muir J.	F/E				
				Sgt Daniel T.W.R.	A/G				
				Sgt Montgomery D.	A/G				
Halifax II	DT777	EY-	78	Sgt Dane G. M.I.D.	Capt	20:57	07:00	01:53	Located by Green markers & visually
				Sgt Goddard R.G.	Nav			6,000 ft	SW corner of 'works'
				Sgt Adams L.	B/A				02:55 combat- JU88 claimed
				Sgt Pople J.W.	W/OP				destroyed near Stockstadt Am Rhein
				Sgt Minnitt A.C.P.	F/E				Dane KIA 13/14th May 5 pow
				Sgt Beatson A.	A/G				Goddard evaded earning DFM
				Sgt Webb F.W.	A/G				

A Shaky do-The Skoda Works Raid of 16/17th April 1943

AIRCRAFT	SERIAL	CODE	SQN	CREW	TRADE	UP	DOWN	BOMBED	NOTES
Halifax II	W7926	EY-P	78	Sgt Bragg R. E.	Capt	20:48	06:39	01:46	I.D.'d by river Cathedral & 'factory' buildings. No green markers until after bombing.
				Sgt Farrell J. RCAF	Nav			7,000 ft	This crew KIA 14th May
				Sgt Gell H.E.	B/A				Sgt Gell pow
				Sgt Matches R.	W/OP				a/c lost 24th May ops Dortmund
				Sgt Williams H.	F/E				
				Sgt Kew A.	A/G				
				Sgt Reed V.	A/G				
Halifax II	JB?	EY-	78	F/O Sells M.	Capt	20:59	06:50	01:48	Early on target. Explosions seen by rear gunner
				Sgt Rogers D.R.	Nav				
				P/O Kelt E.	B/A				
				Sgt Simpson G.	W/OP				
				Sgt Greenlees S.	F/E				
				Sgt Ferris J.S. RCAF	A/G				
				Sgt Hardcastle J.W.	A/G				
Halifax II	JB928	EY-	78	P/O McClelland D.	Capt	20:50	06:33	01:40	I. D.'d by Cathedral in Sq. N.E. of. 'Skoda Works.' Green markers dropped after bombing Captain was on 22nd op. and went to 1663 C.U. May 19th.
				F/S Beals W.	Nav				
				P/O Tingley E.	B/A				
				Sgt Currie E.	W/OP				
				Sgt Ackroyd E.	F/E				
				P/O Stevenson G.	A/G				
				Sgt Brown R.	A/G				
Halifax II Z	DT773	EY-Q	78	F/L Dowse A.P. D.F.C.	Capt	21:00		KIA	Shot down Hofen district of Stuttgart.
				F/S Desjardins R. RCAF	Nav			POW	by Night fighter, Lt. Joseph Nabrich
				Sgt Thompson H.E.	B/A			POW	III./NJG101 03:17 hours.
				Sgt Langsford P. RNZAF	W/OP			POW	
				Sgt Slater T.T.	F/E			POW	
				Sgt Hoare A.W.	M/U			POW	
				F/O Orr A.N.	R/G			POW	4x1000lb RDX 1x500lb MC

A Shaky do-The Skoda Works Raid of 16/17th April 1943

AIRCRAFT	SERIAL	CODE	SQN	CREW	TRADE	UP	DOWN	BOMBED	NOTES
Halifax II	HR659	EY-A	78	F/L Mortenson E.G.	Capt	20:58	FTR	KIA	Trier South of Bitburg. Shot down by
				P/O Dennis R.C.W.	Nav			POW	Fw Paul Faden 11./NJG4 03:07 hrs
				F/O Fisher W.G.	B/A			POW	4x1000 RDX, 1x500lb MC
				Sgt Steven C.A.	W/OP			POW	
				Sgt Bell J.A.	F/E			POW	
				Sgt Pitman D.A.	A/G			KIA	
				Sgt Minshaw L.C.	A/G			POW	
Halifax II	W7930	EY-	78	W/Co Warner G.B.	Capt	20:58	06:35	01:43	AFC DFC
				F/L Blythe K.	Nav				Id'd cathedral & large 'factory'
				F/O King N.	B/A				Bombs aimed at centre of 'factory'
				P/O Ramsey W.	W/OP				partly concealed by smoke.
				P/O Nesbitt J.D.	A/G				
				Sgt Harries E.F.	A/G				
				Sgt Bailey G.T.	F/E				
Lancaster I	W4953	OL-W	83	S/L Shaw W.H.	Pilot	21:13	05:21	01:36	Heavily engaged flak, bombs and
				F/S Dunmore G.	F/E			19,000 ft	flares dropped Munich 01:05. Flak
				F/L Dunk J.H. DFC	Nav			093°	slight damage.
				W/O Bott J.A. DFM	W/op				1x TI Yellow,1xTI Green, 1xTI Grn LB
				F/L Snowden S.J. DFM	B/A				1xTI Red, 1xTI Red LB ,4x4 Wt flares
				F/S Tutton F.M	M/U				1x4000 H.C.
				F/S Morgan R.E.	R/G				
Lancaster I	ED601	OL-T	83	S/L Wellington R.A. DFC	Pilot	21:16	05:37	01:47	Bomb'd with 12 second overshoot on
				F/S Goodwin R.C.	F/E			13,000 ft	Green TIs. Incendiaries & H.E.
				F/L Blair T.W.	Nav			050°	appeared to be short of target
				F/O Reid E.F.	W/op				Very heavy flak after Karlsruhe. Mid-
				F/O Harley V.H.	B/A				Upper turret holed
				F/L Johnson L.G.	M/U				1x TI Yellow,1xTI Green, 1xTI Grn LB
				Sgt Hicks R.B.	R/G				1xTI Red, 1xTI Red LB ,4x4 Wt flares
									1x4000 H.C.

A Shaky do-The Skoda Works Raid of 16/17th April 1943

AIRCRAFT	SERIAL	CODE	SQN	CREW	TRADE	UP	DOWN	BOMBED	NOTES
Lancaster I	R5484	OL-V	83	P/O McNichol G.A. RCAF	Pilot	21:17	FTR	K.I.A.	Shot down Pontavert, Ofw. Kurt
				Sgt Mott G.C.	F/E			P.O.W.	Karsten 7./NJG4 04:45
				P/O Beaupre H.H.F. RCAF	Nav			P.O.W.	
				Sgt McFarlane G.S.	W/op			P.O.W.	
				P/O Lewis T.W. RCAF/USA	B/A			P.O.W.	Bomb load as ED312
				Sgt Willis H.R.	M/U			P.O.W.	
				F/S Hobbs C.E. RCAF	R/G			P.O.W.	Aircraft Hit by flak earlier
Lancaster I	ED312	OL-F	83	S/L Hildyard N.F. DFC	Pilot	21:26	05:26	01:53	Pinpointed on river and lake W. Of
				Sgt Sutton E.	F/E			13,000 ft	'target'
				F/S Hacking J.F.	Nav			035° Mag	
				Sgt Endean J.	W/op				1x TI Yellow,1xTI Green, 1xTI Grn LB
				F/O Coleman S.J. DFM	B/A				1xTI Red, 1xTI Red LB ,4x4 Wt flares
				F/S Meddings	M/U				1x4000 H.C.
				F/S Goldie J. DFM	R/G				
Lancaster I	R5671	OL-K	83	F/L Smith A.B. DFC	Pilot	21:28	05:51	01:45	Saw woods and river clearly on run in
				Sgt Childs E.M	F/E			13,000 ft	Flap jack burst over target, may have
				F/L McMillin J.P. RCAF	Nav			030°mag	been flak.
				Sgt Hirst R.R.	W/op				
				F/S Candlin C.W.	B/A				1x TI Yellow,1xTI Green, 1xTI Grn LB
				F/O Meikle I.C.	M/U				1xTI Red, 1xTI Red LB ,4x4 Wt flares
				Sgt Woollard L.C.	R/G				1x4000 H.C.
Lancaster I	R5622	OL-C	83	F/S Milton F.C.	Pilot	21:29	FTR	KIA	Shot down by flak at 01:52 & crashed
				F/S Beavan R. D.F.M.	F/E			KIA	near Dobrany rail station.
				F/O Wells W.B.	Nav			KIA	The only a/c to go down in the target
				Sgt Podolsky A. RCAF	W/op			KIA	area
				F/O McLellan N.M. RCAF	B/A			KIA	1xTI Yellow,1xTI Green, 1xTI Grn LB
				F/S Rodgers J.	M/U			KIA	1xTI Red, 1xTI Red LB ,4x4 Wt flares
				Sgt Klienhorn M.	R/G			KIA	1x4000 H.C.

AIRCRAFT	SERIAL	CODE	SQN	CREW	TRADE	UP	DOWN	BOMBED	NOTES
Lancaster I	R5686	OL-G	83	P/O McDonald C.P. RCAF	Pilot	21:30	06:12	01:56	Tall 'factory chimneys' seen, TIs &
				Sgt Parrington T.J.	F/E				bombs seen to burst
				P/O Nunn V.W.J.	Nav			030° mag	All this crew shot down up fighter on
				Sgt Coles M.A.	W/op				ops Stettin 20/21 Apr. Ditched &
				Sgt Paley C.M.	B/A				Interned in Sweden
				F/S Ford C.J.	M/U				Also ;crew except Paley crashed on
				F/O Crebbin J.P. DFC	R/G				return from ops Bochum 29/30 Sept.
									Bomb load as R5622
Lancaster I	W4123	OL-A	83	F/O Wilmot T.F.	Pilot	21:32	05:53	01:49	Timed run from Yel. TIs. Thick smoke
				Sgt Roberts G.L.	F/E			13,000 ft	with column up to 3,000 ft.
				F/O Gallienne W.A.G. RCAF	Nav			090° mag	DFC Bar-DSO in excess of 80 sorties!
				Sgt Oates W.	W/op				
				Sgt Duckett O.	B/A				1x TI Yellow,1xTI Green, 1xTI Grn LB
				Sgt Pearce C.P.	M/U				1xTI Red, 1xTI Red LB ,4x4 Wt flares
				Sgt Taylor S.A.	R/G				1x4000 H.C.
Lancaster I	W4905	OL-M	83	F/O Garvey F.J.	Pilot	21:25	05:41	01:45	I.d.'d railway & river Sth of town.
				F/S Webster W.L.	F/E			13,000 ft	Bombs burst centre of fires Ti's
				Sgt Sukthanker S.	Nav			040° mag	jettisoned in sea off Dungeness 05:20
				Sgt Turner B.H.	W/op				Photo flash failed to release
				Sgt Cook J.A.	B/A				1x TI Yellow,1xTI Green, 1xTI Grn LB
				Sgt Thomas L.L.J.	M/U				1xTI Red, 1xTI Red LB ,4x4 Wt flares
				Sgt Ashton H.A.	R/G				1x4000 H.C.
Lancaster I	ED368	OL-L	83	P/O Dundas E.C.	Pilot	21:19	06:04		München attacked off track. Identifi'd
				Sgt Jones A.	F/E				by Amersee. Held in searchlights &
				F/O Craven J.	Nav				engaged by flak. Port Inner develop'd
				Sgt Frost E.H.	W/op				coolant leak near Mannheim.
				Sgt Williamson H.R.	B/A				
				Sgt Ogilvy O.M.	M/U				2x1000 1x4000 H.C.
				F/O Watkins K.B.	R/G				

A Shaky do-The Skoda Works Raid of 16/17th April 1943

AIRCRAFT	SERIAL	CODE	SQN	CREW	TRADE	UP	DOWN	BOMBED	NOTES
Lancaster I	W4955	OL-R	83	F/O Slade I.C.B.	Pilot	21:21	05:28	01:46	Bombed on Green TIs without visual
				F/S Maxwell E. DFM	F/E			12,000 ft	
				F/O McPherson A.N. DFM	Nav				2x1000 1x4000 H.C.
				F/S Baker W.G.C. DFM	W/op				
				Sgt Robinson C.	B/A				
				F/O Turner R.F.W.	M/U				
				Sgt Allen H.E.	R/G				
Lancaster I	W4231	OL-U	83	F/S Murray C. RCAF	Pilot	21:23	05:45	01:55	Flak damage to front of fuselage &
				Sgt Chapman W.G.	F/E			9,600 ft	also to tail unit over Karlsruhe
				Sgt Holt J.	Nav			124° mag	
				Sgt Ainsworth G.	W/op				2x1000 1x4000 H.C.
				Sgt Brown F.	B/A				
				Sgt Davis K.G. RCAF	M/U				
				Sgt Pritchard R.D.	R/G				
Lancaster III	ED561	JA-H	100	F/L Milliken R.E. RNZAF	Capt	21:20	FTR	KIA	South Nalbach, hit by 2cm
		Pos.F		Sgt Jones T.E.	F/E			KIA	flak from Dillingen steel works at
				Sgt George W.H. RCAF	Nav			KIA	00:29 crashed in fields south of river
				Sgt Walton W.H.	B/A			KIA	Prims.
				Sgt Hunt R.E.J.	W/Op			KIA	
				Sgt Good G.J.	M/U			KIA	120x4lbX Type 56x30lb 510x4lb ICB
				Sgt Whitby M.	R/G			KIA	Equipped IFF, Gee
Lancaster III	ED561	JA-F	100	Sgt Thurlow J.R.	Capt	21:17	06:05		PFF markers excellent except for wt
				Sgt Pyle H.	F/E				flares
				Sgt Thompson C.E.	Nav				56x30lb 630x4lb ICB
				Sgt Walters	B/A				
				Sgt Jarman A.	W/Op				
				Sgt Maisner S.	M/U				
				Sgt Norton G.C.W.	R/G				

A Shaky do-The Skoda Works Raid of 16/17th April 1943

212

AIRCRAFT	SERIAL	CODE	SQN	CREW	TRADE	UP	DOWN	BOMBED	NOTES
Lancaster III	ED652	JA-C	100	F/S Cracknell	Capt	21:21	06:00		Whole target area a mass of flames.
				Sgt Dowdall O.D.M.	F/E				One large explosion at 01:53
				Sgt Freckleton J.	Nav				56x30lb 630x4lb ICB
				Sgt Cooke A.W.	B/A				
				Sgt Harvey G.	W/Op				
				Sgt Stericker W.S.	M/U				
				Sgt Reilly N.P.	R/G				
Lancaster III	ED710	JA-D	100	Sgt Townrow L.A. RNZAF	Capt	21:19	06:12		Aircraft hit by flak which entered
				Sgt Fitchett J.P.	F/E				fuselage on Starboard side.
				P/O Bishop S.A. RCAF	Nav				56x30lb 630x4lb ICB
				Sgt Short E.	B/A				
				P/O Bolderson J.	W/Op				
				Sgt Sullivan J.	M/U				
				F/O Wilson K.J.B.	R/G				
Lancaster III	ED709	JA-S	100	P/O McHardy G.L.S.	Capt	21:19	06:20		Short of fuel. Landed Gatwick
				Sgt Kitchen S.	F/E				Sgt Patrick's log entry states, 'low
				Sgt Trafford S.J.	Nav				level,
				F/S Alexander L.F.	B/A				1.3000 ft. 9 hours 15 minutes in air.'
				Sgt Patrick W.	W/Op				56x30lb 630x4lb ICB
				Sgt Bailey E.	M/U				
				Sgt Patrick K.N.K	R/G				Formerly of 12 sqn.
Lancaster III	ED705	JA-P	100	F/O Howgill R.R.	Capt	21:18	06:10		4 crew lost Hamburg ED645 2/3 Aug
				Sgt Marshall A.H.	F/E				56x30lb 630x4lb ICB
				Sgt Best C.H.	Nav				
				P/O Christie W.D.	B/A				
				Sgt Fox C.V.	W/Op				
				Sgt Raven H.R. RCAF	M/U				
				Sgt Gardner E.E.	R/G				

A Shaky do-The Skoda Works Raid of 16/17th April 1943

AIRCRAFT	SERIAL	CODE	SQN	CREW	TRADE	UP	DOWN	BOMBED	NOTES
Lancaster III	ED557	JA-Y	100	Sgt Fletcher L.L.	Capt	21:15	06:25		Clark's log states 'Low level 500-
			3rd Op.	Sgt Clark E.J.	F/E				2000 ft. His first op was Berlin with
				Sgt Franey J.E.	Nav				McKinnon on ED568 'T'.
				Sgt Cooper L.	B/A				56x30lb 630x4lb ICB
				Sgt Jackson R.	W/Op				The only crew of 19 starting in March
				Sgt McRae W.	M/U				to complete tour!
				F/S Cambell W.S.	R/G				
Lancaster III	ED563	JA-G	100	Sgt Atkinson D.K. RNZAF	Capt	21:22	FTR	KIA	Rentrisch. Betw'n Saarbrucken & St.
				Sgt Vanston N.	F/E			KIA	Ingbert. Aircraft was flying very low
				Sgt Brown I.S. RCAF	Nav			KIA	and the pilot was obviously circling
				Sgt Rutter J.	B/A			KIA	area in search of a landing place
				Sgt Clutterbuck R.F.	W/Op			KIA	Hit by flak 00:29 Hours
				Sgt Ruddick P. RCAF	M/U			KIA	120x4lb X Type, 56x30lb, 510x4lb Icb.
				F/S Monk P.V. RAAF	R/G			KIA	
Lancaster III	ED750	JA-V	100	Sgt Morgan T.H. RCAF/US	Capt	21:12	06:38	Last resort	Compass U/S Bombed small factory in
				Sgt Giles W.E.H.	F/E				south Germany between 12 & 1300 E
				Sgt Crossey D.L.	Nav				Morgan killed on an Air Test with a
				Sgt Shyba M.D.	B/A				sprog crew after tour in Oct 43. He
				Sgt Wilson J.	W/Op				Came from New York.
				Sgt Pacquette C.A.	M/U				56x30lb 630x4lb ICB
				F/S Woods M.D.	R/G				
Lancaster III	ED553	JA-R	100	F/L Julian T.A. RCAF/US	Capt	21:16	05:50		Flew some parts of journey at v.low
				Sgt Pickles	2nd Pilot				level
				Sgt Howe M.R.	F/E				56x30lb 630x4lb ICB
				P/O Kirwan L.K.	Nav				
				Sgt Billen L.J.	B/A				
				F/S Magee W.A.	W/Op				
				Sgt Manyweather R.J.	M/U				
				Sgt Crystal R.H.	R/G				

AIRCRAFT	SERIAL	CODE	SQN	CREW	TRADE	UP	DOWN	BOMBED	NOTES
Lancaster	ED370	SR-J	101	F/O Hull W.E.	Pilot	21:10	06:50	02:06	Large explosion before attacking.
				Sgt Cornwall P.J.	F/E			6,000 ft	Smoke obscured ground detail
				Sgt Wilson R.D.	Nav			035°	
				Sgt Hancock W.A.	Wop/Ag				
				Sgt Davies G.D.G.	A/B				
				Sgt McDonald R.J.	M/U				
				Sgt Earl J.C.	R/G				
Lancaster	ED776	SR-U	101	F/S Kelly F.J.	Pilot	21:00	03:55	00:32	Bombed Karlsruhe. Coned between
				Sgt Mooney L.	F/E		3,000 ft		Mannheim/Karlsruhe engaged by flak
				Sgt Wheelwright E.	Nav				Due to damaged stb main plane
				Sgt Home B.T.	Wop/Ag				Karlsruhe was attacked
				Sgt Sparks R.R.	A/B				
				Sgt Wearmouth C.J.	M/U				a/c crashed 5.5.43 on return from
				Sgt Flack D.E.	R/G				Ops to Dortmund, no injuries.
Lancaster	W4275	SR-A	101	Sgt Cunningham T.	Pilot	21:05	23:35	22:44	Turned back from Holbeach area
				Sgt Ward W.A.	F/E			7,000 ft	Bombs jettisoned Nth Sea
				Sgt Wright J.B.	Nav				
				Sgt Hartley J.	Wop/Ag				
				Sgt McNeil J.	A/B				
				Sgt Scaife C.	M/U				
				Sgt Foster J.E.C.	R/G				
Lancaster	ED377	SR-Q	101	F/O Stanford N.J.	Pilot	21:05	00:05	22:56	Turned back from near Chelmsford
				Sgt Clarke A.H.	F/E				Stbd inner U/S jettisoned bombs in
				P/O Patterson R.D.	Nav				North Sea, safe.
				F/O Wood O.W.	Wop/Ag				
				Sgt Lyon A.J.L.	A/B				
				Sgt Reynolds .W.L.	M/U				
				Sgt Hadfield J.M.	R/G				

A Shaky do-The Skoda Works Raid of 16/17th April 1943

AIRCRAFT	SERIAL	CODE	SQN	CREW	TRADE	UP	DOWN	BOMBED	NOTES
Lancaster	ED650	SR-L	101	Sgt Brook D.N.	Pilot	20:05	03:20	00:02	Loss of oil pressure in Port Inner.
				Sgt Keighley A.C.	F/E			8,000 ft	Bombed Saarbrucken some flak
				Sgt Hopkin G.	Nav			170°	damage to fuselage
				Sgt Tippett A.R.	Wop/Ag				
				Sgt Latter T.E.W.	A/B				
				Sgt Smith F.	M/U				
				Sgt Henson K.	R/G				
Lancaster	W4833	SR-C	101	F/L Manahan J.R.	Pilot	21:05	06:35	01:46	By pinpointing and PFF
				Sgt Longston R.E.	F/E			8,000 ft	Smoke haze several fires seen
				P/O Collins L.J.	Nav			020°	including one large fire in target area
				Sgt Mitchell J.H.	Wop/Ag				
				P/O McVitty G.	A/B				
				Sgt Watts W.G.	M/U				
				Sgt Martin F.H.	R/G				
Lancaster	ED775	SR-Z	101	Sgt Edwards I.L.	Pilot	20:50	06:25	01:56	Mid-uppers intercom u/s, flaps u/s
				Sgt Hamilton R.J.	F/E			8,000 ft	both due to flak.
				Sgt Reid B.C.	Nav			030°	
				F/S Bakewell H.W.	Wop/Ag				
				Sgt McAllister E.M.	A/B				
				P/O Badman A.G.	M/U				
				Sgt Maxwell I.D.	R/G				
Lancaster	ED328	SR-S	101	F/S Bowyer R.	Pilot	21:00	06:30	01:43	Many HC bursts 2-3 large fires
				Sgt Kinnear J.A.	F/E			9,000 ft	Superficial damage to windscreen &
				F/S Layton F.	Nav			030°	port aileron by light flak.
				Sgt Nichols T.R.	Wop/Ag				
				Sgt Neal L.	A/B				
				Sgt Ellis N.	M/U				
				Sgt Wright T.	R/G				

A Shaky do-The Skoda Works Raid of 16/17th April 1943

AIRCRAFT	SERIAL	CODE	SQN	CREW		TRADE	UP	DOWN	BOMBED	NOTES
Lancaster	ED379	SR-F	101	F/S Menzies C.K.	RAAF	Pilot	21:21	KIA		Crashed in lake at Dutzendteich near
				Sgt Upton H.A.		F/E		KIA	Outbound	Nazi congress hall Approx 01:00.
				Sgt Evans H.		Nav		KIA		Nürnberg, Flak
				Sgt Green L.		Wop/Ag		POW		Bombs release just before crash.
				P/O Taylor T.M.	RAAF	A/B		KIA		1x4000 HC 3x1000lb
				Sgt Fitch J.H.	RCAF	M/U		KIA		
				Sgt Monks J.		R/G		KIA		Green rescued by German civilian.
Lancaster	ED809	SR-W	101	Sgt Wilkins C.W.			21:00	04:00	00:29	Due to being coned by search lights,
				Sgt Milton G.E.					3,000 ft	and flak damage bombed Karlsruhe
				Sgt Holman H.					101°	ETA.
				Sgt Crabbe E.S.						15 holes in aircraft, trailing aerial
				Sgt Cloud A.						shot away.
				Sgt Turvill E.F.						
				Sgt Cahill E.J.						
Lancaster	W4863	SR-G	101	Sgt Sloper J.L.			21:05	04:35	01:01	Bombed Saarbrucken by dead
				Sgt Gibb S.					6,000 ft	reckoning. Impossible to keep to time
				Sgt Thorn H.C.					325°	
				Sgt Woolmer R.J.						
				Sgt Coy S.D.						
				Sgt Bush L.						
				Sgt Milburn G.						
Lancaster	ED835	SR-T	101	W/Cdr. Reddick A.			21:00	06:00	01:48	Dropped by PFF and pinpoint
				Sgt Howells L.					8,000 ft	Early arrivals dropping ICBs causing
				F/L Greig A.B.					035°	smoke.
				P/O Gates F.W.						1x4000 lb 1x1000 lb
				Sgt Ratcliffe P.A.						
				Sgt Merlin W.D.G.						
				F/S Cox A.K.						

A Shaky do-The Skoda Works Raid of 16/17th April 1943

AIRCRAFT	SERIAL	CODE	SQN	CREW	TRADE	UP	DOWN	BOMBED	NOTES
Lancaster	W4324	SR-M	101	Sgt Margerum C.A.	Pilot	21:10	06:00	01:41	ID by pinpointing and flares
				Sgt Clegg H.	F/E			7,000 ft	Believe bombs fell in South West
				Sgt Dixon R.N.	Nav			040°	corner of works.
				Sgt Park D.J.	Wop/Ag				Duration 8:50
				Sgt Balfour R.D.	A/B				all this crew KIA 27/28th April
				Sgt Stotter J.W.	M/U				on mine laying ops Elderberry area.
				Sgt Veldsman J.J. Rhodesia	R/G				
Lancaster	ED320	SR-R	101	F/L Bigelow A.E.	Pilot	21:00	06:20	01:52	By PFF and flares. Rear turret u/s due
				Sgt Adair C.J.	F/E			7,000 ft	to flak
				Sgt Casely A.T.	Nav			070°	
				Sgt Fryer L.J.	Wop/Ag				
				Sgt Rowlan M.L.	A/B				
				Sgt MacNevin H.F.	M/U				
				F/S Storms D.W.	R/G				
Lancaster	W4888	SR-P	101	P/O Harrower H.G.	Pilot	21:10	06:15	01:48	By PFF & white flares.
				Sgt Lloyd R.P.	F/E			9,000 ft	4000 lb bombs seen to burst. Large
				Sgt Duff B.	Nav			040°	fire seen.
				Sgt Brisbin L.I.	Wop/Ag				
				Sgt Beverige L.W.D.	A/B				
				Sgt Teasdale J.	M/U				
				Sgt Crowhurst F.C.	R/G				
Halifax II Z	JB894	DY-X	102	Sgt Hewlet D.J.	Pilot	20:44	06:25	7,000 ft	Target ID river and Green markers;
				Sgt Blackaller H.A.S.	Nav			214°mag	difficult to ID due to glare from
				F/S Beale N.A.	W/op				flares against ground haze.
				Sgt Hall D.W.V.	A/G				Landed Pershore
				Sgt Reilly A.J.	A/G				
				Sgt Holliday E.	F/E				DFC Evaded 22nd Apr.44 with 76 sqn.
				Sgt Wingham S.T.	B/A				Later flew Mosquitoes.

A Shaky do-The Skoda Works Raid of 16/17th April 1943

AIRCRAFT	SERIAL	CODE	SQN	CREW	TRADE	UP	DOWN	BOMBED	NOTES
Halifax II	W7935	DY-Y	102	Sgt Saywell E.W.	Pilot	20:55	06:19	6,000 ft	ID visually and by markers
				Sgt Moore E.R.	Nav			039°	Landed Harwell
				Sgt Wisson R.W.	W/op				
				Sgt Page K.	A/G				
				Sgt Ward F.F.	A/G				
				Sgt Meldrum E.S.	Eng				
				Sgt Whittaker F.	B/A				
Halifax II	JB782	DY-W	102	F/O Kelly	Pilot	20:50	06:30	8,000 ft	Approached from SW. Saw white
				Sgt Simpkin R.	Nav			039°	flares and Green markers
				F/S Hugill J.	W/op				9 hours 45 minutes in air.
				Sgt McCarthy T.H.	A/G				Hits on Bf110 00:22 49.10N-09:02E
				Sgt Cosford D.	A/G				14k West of Heilbronn.
				Sgt Gerrum E.W.	F/E				Landed New Zealand Farm
				Sgt Fowler R.	B/A				W. Lavington
Halifax II Z	W7912	DY-	102	F/S Quigley R.J.	Pilot	20:45	06:00	4,000 ft	Fires in 'works' and explosion
				P/O St. John J.H.R.S.	Nav				Shot up goods train leaving target
				Sgt Williams F.J.	W/op				
				Sgt White J.	A/G				This a/c in combat 3/4th April
				F/S Rowe E.D.	A/G				
				Sgt Burdon J.	F/E				
				Sgt Carpenter F.R.	B/A				
Halifax II Z	JB869	DY-J	102	W/O Lee L.J.	Pilot	20:52	06:08	8,000 ft	Green TIs seen dropped after
				Sgt Jones G.A.	Nav			000°	bombing
				Sgt Wroughton H.J	W/op				Target more heavily defended than
				Sgt Platt V.S.	A/G				anticipated
				Sgt Traynor F.M.	A/G				
				Sgt Mather R.A.M.	F/E				Landed Pershore
				F/O Baldwin S.A.	B/A				

A Shaky do-The Skoda Works Raid of 16/17th April 1943

AIRCRAFT	SERIAL	CODE	SQN	CREW	TRADE	UP	DOWN	BOMBED	NOTES
Halifax II Z	W7920	DY-	102	F/O Hartley H.S.	Pilot	20:48	06:15	7,500 ft	1x1000 lb hang up, jettisoned in sea
				Sgt Hughes W.H.	Nav			305° mag	Later. Hit by flak Eastbound past
				Sgt Thomson R.	W/op				River Moselle and near Karslruhe
				Sgt Myers J.L.	M/U				
				Sgt Lazenby L.	R/G				
				Sgt Flannery J.R. RCAF	F/E				Landed Harwell
				Sgt Hooper H.	B/A				10 hours 45 min duration
Halifax II	JB799	DY-	102	Sgt Templar A.S.	Pilot	20:47	05:55	8,000 ft	Bursts seen on target
				F/O Ertzinger J.D.	Nav			340°	Had to wait for PFF flares over target
				Sgt Clarke E.	W/op				Landed Pershore
				Sgt Joseph A.A.	A/G				
				Sgt Hirst J.L.	A/G				
				Sgt Strong S.T.	F/E				
				Sgt Clack J.	B/A				
Halifax II	JB867	DY-	102	W/C Coventry H.R.	Pilot	20:57	06:01	7,000 ft	ID'd Built up area by Green markers
				P/O McDonald A.M.	Nav			040°	PFF late
				Sgt Brown R.E.	W/op				
				Sgt Hardy W.	A/G				5 of this crew shot down by Altendorf
				F/L Hogg G.F.	A/G				I./NJG4 14th July. Ops Aachen
				Sgt Pine-Coffin G.T.	F/E				
				P/O Armitage V.W.	B/A				Landed Pershore
Halifax II	DT747	DY-P	102	Sgt Griffiths W.A.	Pilot	20:58	06:53	8,000 ft	No green TIs seen but 2 red markers
				Sgt Marsh G.H.	Nav			040°	This a/c was 2nd nearest to aiming
				F/L Hinchcliffe J.D.	W/op				point in whole command.
				Sgt Weir A.C.	A/G				Rear turret failed just before target
				Sgt White J.	A/G				Port Inner failed just before landing
				Sgt Smith J.	F/E				
				Sgt Campbell J.K	B/A				

A Shaky do-The Skoda Works Raid of 16/17th April 1943

219

AIRCRAFT	SERIAL	CODE	SQN	CREW	TRADE	UP	DOWN	BOMBED	NOTES
Halifax II Z	HR712	DY-M	102	F/S McCormack J.R.	Pilot	20:54	05:50	7,000 ft	Target ID'd by woods & railway
				Sgt Lambert W.T.				035°	Fired at and hit by Lancaster aircraft
				Sgt Lewis J.A.					between starboard inner & main
				Sgt Lee B.					plane 40 Miles NW Mannheim
				Sgt Holder T.M.					
				Sgt Beale N.					
				Sgt Field D.A.					
				Sgt Bennett					Landed Pershore
Halifax II	HR667	DY-O	102	P/O Younger A.S.	Pilot	20:53	06:18	3,500 ft	Green markers SSW of target
				F/S Peltier J.	Nav			000°	Numerous bursts in target area.
				F/S Sharp A.	W/op				Large flash and heavy pawl of black.
				Sgt Bell W.	A/G				smoke
				P/O McArthur T.J.	A/G				
				Sgt Smith E.M.M.	F/E				
				F/S Murphy W.E.J.	B/A				Landed Pershore
Halifax II Z	HR663	DY-T	102	S/L Lashbrook W.I. DFC DFM	Pilot	20:49	FTR	01:50	Evaded
				F/O Bolton K.G.	Nav			4,000 ft	Evaded
				Sgt Laws W.R	W/op				Evaded
				Sgt Neill L.	M/U				P.O.W. wounded in fighter attack.
				P/O Williams G.G. GM	R/G				Williams Killed in fighter attack
				F/S Knight D.C.	F/E				P.O.W.
				F/O Martin A. DFC	B/A				Evaded
				Special reconnaissance a/c					Shot down by Hptm. Wilhelm Herget
				With F14 Mk1 camera					Stb I./NJG4 04:06 Eppe-Sauvage
									5x1000 GP 1x500 GP

A Shaky do-The Skoda Works Raid of 16/17th April 1943

AIRCRAFT	SERIAL	CODE	SQN	CREW	TRADE	UP	DOWN	BOMBED	NOTES
Halifax II	JB835	DY-A	102	S/L Fowle F.R.C.	Pilot	20:41	06:40	5,200 ft	Target ID by Green TI markers and white flares. Believe bombs fell on large sheds.
				Sgt Whittingham S.	Nav			050°	
				Sgt Marsh G.F.C.	W/op				
				P/O Seeley W.J.C.	A/G				
				Sgt Vear K.W.C	A/G				
				Sgt Savell W.M.J.	F/E				Landed Castle Donnington short of fuel.
				Sgt Copeland D.	B/A				
Halifax II	JB864	DY-	102	F/L Ingram G.F.H.	Pilot	20:43	06:12	5,500 ft	Fairly heavy haze up to 2,000 ft
				Sgt Richards S.C.	Nav			060°	Factory ID by Green markers
				Sgt Garlic A.D.	W/op				Bursts felt, but not seen.
				Sgt Moulesong J.	A/G				
				Sgt Pimm H.A.	A/G				
				Sgt White K.	F/E				
				P/O Rushbrook J.	B/A				
Lancaster III	ED731	PM-A	103	S/L England	Pilot	21:03	06:10	01:48	Bombed markers
				P/O Plummer C.J.	Nav			7,000 ft	
				Sgt Parfitt A.J.	A/B				
				Sgt Comer L.J	W/op				
				Sgt Wadsworth J.	F/E				
				Sgt Frey F.J.A.	M/U				
				Sgt Cannon D.	R/G				
Lancaster III	ED713	PM-N	103	F/L Blumenauer C.R. RCAF	Pilot	21:07	06:13	01:52	Bombed markers
				Sgt Proud L.	Nav			7,000 ft	Blumenauer awarded DFC March 43
				Sgt Wardle T.B.	A/B				
				Sgt Whittaker A.	W/op				
				Sgt Taylor G.S.	F/E				
				P/O Whitehouse W.	M/U				
				Sgt Griffiths R.A.	R/G				

A Shaky do-The Skoda Works Raid of 16/17th April 1943

AIRCRAFT	SERIAL	CODE	SQN	CREW	TRADE	UP	DOWN	BOMBED	NOTES
Lancaster III	ED725	PM-P	103	F/L Crich W.R.	Pilot	21:00	06:04	01:42	Bombed markers
				Sgt Beardsall K.B.	Nav			9,000 ft	Crich did 1st tour on 'Battles'
				P/O Wood G.	A/B				Duration 9 hours 10 mins.
				Sgt Manners W.W.	W/op				Stalked by fighter outbound which
				Sgt Spink	F/E				was evaded.
				Sgt Evans R.S.	M/U				
				Sgt Archibald W.G.	R/G				
Lancaster III	ED612	PM-	103	F/L Mck Brown A.	Pilot	21:02	06:01	01:52	Bombed markers
				P/O Lewis H.F.	Nav			7,000 ft	This aircraft and all crew lost 14/15th
				Sgt Greenway J.	A/B				June Ops to Oberhausen
				Sgt Cliffe J.	W/op				
				Sgt Morley E.	F/E				
				Sgt O'Connell E.W. RCAF	M/U				
				Sgt Saville J.H.	R/G				
Lancaster III	ED396	PM-M	103	P/O Ewer H.F. RCAF					Combat with ME210 over Darmstadt
				Sgt Williams D.					at 03:45 4000ft. Hits on own a/c and
				Sgt Robson S.					enemy aircraft underside.
				Sgt Welch S.H.					
				Sgt Wilson J.W.G.					
				Sgt Fitch J.R. RCAF					
				Sgt Lee K.M.					
Lancaster III	ED733	PM-X	103	P/O Crampton L.R.	Pilot	21:05	06:19	01:45	Bombed markers
				P/O Lee E.V. RCAF	Nav			8,500 ft	5 of this crew lost with 156 sqn 27/28
				P/O Crowley J.W. RCAF	A/B				July. Ops Hamburg
				P/O Bagge W.E.	W/op				
				Sgt Leader J.L.	F/E				
				Sgt Scott A.S.	M/U				
				P/O Woodsend H.W.	R/G				

A Shaky do-The Skoda Works Raid of 16/17th April 1943

AIRCRAFT	SERIAL	CODE	SQN	CREW		TRADE	UP	DOWN	BOMBED	NOTES
Lancaster I	ED528	PM-Z	103	Sgt Steel W.A.	RNZAF	Pilot	21:07	03:40	Stuttgart	Coned and hit by flak over Stuttgart
				Sgt Mitchell F.D.		Nav				Bombs dropped and returned early.
				Sgt Fee K.R.	RCAF	B/A				
				P/O Baylis N.		W/Op				13 holes in a/c
				Sgt Beautyman T.W		F/E				
				Sgt Birch A.		M/U				
				Sgt Holland F.L.		R/G				
Lancaster I	ED773	PM-U	103	Sgt Ryan N.J.		Pilot	21:10	07:08	Nr Stuttgart	No navigational aid, couldn't locate
				P/O Gentle E.O.		Nav			7,000 ft	Primary.
				Sgt Stringer C.W.		A/B				
				Sgt Rose K.D.		W/op				
				Sgt Irwin J.		F/E				
				Sgt Wakeham R.		M/U				
				Sgt Waters I.J.		R/G				
Lancaster I	W4848	PM-L	103	Sgt Mooney J.O.B.	RNZAF	Pilot	21:12	FTR	KIA	Crashed Ludwigshafen-Oggersheim
				P/O Gipson A.H.	RCAF	Nav			KIA	on Grossraum Flak
				Sgt Rowse H.J.D.		A/B			POW	battery 1/902 at 00:38 hrs
				P/O Hudson F.J.		W/op			KIA	1x4000 HC3x1000
				Sgt Biggs S.		F/E			POW	
				Sgt Merefield V.J.		M/U			KIA	
				Sgt Harley R.W.		R/G			KIA	
Lancaster I	W4845	PM-Q	103	Sgt Rudge D.W.		Pilot	21:08	06:48	01:57	A/C holed through No.2 port tank by
				Sgt Lancaster G.		Nav			7000 ft	flak. Coned over Saarbrucken by 20 -
				Sgt Catton T.W.		A/B				30 S/L Coned and hit by flak in target
				Sgt Greenwood H.T.		W/op				area 74 holes in aircraft!
				Sgt Robinson S.T.		F/E				Landed Elsham Wolds
				Sgt Baird C.R.		M/U				
				Sgt Kilpatrick J.D.	RAAF	R/G				

A Shaky do-The Skoda Works Raid of 16/17th April 1943

AIRCRAFT	SERIAL	CODE	SQN	CREW		TRADE	UP	DOWN	BOMBED	NOTES
Lancaster III	ED417	PM-	103	P/O Carey D.M.		Pilot	21:04	06:34	01:48	Bombed markers
				Sgt Rowlands D.R.		Nav			7,000 ft	
				Sgt Talbot E.L.		A/B				
				P/O Lewin E.R.		W/op				
				Sgt Breheny F.J.		F/E				
				Sgt Burch J.G.		M/U				
				Sgt Montgomery D.		R/G				
Lancaster III	ED614	PM-G	103	W/O Denwood G.		Pilot	21:01	05:55	02:35	Bombed fires
				P/O Davies T.R.		Nav			7,000 ft	
				F/S Ross J.C.		A/B				
				Sgt Cutter E.J.		W/op				
				Sgt Barlow A.L.		F/E				
				F/S Morrison L.G.		M/U				
				Sgt Pedder D.		R/G				
Lancaster I	W4901	PM-W	103	Sgt Burton S.G.		Pilot	20:58	05:51	01:43	Bombed markers
				F/S Harding J.R.	RCAF	Nav			6,000 ft	
				Sgt Cartwright S.		A/B				
				Sgt Baird P.J.		W/op				
				Sgt Squire R.A.		F/E				
				F/S Brady B.L.		M/U				
				Sgt Mcrae R.		R/G				
Lancaster I	ED389	PM-J	103	Sgt King G.J.D.		Pilot	21:00	06:10	01:44	Bombed markers
				F/O Hemingway R.		Nav			7,000 ft	9hrs 10 duration
				Sgt Jay F.N.		A/B				2,500 ft over land. Perspex blown from
				Sgt Backhurst G.W.		W/op				M/U turret on way back over
				Sgt King C.S.		F/E				Mannheim
				F/S Godden B.M.	RCAF	M/U				
				Sgt Davis G.A.		R/G				

A Shaky do-The Skoda Works Raid of 16/17th April 1943

AIRCRAFT	SERIAL	CODE	SQN	CREW		TRADE	UP	DOWN	BOMBED	NOTES
Lancaster I	W4337	PM-R	103	Sgt Pettigrew G.M.		Pilot	21:24	06:53	Safe over	Turned back. Badly hit by flak almost.
				Sgt Ramsey W.D.		Nav			target	on top of target. Coned by about 30
				Sgt Palfrey L.		A/B				search lights. Jettisoned bombs safe
				Sgt Lane W.H.		W/op				Sgt Lane shrapnel wounds in face.
				Sgt Cooper J.		F/E				Sgt Woolard received a lacerated
				Sgt Elkins R.C.		M/U				wound of right foot.
				Sgt Woolard		R/G				Landed Tangmere.
Lancaster III	ED767	PM-H	103	Sgt Egan A.E.	RAAF	Pilot	21:10	06:26	01:58	Bombedmarkers
				Sgt Elliott S.B.		Nav			7,000 ft	Accurate light flak from aerodromes,
				Sgt Miller W.		A/B				stbd. wing holed by light flak at
				Sgt Brown J.		W/op				French coast. Of this crew 3 pow 4
				Sgt Hedges V.A.M.		F/E				KIA (ED528) Gelsenkirchen 26 June
				Sgt Horrell H.A.		M/U				
				Sgt Britton C.A.		R/G				
Lancaster III	ED819	ZN- U	106	F/O Richardson J.H		Capt.	21:05	06:10	01:56	3 runs over tgt. saw Mannheim
				Sgt Patterson J.B.		F/E			6,000 ft	burning on return
				Sgt Brake G.W.		Nav				1x4000 2x1000
				F/O Blazer A.H.		A/B				
				Sgt Dawson F.		W/op				
				P/O Moxham P.C.		M/U				
				Sgt Wardle J.		R/G				
Lancaster III	ED649	ZN-X	106	P/O Rosner E.L.	RCAF/USA	Capt.	21:05	00:40	Returned	Mission abandoned due to
				Sgt Amor E.W.J.		F/E				shuddering airframe.
				Sgt Bailey W.		Nav				All crew lost ops to Koln 8/9th July
				Sgt Smooker F.H.		A/B				Smooker pow.
				Sgt Hougham J.		W/op				
				Sgt Calder J.R.	RCAF	M/U				
				Sgt Turner D.A.	RCAF	R/G				

A Shaky do-The Skoda Works Raid of 16/17th April 1943

AIRCRAFT	SERIAL	CODE	SQN	CREW	TRADE	UP	DOWN	BOMBED	NOTES
Lancaster III	ED720	ZN-R	106	Sgt Yackman F.W.	Capt.	21:00	05:40	01:49	Evidence of night fighters
				Sgt Worsop S.R.	F/E			10,000 ft	
				Sgt Williams H.	Nav				
				Sgt Morey C.L.	A/B				
				Sgt Gibson J.	W/op				
				Sgt Evans A.E.	M/U				
				Sgt Talbot R.J.	R/G				
Lancaster I	R5611	ZN-W	106	Sgt Howell F.J.	Capt.	21:10	06:35	01:44	damaged over target by light flak
				Sgt Grey D.	F/E				which at times was intense
				Sgt Hill W.H. RCAF	Nav				
				Sgt Beacham E.G.R.	A/B				All crew except Penny
				Sgt Littlefair R.W.	W/op				lost ops Plzen 13th May.
				Sgt Dunmore L.A.	M/U				A/C also lost.
				Sgt Penny I.D.	R/G				
Lancaster I	R5492	ZN-S	106	F/S Foulsham E.J.	Capt.		21:10	06:25	01:50 two runs over tgt. due to ground
				Sgt Bright K.E.	F/E			9,000 ft	haze. Captain's first trip.
				Sgt Coxon H.V.	Nav				
				Sgt Hayward A.E.	A/B				
				Sgt Yeomans L.	W/op				
				Sgt Keenan H.J.	M/U				
				Sgt Black J.	R/G				
Lancaster I	ED409	ZN-	106	Sgt Reid J.A.	Capt.	21:05	06:50	02:12	Plotted photo 6.5 miles from target
				Sgt Lawes D.A.	F/E			9,000 ft	Convinced dummy target was
				Sgt Brown A.J.	Nav				attacked
				Sgt Wardrop W.	A/B				1x400 2x1000
				Sgt Beszant P.T.	W/op				
				Sgt Hatton S.	M/U				
				Sgt Cousens A.	R/G				

A Shaky do-The Skoda Works Raid of 16/17th April 1943

AIRCRAFT	SERIAL	CODE	SQN	CREW	TRADE	UP	DOWN	BOMBED	NOTES
Lancaster I	W4842	ZN-H	106	Sgt Robbins E.A.	Capt.	21:00	06:45	02:03	'factory' in bomb sight
				Sgt Seedhouse J.	F/E			8,000 ft	Defences accurate for height but
				Sgt Carpenter L.C.	Nav				haphazard.
				Sgt Calvert L.	A/B				1x4000 2x1000
				Sgt Calvert G.F.	W/op				
				Sgt Denton J.N.	M/U				
				Sgt Manley B.M.	R/G				
Lancaster I	R5551	ZN-V	106	F/O Stephens C.V.	Capt.	21:20	05:55	01:50	Considerable smoke and haze. Fires at
				Sgt Garbett W.W.	F/E			8,100 ft	aiming point and in open fields
				Sgt Bayne B.R.	Nav				Photo 7 miles SW of target
				Sgt James R.A.V.	A/B				1x4000 2x1000
				Sgt Grimes S.V.	W/op				
				Sgt Holten A.E.	M/U				
				Sgt Tyler G.H.	R/G				
Lancaster I	W4242	ZN-	106	F/O Thompson W.R. RCAF	Capt.	21:00	05:50	01:52	Very large explosion observed 02:00
				Sgt Inman G.	F/E			4,000 ft.	1x40002x1000
				Sgt Bennett A.J.	Nav				
				Sgt Hanratty P.	A/B				
				Sgt Wilkes A.	W/op				
				Sgt Kelly R.G.	M/U				
				Sgt Tolman J.H.	R/G				
Lancaster I	R5573	ZN-B	106	Sgt Munro J.A.G.	Capt.	21:05	06:20	02:00	Bright moonlight. ID by Green TIs
				Sgt Clarke S.R.	F/E				Large explosion at 02:00
				Sgt Cambell J.E.	Nav				1x4000
				F/O Harden G.J.	A/B				Photo 7 miles SW of target
				Sgt Colburn D.K.	W/op				
				Sgt Balmer D.P.	M/U				
				Sgt Lee J.V.	R/G				

AIRCRAFT	SERIAL	CODE	SQN	CREW		TRADE	UP	DOWN	BOMBED	NOTES
Lancaster I	R5677	ZN-A	106	Sgt Burton N.E.		Capt.	21:05	06:15	01:47	Whole area covered with fires
				Sgt Whitby N.K.		F/E			7,000 ft	14 Small bomb containers (SBCs) 30lb
				Sgt Hancock J.		Nav				Brilliant moonlight
				Sgt Rookes A.		A/B				9 hours 20 minutes in the air.
				Sgt Mann F.		W/op				
				Sgt Banks C.A.		M/U				
				Sgt Hall J.		R/G				
Lancaster I	ED451	ZN-G	106	Sgt Abell S.		Capt.	21:05	06:15	02:10	Attacked by two fighters, both these
				Sgt Alderson J.G.	RCAF	F/E				were driven off. 23:44 15,000 ft
				P/O Nono V.A.		Nav				Photo 7 miles from A.P
				Sgt Plaskett S.		A/B				1x4000 2x1000
				Sgt Harrower C.M.		W/op				All crew and a/c lost Essen 1.5.43
				Sgt Brown D.		R/G				
				Sgt Barber A.L.		M/U				
Lancaster III	ED708	ZN-	106	S/L Young A.M.		Capt.	21:10	06:30	01:53	No detail seen on target due to
				Sgt Hayle J.R.		F/E				smoke and dust.
				F/O McIver M.		Nav				1st trip as captain B flight c/o
				Sgt Dickison A.W.	RCAF	A/B				
				F/S Mallett C.L.	D.F.M.	W/op				
				Sgt Peel G.H.		M/U				
				F/O Bell J.	D.F.M.	R/G				
Lancaster III	ED801	ZN-N	106	F/L Browne W.D.		Capt.	21:00	05:55	01:48	Photo 8 Miles from A.P. practically no
				Sgt Allen G.		F/E				Flak, search lights useless.
				Sgt Lynn T.		Nav				
				Sgt Pepworth S.A.		A/B				
				Sgt Hayhurst J.		W/op				
				Sgt Williams R.		M/U				
				Sgt Berry W.T.		R/G				

A Shaky do-The Skoda Works Raid of 16/17th April 1943

AIRCRAFT	SERIAL	CODE	SQN	CREW		TRADE	UP	DOWN	BOMBED	NOTES
Lancaster II	DS617	KO-N	115	S/Ldr D.P. Fox DFC		Pilot				
				F/Sgt S Spring		Nav				sqn crews are made up of regulars
				F/Sgt P Chapman		B/A			Note;115	
				Sgt A Johnson		W/T				only captains were listed in ops record.
				F/Sgt A Spires	DFM	R/G				
				Sgt A Bulmer		M/U				
				Sgt P Nixon		F/E				
Lancaster II	DS627	KO-R	115	F/Lt W. Farquharson		Pilot				
				Sgt J Willis		Nav				
				F/Sgt A Stringer		B/A				
				Sgt J Rosenbloom		W/T				
				F/Sgt G Graham		R/G				
				Sgt W Mason		M/U				
				Sgt K Pearson		F/E				
Lancaster II	DS622	KO-Q	115	P/O H Prager		Pilot				
				Sgt W Snook		Nav				
				P/O T Angus		B/A				
				Sgt B West		W/T				
				Sgt G Fairless		R/G				
				Sgt J McCarthy		M/U				
				Sgt L Milner		F/E				
Lancaster II	DS618	KO-P	115	P/O M Coles		Pilot				
				P/O J Woof		Nav				
				Sgt W Coton		B/A				
				Sgt F Proud		W/T				
				Sgt G Hall		R/G				
				Sgt E Sharpe		M/U				
				Sgt A Marshall		F/E				

A Shaky do-The Skoda Works Raid of 16/17th April 1943

AIRCRAFT	SERIAL	CODE	SQN	CREW	TRADE	UP	DOWN	BOMBED	NOTES
Lancaster II	DS612	KO-F	115	F/O W Thomas	Pilot			Note;115	sqn crews are made up of regulars
				F/O H Beckett	Nav				only captains were listed in ops record
				Sgt I Watt	B/A				
				Sgt A Vallins	W/T				
				Sgt A Jones	R/G				
				Sgt A Chalk	M/U				
				Sgt A Maguire	F/E				
Lancaster II	DS616	KO-G	115	Sgt F Plum	Pilot				Shot up airfield
				F/Sgt R Newton	Nav				This crew's names are certain
				Sgt F McKay	B/A				
				Sgt E Eaglebury	W/T				
				Sgt G Bentley	R/G				
				Sgt E Bean	M/U				
				Sgt C F Trott	F/E				
Lancaster II	DS626	KO-J	115	Sgt G Finnerty	Pilot				
				Sgt C Boyes	Nav				
				Sgt A Jones	B/A				
				Sgt J Bellamy	W/T				
				F/Sgt T Page	R/G				
				Sgt W Baker	M/U				
				Sgt D Cowling	F/E				
Lancaster II	DS624	KO-L	115	F/Lt A Avant DFC	Pilot				
				F/O G Edwards	Nav				
				F/Sgt L Kennedy	B/A				
				P/O F Skinner	W/T				
				Sgt E Smith	R/G				
				Sgt W Hocking	M/U				
				Sgt J Hargreaves	F/E				

A Shaky do-The Skoda Works Raid of 16/17th April 1943

AIRCRAFT	SERIAL	CODE	SQN	CREW	TRADE	UP	DOWN	BOMBED	NOTES
Lancaster I	W4854	GT-D	156	W/O Andersen H.R. DFC	Capt.	21:26	FTR	1x4000	Hit by Flak from Reims-Courcy
				P/O Bordycott K.W. DFC DFM	Nav		All crew KIA		airfield crashed NW Brimont. Bordycott Injured in Wimpy crash
				P/O Smith F.	W/Op			4x250 TI	L7775 nav sortie Lossiemouth. 24th
				Sgt Brougham-Faddy P.L.	F/E			16 flares	October 1940
				Sgt Gooding B.H.	A/B				Bordycott was 19 years old when KIA
				Sgt Stephens J.T.	M/U				
				Sgt Woolnough W.O.	R/G				Equipped TR1335
Lancaster I	W4851	GT-	156	F/L Kearns R.S.D. RNZAF	Capt.	21:25	05:45	01:55	Bombed on TI Green
				P/O Barclay W.J. RNZAF	Nav			13,000 ft	
				Sgt Barnham J.E RNZAF	W/Op				1 TI Yellow, 1 TI Green, 1 LB TI Green
				Sgt Evans D.H. 'Taffy'	F/E				1 TI Red, 1 LB TI Red, 4x4flares Wight
				P/O Moller J.A. RNZAF	A/B				1x4000 HC
				F/S Crankshaw K.A. RNZAF	M/U				
				Sgt Dowman M.G. RNZAF	R/G				
Lancaster I	W4943	GT-	156	F/L Lang A.G.		21:20	05:50	01:49	12 search lights ineffective at target. At 22:24 A/C held in 4 search lights
				Sgt Marson J.A.					at Beauvais airfield, also over Roge
				F/L Grey E.M.				13,000 ft	at 4:08 hrs. Rear gunner extinguished
				F/S Rydings D.G.				On Green TI	light. No damage from
				Sgt Clark J.L.				Load	accompanying flak.
				F/S Lee R.J.					
				Sgt Wood N.H.					1 TI Yellow, 1 TI Green, 1 LB TI Green
				F/S Venn F.M.					1 TI Red, 1 LB TI Red, 4 x flare Wight
									1x4000 HC

232

AIRCRAFT	SERIAL	CODE	SQN	CREW	TRADE	UP	DOWN	BOMBED	NOTES
Lancaster III	ED822	GT-	156	P/O Horan J.M.	Capt.	21:20	05:35	01:45	Moderate hvy predicted flak with 30
				F/S Atkin R.J.	Nav			11,000 ft	search lights and 7 balloons W. of
				F/S Fast E.P.	W/Op				Skoda works.
				Sgt Chapman J.C.	F/E				01:12 JU88 sighted no action.
				W/O Saunders D.C.A.	A/B				Blast furnaces seen at Metz.
				Sgt Forbes G.G.	M/U				Flame track photo. No TI seen
				Sgt Curtis J.R.	R/G				Bomb load as ED715
Lancaster I	ED715	GT-A	156	S/L Duigan B.L. RAAF		21:20	05:55	01:37	Moderate accurate heavy and light
				S/L MacKintosh				9,000 ft	flak.12 S/Ls were very tenacious
				S/L Mitchell H.C.					Did four runs over target!
				F/O Eade J.C.					1 TI Yellow, 1 TI Green, 1 LB TI Green
				Sgt Hammond H.					1 TI Red, 1 LB TI Red, 4 x flare Wight
				F/O Drake D.J.					1x4000 HC
				Sgt Dawson K.E.					
				F/L Rodgers J.A.					
Lancaster III	ED841	GT-	156	S/L White J.H.	Capt.	21:30	06:00	01:55	On five separate occasions a/c were
				P/O Roberts R.	Nav				seen falling in flames en route and
				Sgt Stoneley M.J.E.	W/Op				over the target. Slight Heavy & light
				Sgt Wilkinson W.	F/E				flak over target. Well predicted
				Sgt Otter J.C.	A/B				heavy. flak Nürnberg 01:10 hours
				P/O Thompson E.M.	M/U				1 TI Yellow, 1 TI Green, 1 LB TI Green
				Sgt Silverman D.M.C.	R/G				1 TI Red, 1 LB TI Red, 4 x flare Wight
									1x4000 HC
Lancaster III	ED837	GT-	156	P/O Thomson J.F. RNZAF	Capt.	21:40	05:50	01:48	Moderate/heavy flak 20-30 search
				Sgt Wilkin F.J.	Nav			13,300 ft	lights. ME110 seen over target at
				Sgt Farnell H.A.	W/Op				01:48 no action. ID by river & Green
				Sgt Rowe W.J.	F/E				TI
				Sgt Hamilton C.F.	A/B				1 TI Yellow, 1 TI Green, 1 LB TI Green
				Sgt Baxter J.C.	M/U				1 TI Red, 1 LB TI Red, 4 x flare Wight
				Sgt Craighead J.	R/G				1x4000 HC

A Shaky do-The Skoda Works Raid of 16/17th April 1943

AIRCRAFT	SERIAL	CODE	SQN	CREW	TRADE	UP	DOWN	BOMBED	NOTES
Lancaster III	ED734	GT-H	156	Sgt Lay K.L.W.	Capt.	21:30	05:40	01:55	Target area 01:53 ME210 seen 300 yd
				P/O Bryant R.M.	Nav			14,000 ft	no action.
				Sgt Drake W.J.	W/Op				An a/c seen to fall in flames at 01:50
				Sgt Ratcliff R.E.	F/E				with TIs & flares going off
				Sgt Bauman W.J.	A/B				(R5622 83 sqn.)
				Sgt Webb P.D.	M/U				
				Sgt Foster W.	R/G				
Lancaster III	ED842	GT-	156	F/O Smith B.F.	Capt.	21:45	05:30	01:48	20 miles N.E. Saarbrucken twin eng.
				P/O Smith W.J.	Nav				enemy A/C was seen. Evasive action
				F/O Goodwin R.E.	W/Op				taken to Port, E/A a/c came over top,
				Sgt Marshall B.	F/E				tracer went under own a/c.
				F/O Philpe J.A.	A/B				
				Sgt Jones L.J.	M/U				
				F/O Hayes S.	R/G				
Lancaster I	W4930	GT-	156	Sgt Gonce H.B	Capt.	21:25	FTR		Crashed at Aigny (Marnes)
				Sgt Dean J.C.	Nav				
				Sgt Rowe H.D.	W/Op				
				Sgt Muirhead M.M.	F/E				
				P/O Anastassiades M. Cyp.	A/B				1x4000 4x250 ICB
				Sgt Boyd J.	M/U				16 flares
				Sgt Corley L.E. RCAF/USA	R/G				Equiped Gee
Halifax II	HR720	NP-B	158	W/Co Hope T.R.DFC Sqn C/O	Capt.	20:59	06:25	01:48	Ground detail ID'd at Yellow marker
				Gp.Cpt. Seymour-Lucas	Official Obs			7,500 ft	last turning point. Timed run to target
				F/O Garrett E.A. RCAF	Nav				270°Target lit by Green markers
				P/O Kennedy P.J.	A/B				
				Sgt Cottrell K.G.	W/Op				450 x 4lb, 90x4lb X type 24x30lb ICB
				Sgt Warburton F.	M/U				
				F/S O'Handley J.J. RCAF	R/G				
				F/L Hope V.G.	F/E				Hope was Eng.Section Ldr.

A Shaky do-The Skoda Works Raid of 16/17th April 1943

AIRCRAFT	SERIAL	CODE	SQN	CREW	TRADE	UP	DOWN	BOMBED	NOTES
Halifax II	HR776	NP-O	158	W/O Smith F.S. RCAF	Capt.	20:36	03:02	00:16	Engine failure Saarbrucken attacked
				W/O Crawley F.W.	Nav			11,000 ft	Concentration of flak and S/Ls
				Sgt Porter M.S.J.	A/B			275°	Glimpse of river Saar
				Sgt Wooldridge H.T.	W/Op				
				Sgt Scroggie J.	M/U				450 x 4lb, 90x4lb X type 24x30lb ICBs
				Sgt Eastwick R.L.	R/G				
				Sgt Ayton G.	F/E				
Halifax II	HR785	NP-G	158	S/L Williams R.S. D.F.C.	Capt.	20:44	06:36	02:01	Timed run from Yellow markers.
				P/O Kerr L.	Nav			4,500 ft	Long roof with chimneys seen.
				Sgt Ward G.	A/B			150° mag	White flares lit up area. Bombed on 5
				Sgt Gosling A.R.	W/Op				large chimneys in a group. Rear
				Sgt Binnington W. R.	M/U				gunner saw two fires coming away,
				Sgt Edmond W.	R/G				one red, one white
				Sgt Watts S.H.C.	F/E				
Halifax II	HR717	NP-E	158	P/O Sandgren W.H. RCAF	Capt.	20:28	06:59	01:45	Yellow markers dropped just after a/c
				P/O Stanyard F.	Nav			7,000 ft	Turned onto target at 01:35 hours.
				F/S DeMarco F.V RCAF	A/B			330° mag	Green markers to port just prior to
				P/O Dobson W. RCAF	W/Op				bombing. Saw building with peaked
				P/O Bristow H.W.	M/U				roofs and railway. Several large
				Sgt Harding M.A. RCAF	R/G				explosions.
				Sgt Shaw P.E.	F/E				450 x 4lb, 90x4lb X type 24x30lb ICB
Halifax Ia	HR722	NP-C	158	F/L Donaldson D.J.	Capt.	20:37	06:44	01:55	Target ID'd by Yellow markers
				Sgt Lay H.F.D.	Nav			5,000 ft	Several large fires.
				Sgt Banks D.F.R.	A/B			190° mag	450 x 4lb, 90x4lb X type 24x30lb ICB
				Sgt Cole G.W.	W/Op				Stalked by two, Ju88 23:55 and at
				Sgt Fitzgerald M.J.	M/U				00:08 with JU88 rear gunner fired
				P/O Willis G.H.	R/G				burst +again an E/A South of
				Sgt Whyatt L.	F/E				Luxemburg.

A Shaky do-The Skoda Works Raid of 16/17th April 1943

AIRCRAFT	SERIAL	CODE	SQN	CREW	TRADE	UP	DOWN	BOMBED	NOTES
Halifax II	HR735	NP-N	158	F/L Reynolds K.H.	Capt.	20:42	06:28	01:43	Yellow markers seen. White flares &
				P/O Worsnop F.	Nav			3,000 ft	Green TIs at target. Explosions seen
				P/O Harbottle J.	A/B			270°	buffeted all the time by HE
				F/O Winship T. RCAF	W/Op				explosions.
				Sgt Weatherill D.A.	M/U				
				Sgt Buckland C.R.	R/G				450 x 4lb, 90x4lb X type 24x30lb ICB
				Sgt Wilson W.J.	F/E				
Halifax II	HR719	NP-M	158	Sgt Williamson J.	Capt.	20:30	07:05	01:55	Map read from Yellow markers at
				W/O Cridge J.H.	Nav			7,000 ft	turning point up to target. Bombed
				Sgt McQuaker R.G.	A/B			260° mag	just before long building with
				Sgt Hasleton P.	W/Op				smoking chimneys.
				Sgt Brundle H.F.	M/U				
				Sgt Kinsey W.E.	R/G				450 x 4lb, 90x4lb X type 24x30lb ICB
				Sgt Hampson K.C.	F/E				
Halifax II	HR724	NP-W	158	Sgt Laver E.A.J.	Capt.	20:29	06:56	01:48	Target ID'd by bomb flashes. White
				Sgt Plumridge E.J.	Nav			7,000 ft	and green markers going down after
				Sgt Clelland H.J.	A/B			335° mag	bombing. Many fires. Smoke
				Sgt Johnson F.R.	W/Op				beginning to blot out the works
				Sgt McVitie A.	M/U				
				Sgt Adams F.T.	R/G				450 x 4lb, 90x4lb X type 24x30lb ICB
				Sgt MacRae G.J.	F/E				
Halifax II	HR775	NP-V	158	P/O Smith N. RCAF	Capt.	20:39	06:39	01:45	Visibility clear, but ground haze and
				F/O Rowe J.M.	Nav			9,000 ft	drifting smoke. Green markers seen
				Sgt Brown F.W.	A/B			000°mag	After bombing 1/3rd SBCs hung up &
				Sgt Hatch C.F	W/Op				later jettisoned off French coast.
				Sgt Edwards T.W.	M/U				
				Sgt Smith E.J.	R/G				450 x 4lb, 90x4lb X type 24x30lb ICB
				Sgt Ginger W.	F/E				

A Shaky do-The Skoda Works Raid of 16/17th April 1943

AIRCRAFT	SERIAL	CODE	SQN	CREW		TRADE	UP	DOWN	BOMBED	NOTES
Halifax II	HR758	NP-Y	158	F/O Jay B.P.	RAAF	Capt.	20:32		KIA	Crashed woodland at Hahnweilerhof
				Sgt Scholes G.D.W.		Nav			pow	woods 2 miles nth Borrstadt shot
				P/O Barratt K.A.		A/B			KIA	down by night fighter just after
				Sgt Ford A.		W/Op			pow	midnight flying east.
				Sgt Newdick R.		M/U			pow	Returned fire shot down E/A
				Sgt Fawcett C.D.	RCAF	R/G			pow	450x4, 90x4 X type, 24x30 ICB
				Sgt Holmes F.E.		F/E			pow	Equipped, Mandrel, Tinsel, TR.1335
Halifax II	HR752	NP-T	158	Sgt Sugden J.S.		Capt.	20:45	06:41	01:45	Yellow markers not seen when
				Sgt Parry W.E.A.		Nav			8,000 ft	expected at last turning point. Did
				Sgt Black D.M.		A/B			270°mag	orbit, yellows were then seen. ID'd
				Sgt Hawkins A.	RCAF	W/Op				bend in river Danau. At tgt Bombed
				Sgt Leighton R.		M/U				railway sidings. Rear gunner reported
				Sgt Ross J.T.		R/G				large explosion at 01:49
				Sgt Rudrum G.H.		F/E				450 x 4lb, 90x4lb X type 24x30lb ICB
Halifax II	HR751	NP-J	158	P/O Bond H.		Capt.	20:43	06:54	01:46	Saw green markers & white flares at
				F/O Burt P.R.		Nav			8,000 ft	Target. Bombs down immediately
				Sgt Allen G.		A/B			330°mag	Nth of green TI.
				Sgt Rowsell C.R.		W/Op				
				Sgt Wright S.		M/U				
				F/S Oman S.W.		R/G				
				Sgt McGuigan J.H.		F/E				450 x 4lb, 90x4lb X type 24x30lb ICB
Halifax II	HR740	NP-K	158	Sgt Brown S.C.	RNZAF	Capt.	20:33	06:22	01:47	Target ID'd by bend in river & white
				W/O Barnard A.		Nav			9,000 ft	Flares. Aircraft shaken over target.
				P/O Fyfe J.G.		A/B			220° mag	Lost 50 gallons of petrol through vent
				Sgt Holroyd S.G.		W/Op				on take off.
				Sgt Leary H.		M/U				
				Sgt Robinson R.W.		R/G				6 SBC 8x30lb 6 SBC 90x4 lb
				Sgt Martin L.V.		F/E				Landed Chipping Warden

A Shaky do-The Skoda Works Raid of 16/17th April 1943

AIRCRAFT	SERIAL	CODE	SQN.	CREW		TRADE	UP	DOWN	BOMBED	NOTES
Halifax II	HR755	NP-X	158	Sgt Brown W.T.	RNZAF	Capt.	20:38	07:02	01:47	ID'd by Yellow markers at last turning point and river there. Bombed on position Nth. Of green markers on
				Sgt Whitelaw A.	RNZAF	Nav			8,800 ft	
				Sgt Doel H.C.		A/B			180° mag	Target.
				Sgt Owen W.A.		W/Op				Smoke obliterated target.
				Sgt Austen J.		M/U				
				Sgt Parkes J.	NZAF	R/G				450 x 4lb, 90x4lb X type 24x30lb ICB
				Sgt Evans S.		F/E				
Halifax II	HR734	NP-P	158	S/L Viney J.M. B Flight c/o		Capt.	20:40	06:49	01:47	7/10ths cloud 5,000 ft.
				P/O Heaton P.	RCAF	Nav			6,000 ft	Saw Yellow markers at turning point,
				F/L Reid J. Bombing Sect Ldr		A/B			290° mag	green over target. Made two runs.
				P/O Morgan E.E.	RCAF	W/Op				Fire & smoke obscured all buildings.
				Sgt Kemp W.G	RCAF	M/U				Rear Gnr. saw building collapse
				P/O Clark R.J.	RCAF	R/G				north of River. Smoke up to 4,000 ft.
				Sgt Smith W.S.		F/E				450 x 4lb, 90x4lb X type 24x30lb ICB
										Large explosion seen when 60 miles
										away.
Halifax II	HR780	NP-D	158	F/S Roberts R.D. D.F.M.		Capt.	20:34	23:53	Returned	a/c wouldn't climb 40 miles
				Sgt Schofield A.R.		Nav				S.E. Felixstowe
				F/S Pridden W.E.E.B.	RCAF	A/B				
				F/S Hand H.F.		W/Op				
				Sgt Culley E.J.		M/U				
				Sgt Gibson H.A.		R/G				
				Sgt Dent W.G.	RCAF	F/E				

A Shaky do-The Skoda Works Raid of 16/17th April 1943

AIRCRAFT	SERIAL	CODE	SQN	CREW	TRADE	UP	DOWN	BOMBED	NOTES
Lancaster I	W4952	EM-T	207	P/O Herrin P.G.	Pilot	21:27	06:10	01:44	ID visually after two runs. One SBC hung up.
				Sgt Mills P.	F/E			7,500 ft	Half port elevator missing. Port fin &
				P/O Flatt W.H.	Nav			020 °mag	Rudder holed 10 inch sq. hole port
				P/O Kleinberg G. (Belgium)	A/B				main plane-due to light flak.
				Sgt Payton S.	Wop/Ag				14 SBC
				Sgt Male G.A.H.	M/U				Landed Tangmere
				Sgt Bradshaw R.	R/G				
Lancaster I	ED412	EM-Q	207	Sgt Stephens J.A.	Pilot	21:33	05:45	01:48	Target ID'd by river & green TIs.
				Sgt Bury N.R. 'Blondie'	F/E			8,000 ft	Holed in Starboard wing & bomb dr.
				Sgt Love J.N.	Nav			050°	Dent in starboard side M/U turret all
				Sgt Llewellyn W.J.	A/B			8 hrs 25 min	due to flak
				Sgt Pegrum A.J.C. 'Lucky'	Wop/Ag				12 SBC 90x4lb 2 SBC 90x4 icb Type X
				Sgt Barfoot A.	M/U				Landed Tangmere Xd
				Sgt McDavitt A.T.	R/G			Sgt Barfoot	Injured in crash of Hampden PT081
									14Feb 1942 16 OTU
Lancaster I	W4945	EM-Z	207	F/O Balme D.M.	Pilot	21:23	00:32	Returned early	Inter-com to rear turret u/s
				Sgt Bashford G.J.	F/E				
				Sgt Lawes C.M.	Nav				
				Sgt Rumgay J.L.	A/B				
				Sgt Thomas H.	Wop/Ag				
				Sgt Cordon A.	M/U				
				Sgt Mitchell L.W.	R/G				
Lancaster I	W4174	EM-V	207	Sgt Tombs J.	Pilot	21:26	00:30	Returned early	Air pressure system u/s shortly after take off.
				Sgt Brookes A.E.	F/E				
				Sgt Lance A.C.E.	Nav				
				Sgt Deschaine G.E.	A/B				
				Sgt Faux R.G.	Wop/Ag				
				Sgt Cook C.S.	M/U				
				Sgt Jones B.	R/G				Landed Wittering

A Shaky do-The Skoda Works Raid of 16/17th April 1943

AIRCRAFT	SERIAL	CODE	SQN	CREW	TRADE	UP	DOWN	BOMBED	NOTES
Lancaster I	W4171	EM-J	207	Sgt Jones I.B.	Pilot	21:28	06:00	01:46	ID'd by PFF flares and visually from river.
				Sgt Gillespie J. RCAF	F/E			8,000 ft	
				Sgt Glare G.J.	Nav			090°	14 SBC 8x30lb
				F/O Hyland B.P.M.	A/B				
				Sgt Hollett W.A.	Wop/Ag				This aircraft & all but R/G lost
				Sgt Davies F.W.	M/U				27.4.43.
				Sgt Mortlock K.G.	R/G				Ops. Duisberg
Lancaster I	ED361	EM-R	207	P/O Mappin H.	Pilot	21:30	06:05	01:45	ID'd by PFF and white flares. River
				Sgt Wigget C.E.	F/E			8,000 ft	visible 5 large explosions seen.
				Sgt Boar A.J.	Nav			055° mag	
				Sgt Livett G.A.	A/B				12 SBC 90x4lb 2 SBC 90x4lb X type.
				Sgt Crank A.A.	Wop/Ag				
				Sgt Anderson W.	M/U				
				Sgt Turner F.W.	R/G				
				Sgt Williams					Landed Tangmere
Lancaster I	ED537	EM-O	207	W/O Hawkes W.D.	Pilot	21:25	05:50	01:48	ID'd visually by white flares
				Sgt Tompkins E.S.	F/E			7,000 ft	Fires in target area seemed to merge
				Sgt Whiteoak A.W.	Nav			047° mag	
				Sgt Mcnair W.A.	A/B				
				Sgt Nipper G.R.	Wop/Ag				
				Sgt Lambert R.	M/U				
				F/S Etherton H.J.	R/G				Landed Tangmere
Lancaster I	W4938	EM-A	207	W/O King K.A.	Pilot	21:31	06:10	01:42	ID'd visually by PFF flares, also join in
				Sgt Broadhead G.	F/E			9,000 ft	two rivers. Large square building in
				P/O Gallagher E.D.	Nav			020°	bomb sight. Bombs seen to explode
				Sgt Gainsboro'Allen J.H.	A/B				
				F/O Grey W.	Wop/Ag				14 SBC 8x30lb
				Sgt Brown W.T.	M/U				
				Sgt Jamieson W.	R/G				Landed Tangmere

A Shaky do-The Skoda Works Raid of 16/17th April 1943

239

240

AIRCRAFT	SERIAL	CODE	SQN	CREW	TRADE	UP	DOWN	BOMBED	NOTES
Lancaster I	ED692	EM-W	207	Sgt Stubbs LE	Pilot	21:24	05:48	01:55	ID'd by TI markers & white flares.
				Sgt Mitchell R.C.	F/E			8,000 ft	Bombs seen to burst
				Sgt Coates A.H.	Nav			026°	12 SBC 90x4lb 2 SBC 90x4lb X type.
				P/O Mawson E.	A/B				
				Sgt Lucan R.D.	Wop/Ag				Landed Ford
				Sgt Furman R.M.	M/U				
				Sgt O'Brien W.	R/G				
Lancaster I	ED304	PO-C	207	Sgt McIntosh J.		21:32	05:35	01:44	White flares seen but no green TIs
	borrowed		467 sq	Sgt Sooley R.C.				7,000 ft	Fires seemed to start when
				Sgt Nicholson I.H.				038°	left target. Camera failed.
				Sgt Ball D.A.J.W.					1x4000 2x1000
				Sgt Hyde J.					
				Sgt Simmons J.					
				Sgt Middleton R.					
				Sgt Davidson					Landed Tangmere
Halifax II	JB925	EQ-R	408	F/L Hatle C.O. RCAF	Capt	21:04	FTR	KIA	28k s.e.Trier/Bierfeld Nonnweiler
				P/O Holmes L.H.	Nav/B			KIA	Shot down by Uffz.Depperman
				Sgt Osmond S.F.	Nav/B			KIA	12./NJG4 03:01
				Sgt Richmond H. RCAF	Wop/Ag			KIA	1x2000 MC 2x1000 GP
				Sgt Gibson J.W. RCAF	Wop/Ag			KIA	16x30 150x4 30x4 x type
				Sgt Tschantre A.A. RCAF/US	A/G			KIA	
				Sgt Kapuscinski W.G. RCAF	F/E			KIA	
				P/O O'Connell T.N. RCAF	2nd Pilot			KIA	

A Shaky do-The Skoda Works Raid of 16/17th April 1943

AIRCRAFT	SERIAL	CODE	SQN	CREW	TRADE	UP	DOWN	BOMBED	NOTES
Halifax II	DT752	EQ-W	408	F/O Sergent J.R.L. RCAF	Capt	21:00	FTR		St Hubert. Night fighter Ludwig Meister I./NJG4 04:08
				Sgt Hill G.M.	Nav/B				
				Sgt Cocks F.R.	Nav/B				1x2000 HC, 2x1000 GP 16x30 ICB
				Sgt Gargrave D.F.	Wop/Ag				
				Sgt Kwasney W. RCAF/US	Wop/Ag				150x4 ICB, 30x4 X type
				Sgt Heming C.D. RCAF	A/G				
				Sgt Machell H.G. RCAF	F/E				
Halifax II	BB343	EQ-X	408	W/O Guay J.A. RCAF	Capt	21:05	FTR		Crashed Lesquielles St Germain.
				Sgt Pilon F.R. RCAF	Nav/B				Shot down by Ofw.Adolf
				Sgt Haines L.G. RCAF	Nav/B				Brandstetter of 3./NJG 4 04:37 hours
				Sgt Winter R.H.	Wop/Ag				
				Sgt McDonald I. RCAF	Wop/Ag				1x2000 MC 2x1000 GP
				Sgt Gielty A.P. RCAF	A/G				16x30, 150x4, 30x4 X type Inc.
				Sgt Fill H.W. RCAF	F/E				
Halifax II	JB854	EQ-D	408	Sgt Heming G.C. RCAF	Capt	21:05	FTR		Louppy-le-Chateau, Bar le Duc
				F/S Birchall R. RCAF	Nav/B				Shot down by Lt .Friedrich Tober
				Sgt Zaleschuk D. RCAF	Nav/B				II./NJG4 at 00:03 2500 metres
				Sgt Mason R.W.	Wop/Ag				5k NE Laimont
				Sgt Jorgensen S.J. RCAF	Wop/Ag				
				Sgt Archie S. RCAF	A/G				4x1000 GP, 16x30, 150x4, 30x4 X type
				Sgt Cantley A.C. RCAF	F/E				ICB
Halifax II	JB959	EQ-K	408	S/L Newson W.F.M.	Capt	21:02	06:43	01:48	Fires starting, target in sights.
				F/O Harris W.J.	Nav/B			9,500 ft	1x2000 2x1000 150x4lb 30x4lb X type
				Sgt Naylor W.K.	Nav/B			060° mag	16x30lb. 4x30lb ICB hung up
				Sgt O'Connor P.C.	Wop/Ag				
				Sgt ConleyW.	Wop/Ag				
				Sgt Mcarter D.M.	A/G				
				Sgt Martin R.	F/E				
				F/O Colvin J.M.	2nd Pilot				

A Shaky do-The Skoda Works Raid of 16/17th April 1943

AIRCRAFT	SERIAL	CODE	SQN	CREW	TRADE	UP	DOWN	BOMBED	NOTES
Halifax II	DT677	EQ-P	408	P/O Stovel C.C.	Capt	21:03	05:27	01:42	Centre of 'factory' in bomb sights
				F/S Bemister J.E.	Nav/B			12,000 ft	
				Sgt McDougal G.H.	Nav/B			021° mag	4x1000 150x4lb 30x4lb X type
				Sgt Richardson W.B.J.	Wop/Ag				16x30lb
				Sgt Parker E.F.	Wop/Ag				Mandrel used.
				F/O Macdonald H.W.	A/G				
				Sgt Borley J.H.	F/E				
				Sgt Johnston G.	2nd Pilot				Landed West Malling short fuel
Halifax II	JB858	EQ-S	408	Sgt Milligan B.R.	Capt	20:56	06:55	01:48	Flares in bomb sight, no results seen
				P/O Culbert F.	Nav/B			9,000 ft	
				Sgt Dally N.J.B.	Nav/B			340°mag	
				Sgt Aiken D.	Wop/Ag				
				Sgt Hunter J.D.B.	Wop/Ag				
				Sgt Giffin E.M.	A/G				
				Sgt Wright R.B.	F/E				
Halifax II	JB898	EQ-Q	408	Sgt Blackhall R.O. RCAF	Capt	20:58	08:05	01:56	ID'd visually & by PFF. Pinpoint
				F/S Norton C.B.	Nav/B			9,500 ft	obtained. Fires in bomb sight
				Sgt Semper G.I.	Nav/B			030 °mag	4x1000 150x4lb 30x4lb X type
				F/S Godfrey K.E.	Wop/Ag				16x30lb
				Sgt Sutton A.J. RCAF	Wop/Ag				This a/c shot down by fighter4/5th
				Sgt Horn C.L.	A/G				May Ops Dortmund.
				Sgt Emmons K.E. RCAF	F/E				Blackhall, Emmons & Sutton
				F/O Smith C.W.	2nd Pilot				were KIA. Norton, Semper & Godfrey
									were P.O.W.

A Shaky do-The Skoda Works Raid of 16/17th April 1943

AIRCRAFT	SERIAL	CODE	SQN	CREW	TRADE	UP	DOWN	BOMBED	NOTES
Halifax II	DT749	EQ-C	408	F/O Harriss B.E.	Capt	21:02	06:32	01:51	Bombs seen to burst in SW corner of
				P/O Sharman G.B.	Nav/B			10,000 ft	'Skoda works'
				P/O Harris T.W.	Nav/B			045 °mag	4x1000 150x4lb 30x4lb X type
				Sgt Shellington W.R.	Wop/Ag				16x30lb
				Sgt Dimma T.W.	Wop/Ag				
				Sgt Willis G.E.	A/G				
				Sgt Skebo T.H.	F/E				
				Sgt Brooke D.	2nd Pilot				
Halifax II	JB913	EQ-F	408	Sgt Dungey E.B.	Capt	21:06	06:22	01:50	Bombed immediately beyond green
				F/O Foster J.W.G.	Nav/B			9,500 ft	Markers. 1x2000 2x1000
				P/O Lowrey T.	Nav/B			050°	150x4lb 30x4lb X type 16x30lb
				Sgt Evans R.	Wop/Ag				
				Sgt Bowlby A.T.	Wop/Ag				
				Sgt Speller R.H.	A/G				
				Sgt James L.K.	F/E				
Halifax II	DT769	EQ-J	408	P/O Smuck A.O. RCAF	Capt	20:59	07:00	01:58	Sheds were in centre of
				P/O Kelly J.J.	Nav/B			10,000 ft	bomb sight. Astro hatch blown off
				P/O Bilsen F.W.	Nav/B			041°	over target. Pilot's escape hatch
				Sgt Barneveld R.	Wop/Ag				blown off during flak attack at 00:20
				Sgt Mckay D.G. RCAF	Wop/Ag				at Saarbrucken. Fighter contact
				Sgt Brown D.L.G. RCAF	A/G				00:40 hrs 49.18N 07.32E short distance
				Sgt Foggon J.	F/E				east of Homburg. R/G fired at enemy
								Load 4x1000	150x4lb 30x4lb X type 16x30lb
Halifax II	DT674	EQ-A	408	F/S Leaver F.H.	Capt	21:11	05:35	01:46	Bombs thought to have fallen on
				Sgt Burgess C.S.	Nav/B			7,000 ft	south side of works.
				Sgt Kerr L.W.	Nav/B			029°	Mandrel used
				Sgt Smith R.L.M.	Wop/Ag				
				Sgt Saprunoff S.	Wop/Ag			Load 4x1000	150x4lb 30x4lb X type 16x30lb
				Sgt Young S.G.	A/G				
				Sgt Box J.	F/E				Landed Gatwick short fuel

AIRCRAFT	SERIAL	CODE	SQN	CREW	TRADE	UP	DOWN	BOMBED	NOTES
Halifax II	W7817	VR-A	419	F/O Vaillancourt C.J.	Capt	20:40	06:51		ID'd by river & markers.
				P/O Grimshaw D.	Nav/B				Bombed on white flares & fires. Hvy
				Sgt Douglas M.W.	Nav/B				Smoke & large fires. One huge
				Sgt Morrison A.S.	Wop/Ag				explosion seen to rise to 15,000 ft.
				Sgt Jaynes A.	Wop/Ag				Mannheim mass of flames on return
				Sgt Peck J.L.	A/G				1x2000 2x1000 fused T.D.O .25
				Sgt Stanley F.T.	F/E				SBC 90x4lb 20% X type.2 SBC 80x30lb
Halifax II	JB912	VR-B	419	P/O Jackson T.E. RCAF	Capt	20:51	06:38		Woods & fires ID'd.
				F/S Carlton J.M. RCAF	Nav/B				Nr collision with Lanc over tgt area
				P/O Fry J.R. RCAF	Nav/B				Bomb load as W7817 above.
				Sgt Crandell T.M. RCAF	Wop/Ag				Pilot & 5 of this crew shot down on
				Sgt Sebastian C.J. RCAF	Wop/Ag				Ops Stettin 20/21 April. Gourde KIA
				Sgt Jury E.	A/G				28/29 Apr. Gardening, Silverthorne.
			Odd bd	Sgt Gourde R.R. RCAF/US	F/E				He was from Longview Washington.
Halifax II	JB861	VR-C	419	F/S Palmer J.	Capt	20:57	06:46	8,000 ft	ID'd by river and markers.
				Sgt Walsh H.W.	Nav/B				Dense smoke
				P/O Brown T.	Nav/B				
				Sgt Weedy R.	Wop/Ag				1x2000 2x1000 fused T.D.O .25
				Sgt Simonett W.A.	Wop/Ag			2SBC 90x4lb	20% X type. 2SBC 80x30lb
				Sgt Ratelle R.E.L.	A/G				
				Sgt Gearing A.J.	F/E				
Halifax II	DT672	VR-D	419	P/O Dickson J.D.	Capt	20:46	06:42	8,000 ft	Bombed by markers & ground detail
				F/L Parnall A.L.	Nav/B				Heavy pall of black smoke over target
				Sgt Harris A.C.	Nav/B				Load as JB861
				Sgt Bright T.J.	Wop/Ag				
				Sgt Allan J.C.	Wop/Ag				
				P/O Wagner R.J.	A/G				
				Sgt Weeks J.A.	F/E				

A Shaky do-The Skoda Works Raid of 16/17th April 1943

AIRCRAFT	SERIAL	CODE	SQN	CREW	TRADE	UP	DOWN	BOMBED	NOTES
Halifax II	JB900	VR-	419	P/O Heintz B.F.	Capt	20:56	07:20	10,000 ft	Bombed on markers. Most of target
				P/O Hart J.E.	Nav/B				Covered with pall of smoke. Glowing
				F/S Youngblut S.E.	Nav/B				Fires underneath.
				Sgt Tompkins C.	Wop/Ag				
				Sgt Empson E.	Wop/Ag				1x2000 2x1000 fused T.D.O .25
				Sgt Morrison S.R.	A/G				2SBC90x4lb 20% X type.2SBC80x30lb
				F/S Dell O.H.	F/E				
Halifax II	JB859	VR-	419	P/O Weedon P.G.	Capt	21:00	06:34		ID'd by markers. Building seen to be
				F/O Campbell P.	Nav/B				hit
				F/O Shields R.K.	Nav/B				
				Sgt Wigelsworth M.	Wop/Ag				Bomb load as JB900 above
				Sgt Nevins C.W.	Wop/Ag				
				Sgt Poole S.	A/G				
				Sgt Plyley D.G.	F/E				
Halifax II	JB929	VR-	419	S/L Kenney D.H.	Capt	20:59	06:53		Smoke & haze over target bombed
				Sgt Wother G.J.	Nav				visually
				Sgt Doolan W.	A/B				
				F/O Rice W.G.	Wop.AG				
				Sgt Goodman G.M.	F/E				Bomb load as JB900 above
				Sgt Rock B.J.	2nd Gun				
				Sgt Batkin W.C.	R/G				Westerman from Pittsburgh shot
				Sgt Westerman J.F. RCAF/US	2nd pilot				down Stettin P.O.W. on Halifax JB912
Halifax II	DT616	VR-K	419	F/O Boyce W.J.	Capt	21:01	Colerne		ID'd by river & markers 'works' in
				P/O Black D.I.	Nav				Bombsight.
				P/O Buck C.L.	A/B				
				Sgt Chambers D.E.C.	Wop.AG				Bomb load as JB900 above
				Sgt Stewart D.M.	F/E				
				Sgt Hall R.M.	2nd Gun				
				Sgt Gray J.D.	R/G				Landed Colerne

A Shaky do-The Skoda Works Raid of 16/17th April 1943

AIRCRAFT	SERIAL	CODE	SQN	CREW	TRADE	UP	DOWN	BOMBED	NOTES
Halifax II	JB862	VR-U	419	F/S Goddard R.G.	Capt	20:52	07:11		Target ID's by flares & fires
				F/S Johnson R.	Nav				
				F/S Sherman H.M.	A/B				Attacked twice by JU88 no claim or
									damage
				Sgt Deane K.I.J.	Wop.AG				1x2000 2x1000 fused T.D.O.25
				Sgt Joy W.N.	F/E				2SBC 90x4lb 20% X type. 2SBC
				Sgt McKenzie J.J.	2nd Gun				80x30lb
				Sgt Clarke G.F.	R/G				
				F/O Elliot G.W.	2nd pilot				
Halifax II	DT794	VR-Y	419	F/S Bell R.A.H.	Capt	20:50	Colerne		Bomb bursts & icb strikes seen
				F/S White W.L.	Nav				
				F/S Williston R.O.	A/B				Load as JB862 above
				Sgt Arseneau J.D.	Wop.AG				
				Sgt Taylor W.B.	F/E				
				Sgt Graham J.F.	2nd Gun				
				F/S Aitken G.E.	R/G				Landed Colerne
				F/O Tyler J.W.E.	2nd pilot				
Halifax II	DT689	VR-N	419	F/S Gray M.F.	Capt	21:05	00:31	RTN	Returned from 50.26N 01.20E 22:53
				F/S Hancock C.O.	Nav				3gns in rear u/s 12 miles off French
				F/O McNicol W.J.	A/B				coast S.W. from Etaples.
				Sgt Low C.N.	Wop.AG				
				Sgt Wilby C.	F/E				Load as JB862 above
				F/S Braniff M.S.	2nd Gun				
				P/O Gray G.E.	R/G				

A Shaky do-The Skoda Works Raid of 16/17th April 1943

AIRCRAFT	SERIAL	CODE	SQN	CREW	TRADE	UP	DOWN	BOMBED	NOTES
Halifax II	W1271	VR-P	419	S/L Clark D.W.S. RNZAF	Capt	20:53	07:06		Target ID'd by markers & river.
				F/S Williams R.J.	Nav				Heavy flak on way out. Hit by flak ov'r
				F/O Duncan I.G.	A/B				Mannheim on way back. Starboard
				Sgt Jackson F.	Wop.AG				Outer failed.
				Sgt Lee V.	F/E				Fuel 1880 gallons+230 gals overload
				Sgt Thompson J.N.	2nd Gun				1x2000 HC 2x1000 RDX fuse T.D.O.25
				F/S Brunet J.A.L.	R/G				2SBC 90x41b 20% X type 2SBC 80X30lb
				F/O Quaile A.N.	2nd pilot				
Halifax II	JB923	VR-Q	419	W/O McMillan G.A.	Capt	20:48	06:57		Works in bomb sight. Clouds of
				P/O Lowry R.W.	Nav				smoke, explosions and incendiaries
				P/O Enever H.	A/B				all over the target area.
				Sgt Alison W.H.D.	Wop.AG				1x2000 2x1000 fused T.D.O.25
				Sgt Howell W.J.	F/E2				
				P/O Wallace A.R.	2nd Gun				
				Sgt Bees H.G.	R/G				
Halifax II	BB323	VR-R	419	F/O Keddie W.N.	Capt	21:16	07:02		Much flak & search lights Mannheim
				P/O Hair F.S.	Nav				area, little over target.
				P/O Winskill A.S.	A/B				
				Sgt Coburn C.S.	Wop.AG				1x2000 2x1000 fused T.D.O.25
				Sgt Kirkham E.R.	F/E				2SBC 90x4lb 20% X type. 2SBC
				Sgt Hurst G.A.	2nd Gun				80x30lb
				Sgt Lesage J.A.	R/G				
Halifax II	DT798	VR-T	419	F/O MacIntosh C.E.	Capt	20:54	05:38		Target bombed by markers. Fires
				P/O Harrold K.V.	Nav				Growing. Fires seen when 100 miles
				Sgt Hancock E.J.G.	A/B				from target. Large number. Aircraft
				Sgt Davison N.E.	Wop.AG				seen..
				Sgt Mulholland E.S.	F/E				Bomb load as BB323 above
				Sgt Lemire A.J.	2nd Gun				
				F/O Noble W.L.	R/G				Landed Newmarket

AIRCRAFT	SERIAL	CODE	SQN.	CREW	TRADE		UP	DOWN	BOMBED	NOTES
Lancaster III	ED711	UV-U	460	Sgt White D.E. DFM	Pilot	RAAF	20:59	FTR		Heukopf, Stuttgart 00:55 Hit by light flak. Released Bombs in emergency Upper Rosenberg Street. Gunners returned fire wounding flak gunner. 1x4000 3x1000
				Sgt Stewart J.S	2nd Pilot	RAAF				
				W/O Charlton W.R.K.	Nav	RAAF				
				F/S Ward F.H.	B/A	RAAF				
				F/S Parker A.K.	Wop/Ag	RAAF				
				Sgt Knilands B.	F/E	RAAF				
				F/S Baker R.H.	M/U	RAAF				
				F/S Smith A.K.	R/G	RAAF				
Lancaster	ED525	UV-N	460	F/S Cope G.R.	Pilot	RAAF	21:07	05:54	02:24	Bombed believed Erlangen. Circled Primary at 01:40 for 20 mins, no flares seen
				F/O Gordon H.L.	Nav	RAAF			6,000 ft	
				Sgt Douds D.	B/A	RAAF			270 °	
				Sgt Crouch D.H.	Wop/Ag	RAAF				
				Sgt Hartfield	F/E					
				Sgt Matheson W.R.	M/U	RCAF				1x4000 3x1000
				Sgt Finlason D.S.	R/G	RAAF				
Lancaster I	W4844	UV-D	460	Sgt Coldham P.A.	Pilot	RAAF	21:03	05:33	01:40	Target ID'd by PFF flares. Coned north of target but dowsed lights when fired at.
				P/O Stevens P.A	Nav	RAAF			6,000 ft	
				Sgt Robinson G.H.	B/A					
				Sgt Bland A.P.	Wop/Ag	RAAF				1x4000 3x1000
				Sgt Coles G.H.	F/E					
				Sgt Warrick N.	M/U					
				Sgt Pascoe G.H.	R/G	RAAF				
Lancaster I	W4941	UV-E	460	Sgt Fuhrmann H.L.	Pilot	RAAF	21:05	06:23	01:50	ID'd by PFF flares Mannheim still burning as aircraft passed on return leg.
				F/O Anderson C.B.	Nav	RAAF			7,500 ft	
				Sgt Scott S.M	B/A	RAAF			010 °	
				Sgt Gliddon	Wop/Ag					
				Sgt Woods D.W.	F/E					
				Sgt Doyle J.P.	M/U					1x4000 3x1000
				Sgt Bent D.E.	R/G					

A Shaky do-The Skoda Works Raid of 16/17th April 1943

AIRCRAFT	SERIAL	CODE	SQN.	CREW		TRADE	UP	DOWN	BOMBED	NOTES
Lancaster I	ED369	UV-A	460	Sgt Hewerdine J.J.	RAAF	Pilot	20:54	06:10	01:41	ID'd by PFF flares. Many explosions
				Sgt Dallimore L.W.		Nav			6,000 ft	Pilot & 4 of this crew lost , 156 sqn
				Sgt Stokes G.J.H.		B/A			045°	12/13th July Ops Torino.
				Sgt Callum J.F.W.		Wop/Ag				
				Sgt Dickins T.E.		F/E				
				Sgt Buckle R.O.	RAAF	M/U				
				Sgt Archibald J.	RAAF	R/G				1x4000 3x1000
Lancaster I	ED315	UV-P	460	F/L Simpson L.J.	RAAF	Pilot	21:00	06:35	02:45	Attacked Nürnberg off track. D.R.
				F/S Kennedy A.	RAAF	2nd Pilot			6,000 ft	from Augsburg & Munich.
				F/S McLeod C.W.	RAAF	Nav			290°	Captain stated that 150 to 200 feet
				F/S Searle R.	RAAF	B/A				Was too high. 100 ft would have been
				Sgt King F.J.	RAAF	Wop/Ag				better!
				Sgt Maltby W.T.		F/E				
				Sgt Sutton K.		M/U				
				Sgt Christie R.S.	RAAF	R/G				1x4000 3x1000
Lancaster I	W4325	UV-O	460	F/S Hogben R.S.	RAAF	Pilot	21:04	06:28	01:43	ID'd by flares, river & railway.
				Sgt Pomfret J.		Nav			6,500 ft	This a/c amongst 1st over target. Lost
				Sgt Boland T.		B/A			050°	Stettin 21 Apr
				Sgt Smith R.E.		Wop/Ag				
				Sgt Cousins A.J.	RAAF	F/E				
				Sgt Dixon H.E.		M/U				
				Sgt Pascoe G.H.		R/G				1x4000 3x1000
Lancaster I	W4927	UV-C	460	P/O Hudson E.A DFC	RAAF	Pilot	21:10	06:19	01:41	One burst on shed probably 4000lb
				P/O Friend R.F.	RAAF	Nav			5,500 ft	Incendiaries over concentrated area.
				Sgt Young		B/A			350°	This aircraft was the only one plotted
				Sgt Austin J	RAAF	Wop/Ag				On the target.
				Sgt Rose C.A.	RAAF	F/E				Good photo taken by Hudson's crew.
				Sgt Wards J.F.	RAAF	M/U				
				Sgt Mardell J.A.V.		R/G				1x4000 3x1000

A Shaky do-The Skoda Works Raid of 16/17th April 1943

250

AIRCRAFT	SERIAL	CODE	SQN.	CREW		TRADE	UP	DOWN	BOMBED	NOTES
Lancaster I	W4331	UV-R	460	Sgt Miller I.G.	RAAF	Pilot	21:06	FTR	KIA	Ludwigshafen Oggersheim 03:07 flak
				Sgt Richmond R.P.		Nav			KIA	Wreck discovered 15 July 1999
				Sgt Capon M.G		B/A			KIA	
				Sgt Wilson G.J.		Wop/Ag			KIA	1x4000 3x1000
				Sgt Curtis D.		F/E			KIA	
				Sgt Hall R.A.		M/U			KIA	
				Sgt Beaumont R.		R/G			KIA	
Lancaster III	W4783	UV-G	460	F/S Murray J.N.	RAAF	Pilot	21:08	05:29	02:35	Own bombs burst in built up area.
				Sgt. Pridgeon W. F.		2nd Pilot			6,000ft	Circled primary 25 mins 8000ft, no
				W/O Taylor C. L.	RAAF	Nav			284°	flares. Bombed Koblenz on return.
				W/O Osborn T.E.	RAAF	B/A			Saw	4 A/C shot down+3 E/A. Contact with 1
				F/S Dodds J.A.	RAAF	Wop/Ag				G George now in Australian Museum,
				Sgt Bentham C.		F/E				completed 89 Ops. and was
				F/S Hodgen O.F.	RAAF	M/U				flown to Australia by Hudson Oct'44
				F/S Kirkby J.A.	RAAF	R/G				1x4000 3x1000 GP- 1700 miles flown
Lancaster I	ED774	UV-S	460	S/L Campling E.F.K.	DFC	Pilot	21:09	06:44	02:05	ID'd by PFF & visually. Target well
				F/O Dollar E.	RAAF	Nav			7,500 ft	alight & completely covered in
				P/O Ward P.W.	RAAF	B/A			015°	billowing smoke up to 5,000 ft
				P/O Mould R.M. DFM	RAAF	Wop/Ag				1x4000 3x1000
				P/O Bennett B.W.	RAAF	F/E				Made return trip at 100ft. Search
				P/O Stephenson		M/U				lights worried aircraft south of
				F/S Osborn A.G.	RAAF	R/G				Mannheim. Two shot out by this a/c
Lancaster I	W4939	UV-L	460	Sgt Giles K.W.	RAAF	Pilot	20:58	05:53	01:46	Target ID'd by PFF & large fires.
				Sgt Morgan R.W.	RAAF	Nav			9,000 ft	PFF flares dazzled making ID difficult
				F/S Gordon S.W.	RAAF	B/A			075°	Large fires seen 40 miles away from
				Sgt Mohr A.J.		Wop/Ag				target. Small flak holes in fuselage
				Sgt Brimelow W.B.		F/E				and tail plane.
				F/S Delohery A.W.		M/U				
				Sgt Smith G.R.		R/G				1x4000 3x1000

A Shaky do-The Skoda Works Raid of 16/17th April 1943

AIRCRAFT	SERIAL	CODE	SQN.	CREW		TRADE	UP	DOWN	BOMBED	NOTES
Lancaster I	W4330	UV-H	460	F/S Moodie D.B.	RAAF	Pilot	20:57	05:57	02:25	Bombed SE Nürnberg 02:25 hrs.
				F/S Aitken A.L.	RAAF	Nav			8,000 ft	primary not reached, lack of detail.
				Sgt Bethel S.J.	RAAF	B/A				Attacked by fighters. R/G scored
				F/S Stain R.R.	RAAF	Wop/Ag				hits on fuselage of enemy aircraft.
				Sgt Sutton G.	RAAF	F/E				
				Sgt Williams S.C.		M/U				1x4000 3x1000
				Sgt Macwaters H.J	RAAF	R/G				
Lancaster I	W4942	UV-F	460	Sgt Williams J.N.	RAAF	Pilot	21:06	FTR		Worms shot down 00:34 by Ofw..
				Sgt King E.R.	RAAF	Nav				Richard Launer:10./NJG4 on the
				Sgt Ebott E.C.	RAAF	B/A				Worms –Horchheim road
				Sgt Smith L.C.		W/OP				Also coned at low level. Flak hits
				Sgt Bell J.C.	RAAF	F/E				
				Sgt Clark A.W.		M/U				1x4000 HC 3x1000
				Sgt Ablethwaite E.J.		R/G				
Lancaster	W4818	UV-B	460	S/L Baird K.D.	RAAF	Pilot	21:02	06:06	01:46 9,500 ft 035°	Target ID'd by PFF flares
				W/O Cox A.E.		Nav				
				Sgt Jackson		B/A				Mannheim well alight 02:55 when
				P/O Liddle J.	RAAF	W/OP				this aircraft passed by.
				Sgt Macintyre	RAAF	F/E				
				Sgt Wilson R.M.		M/U				
				F/S Borcherds P.D.		R/G				
Lancaster I	ED780	PO-E	467	Sgt Stuart R.C.	RAAF	Pilot	21:33	FTR		La Haie Mouret,Thieulloy l'Abbaye 6k
				Sgt Martin T.		F/E				NW Poix-de-la-Somme about 04:00
				Sgt McDonald A.F.		A/B				Probably due to flak
				F/O McNair B.R. DFC		Nav				
				Sgt Anderson R.C.	RNZAF	W/op				
				Sgt Boase P.L.	RAAF	M/U				
				Sgt Johnson R.J.		R/G				Bomb load 1x4000 HC 2x1000 Gp

A Shaky do-The Skoda Works Raid of 16/17th April 1943

AIRCRAFT	SERIAL	CODE	SQN	CREW	TRADE	UP	DOWN	BOMBED	NOTES
Lancaster III	ED803	PO-B	467	F/S Tillotson G.F.	Pilot	21:23	05:20	01:55	No flares seen at turning point.
				Sgt Winston A.L.	F/E			7,000 ft	Saw green & white Tis at target
				Sgt Gervers T.K.	A/B			1x4000	Flak met with along whole route
				Sgt Graham G.E.M.	Nav			2x1000	Two contacts with fighters evaded
				Sgt Steele J.A.	Wop/Ag				At the Rhine a searchlight with blue &
				Sgt Mantock R.G.W.	M/U				red rays pointed at aircraft.
				Sgt Parkhurst W.P.	R/G				Landed Boscombe Down
Lancaster III	ED545	PO-J	467	Sgt Ball A.	Pilot	21:32	06:26	02:03	Overshot markers, bombed long
				Sgt Craham D.G.	F/E				buildings. 10 active search lights over
				Sgt White W.H.	A/B				target mainly obscured by smoke
				F/O Berrisford N.C.	Nav				
				Sgt Anderson E.F.	Wop/Ag				1x4000 HC 2x1000 gp
				Sgt Patty A.	M/U				
				Sgt Belshaw R.	R/G				Landed Boscombe Down
Lancaster III	ED547	PO-M	467	W/C Gomm G.L. DSO DFC	Pilot	21:30	06:14	02:01	Numerous bursts 'factory' area
				Sgt Lee J.R.	F/E			6,000 ft	reported PFF flares ignited too low
				P/O Campbell F.G.	A/B				and caused effective smoke screen
				P/O Gibson K.	Nav				Defences stronger than expected.
				P/O Reardon A.H.	Wop/Ag				Coned in target area and 2x on return
				P/O Hare W.R.	M/U				1x4000 HC 2x1000 gp
				F/S McKenny L.L.	R/G				Landed Boscombe Down
Lancaster III	ED539	PO-V	467	P/O Manifold W.G. RAAF	Pilot	21:43	05:35	01:45	Factory rail siding in bomb sight
				Sgt Jarvis F.P.	F/E			6,000 ft	Navigator was sure they had bombed
				Sgt Brown A.C.F.	A/B				wrong place as they used the TIs
				P/O Moppett T.W RAAF	NAV				as a guide.
				Sgt Hernaman H.C	Wop/Ag				
				P/O Currie G.D. RAAF	A/G				1x4000 HC 2x1000 gp
				Sgt Rosie E.M.P.	A/G				Landed Boscombe Down

A Shaky do-The Skoda Works Raid of 16/17th April 1943

AIRCRAFT	SERIAL	CODE	SQN	CREW		TRADE	UP	DOWN	BOMBED	NOTES
Lancaster III	ED651	PO-Y	467	Sgt Wilson B.C.	RAAF	Pilot	21:25	POW		Coned and shot down by night fighter
				Sgt Pallender R.H.		F/E		KIA		on return journey.
				P/O Boswell F.C.		A/B		POW		Crash landed believed in the Koln
				P/O Stitt R.		Nav		POW		area flying 'on the deck!'
				Sgt Goode H.F.		Wop/Ag		Injured		Goode died in hospital
				Sgt Dunn R.		M/U		KIA		
				Sgt Bannatyne W.W.		R/G		KIA		1x4000 HC 2x1000 GP
Lancaster III	ED546	PO-W	467	F/S Parsons J.M. RAAF		Pilot	21:34	05:56	01:45	Bomb'd visually 1x4000 HC 2x1000 gp
				Sgt Spencer B.		F/E			7,000 ft	Results of Mannheim raid seen 03:10
				Sgt Vaulkhard N.J.		A/B				Fairly concentrated flak at target .
				Sgt Egan J.P.		Nav				Search lights & flak at Rhein. Crew
				Sgt Selman RCAF		Wop/Ag				shot down Düsseldorf 26/27 May-
				Sgt Hunt B.A.		M/U				Flak. Parsons, Spencer + Chalmers KIA
				Sgt Chalmers T.		R/G				Landed Boscombe Down
Lancaster III	ED534	PO-R	467	F/S Hooper S.R.		Pilot	21:27	05:52	01:55	ID'd by light of flares green TI seen
				Sgt Gittings J.		F/E			4,800 ft	Own bombs not seen. Three bombs
				Sgt Fridgen J.C.L.		A/B				seen to explode. Plenty flak + S/Ls
				Sgt Anderson S.R.		Nav				en route. Shot at x-ing coast.
				Sgt Todd A.		Wop/Ag				Returned fire. Small amount
				Sgt Clark R.M.		M/U				effective flak over target.
				Sgt Burns A.W.J.		R/G				1x4000 HC 2x1000 gp
										Landed Boscombe Down
Lancaster III	ED538	PO-O	467	F/L Mackenzie D.C.		Pilot	21:21	05:20	01:58	Bombed Red TI
				Sgt McClusky J.F.		F/E			6,000 ft	Numerous fires and explosions.
				Sgt Moore A.D.		A/B				
				W/O Carroll M.W.		Nav				
				F/O Joseph C.H.		Wop/Ag				1x4000 HC 2x1000 gp
				F/S Haywood J.R.		M/U				
				Sgt Donohue J.W.		R/G				Landed Boscombe Down

A Shaky do-The Skoda Works Raid of 16/17th April 1943

AIRCRAFT	SERIAL	CODE	SQN	CREW	TRADE	UP	DOWN	BOMBED	NOTES
Lancaster III	ED531	PO-T	467	Sgt Marks D.J.	Pilot	21:26	05:44	01:46	Pinpointed river & ID'd target by light of flares. Three bombs seen to explode. Did dummy run. Light flak to North west. Searchlights quite good but working individually.
				Sgt Fentiman D.C.	F/E			5,000 ft	
				Sgt Dunbar J.A.	A/B				
				P/O Hammond G.N.	Nav				
				Sgt McDonald D.	Wop/Ag				
				Sgt Unwin P.H.	M/U				1x4000 HC 2x1000 gp
				Sgt Cumming J.	R/G				Landed Boscombe Down, Crew lost Hamburg ED862 97 sqn 29/30 July
Lancaster III	ED504	PO-K	467	F/L Desmond J.M. RAAF	Pilot	21:24	05:37	01:49	Fire and smoke at target. A dozen or so bombs seen far away from target.
				Sgt Davis E.S.	F/E			5,500 ft	
				Sgt Lockwood J.N.	A/B				1x4000 HC 2x1000 gp
				Sgt Cribben G.	Nav				
				F/S Padden	Wop/Ag				
				P/O Cazaly K.C.	M/U				Landed Boscombe Down
				F/S Ryalls J.R. RAAF	R/G				a/c and crew lost 27/28 May 43 Essen
Lancaster III	ED772	PO-	467	Sgt Heavery F.G.	Pilot	21:22	05:59	01:45	Own Cookie seen to burst centre of target.
				Sgt Rodgers F.	F/E			6,000 ft	
				Sgt Murray R. M. 'Nick'	A/B				Light flak shell through nose when
				Sgt Foster E.	Nav				crossing French coast on return trip.
				Sgt Lloyd B.P.H.	Wop/Ag				
				Sgt Butterworth K.	M/U				1x4000 HC 2x1000 gp
				Sgt Knott S.J.	R/G				Landed Boscombe Down

A Shaky do-The Skoda Works Raid of 16/17th April 1943

AIRCRAFT	SERIAL	CODE	SQN	CREW	TRADE	UP	DOWN	BOMBED	NOTES
Lancaster III	ED771	PO-	467	Sgt Claxton D.B.	Pilot	21:29	06:21	01:43	White flares right over target
				Sgt Wilson J.S.	F/E			7,000 ft	Arrived early made orbit waiting for.
				Sgt Evans D.	A/B				flares. Smoke pall on leaving target
				Sgt Dishington A.E.	Nav				Flak moderate
				Sgt Fitt G.E. 'Peter'	Wop/Ag				1x4000 HC 2x1000 gp
				Sgt Williams T.B.	M/U				
				Sgt Clark J,M.	R/G				Landed Boscombe Down
Lancaster III	ED737	PO-F	467	Sgt Wilson W.L.	Pilot	21:31	06:28	01:53	Bombed on ETA from Yellow markers
				Sgt Cawthorne D.A.	F/E			6,000 ft	at position 'C' also by Green & yellow
				Sgt White K.	A/B				Flares in target area.
				Sgt Crumplin H.P.	Nav				Top of Perspex in rear turret holed.
				Sgt Booth D.	Wop/Ag				believed flak
				Sgt Oliver P.G.	M/U				1x4000 HC 2x1000 gp
				Sgt Barry T.P.	R/G				Landed Boscombe Down. 9 hours.
Lancaster III	ED543	PO-H	467	F/L Sinclair E.K.	Pilot	21:28	?	01:55	Target obscured by smoke and fires.
				Sgt Traynor P. 'Paddy'	F/E			6,000 ft	Ground defences en route to and
				Sgt Loveday G.A.	A/B				from target very active and accurate
				F/S Gordon J.I.	Nav				A/C Lost ops to Plzen 13/14 MAY 43
				F/S Hall E.G.	Wop/Ag				
				Sgt Crall A.J.A.	M/U				
				F/S Hall E.T.	R/G				Landed Boscombe Down

A Shaky do-The Skoda Works Raid of 16/17th April 1943

Operation Chub Mannheim Losses 16/17th April 1943

Type	Serial	Code	Sqn	Base	Crash	Time	Cause
Stirling	BF474	LS-H	15	Mildenhall	Brunehamel	23:31	Lt Bergmann Stb.III/NJG4
Stirling	BK691	LS-F	15	Mildenhall	Hetzerath/Rapperath	00:20	Lt Heinz Hadeball 12./NJG4
Stirling	W7469	AA-O	75	Newmarket	Katzenbach	01:15	Hptm Wohlers Stb.IV./NJG4
Stirling	BF451	AA-Z	75	Newmarket	Rilly la Montagne	03:48	Hptm Materne 4./NJG4
Stirling	BK664	AA-M	75	Newmarket	Base		Flak/Crash at base
Halifax	JB870	MP-F	76	Linton On Ouse	Goyencourt	02:15	Lt Bergmann Stb III./NJG4
Stirling	BK725	WP-M	90	Ridgewell	Commenchon	02:14	Ofw Macke 9./NJG4
Halifax	HR779	NP-Z	158	Lissett	Void/Vaucouleurs	00:35	Hptm Matterne 4./NJG4
Wellington	HE862	AS-L	166	Kirmington	Cayeaux ditched	23:00	Ditched In Channel/Engine
Wellington	HE387	ZO-Z	196	Leconfield	St Pierre Aigle	02:09	Hptmn H-K Kamp 7./NJG4
Wellington	HE469	ZO-	196	Leconfield	Croyden	04:00	Abandoned Fuel shortage
Stirling	BK653	BU-A	214	Chedburg	Bonneuil les eaux ?	00:30	Poss.Lt Pietrek 2./NJG4
Stirling	BF514	HA-X	218	Downham Market	Raucourt et Flaba	00:14	Maj Holler NJG4
Wellington	HE682	PT-T	420	Middleton St G	Froid lieu	00:20	Ofw Rahner 3./NJG4
Wellington	HE475	KW-E	425	Dishforth	Lotzbeuren	00:49	Lt Heinz Hadeball 12./NJG4
Wellington	HE591	OW	426	Dishforth	Kyll, Bitburg	01:51	Fw Faden11./NJG4
Wellington	HE547	ZL-D	427	Croft	Kirf	01:00 Approx	Flak
Wellington	HE745	ZL-E	427	Croft	Crash landed base	23:30	Crashed at base
Wellington	BK162	AL-B	429	East Moor	Septmonts, Aisne	02:1	Oblt. K Fladrich 9./NJG4
Wellington	HE379	SE-H	431	Burn	Hochspeyer	01:00	Flak
Wellington	HE501	HD-J	466	Leconfield	Serraincourt Ardennes	23:56	Lt Bergmann Stb.III/NJG4

Total airframe losses 21, for Mannheim operation

A Shaky do. The Plzen raid April 16/17th April 1943